Social Movements in Latin America

SOCIAL MOVEMENTS AND TRANSFORMATION

This series tackles one of the central issues of our time: the rise of large-scale social movements and the transformation of society over the last thirty years. As global capitalism continues to affect broader segments of the world's population—workers, peasants, the self-employed, the unemployed, the poor, indigenous peoples, women, and minority ethnic groups—there is a growing mass movement by the affected populations to address the inequities engendered by the globalization process. These popular mass movements across the globe (such as labor, civil rights, women's, environmental, indigenous, and anti-corporate globalization movements) have come to form a viable and decisive force to address the consequences of the operations of the transnational corporations and the global capitalist system. The study of these social movements—their nature, social base, ideology, and strategy and tactics of mass struggle—is of paramount importance if we are to understand the nature of the forces that are struggling to bring about change in the global economy, polity, and social structure. This series aims to explore emerging movements and develop viable explanations for the kind of social transformations that are yet to come.

Series Editor:

Berch Berberoglu is Professor of Sociology and Director of Graduate Studies in Sociology at the University of Nevada, Reno.

Titles:

Social Movements in Latin America: Neoliberalism and Popular Resistance
James Petras and Henry Veltmeyer

Social Movements in Latin America

Neoliberalism and Popular Resistance

James Petras and Henry Veltmeyer

SOCIAL MOVEMENTS IN LATIN AMERICA
Copyright © James Petras and Henry Veltmeyer, 2011.

First published in 2011 by
PALGRAVE MACMILLAN®
in the United States—a division of St. Martin's Press LLC,
175 Fifth Avenue, New York, NY 10010.

Where this book is distributed in the UK, Europe and the rest of the world,
this is by Palgrave Macmillan, a division of Macmillan Publishers Limited,
registered in England, company number 785998, of Houndmills,
Basingstoke, Hampshire RG21 6XS.

Palgrave Macmillan is the global academic imprint of the above companies
and has companies and representatives throughout the world.

Palgrave® and Macmillan® are registered trademarks in the United States,
the United Kingdom, Europe and other countries.

ISBN: 978–0–230–10411–2

Library of Congress Cataloging-in-Publication Data

Petras, James F., 1937–
    Social movements in Latin America : neoliberalism and popular
resistance / James Petras, Henry Veltmeyer.
        p. cm.—(Social movements and transformation)
    ISBN 978–0–230–10411–2 (alk. paper)
        1. Social movements—Latin America. 2. Anti-imperialist
movements—Latin America. 3. Anti-globalization movement—Latin
America. 4. Neoliberalism—Latin America. 5. Economic development—
Political aspects—Latin America. 6. Latin America—Social conditions—
21st century. 7. Latin America—Politics and government—21st century.
I. Veltmeyer, Henry. II. Title.

HN110.5.A8P463 2010
303.48'4098—dc22   2010031398

A catalogue record of the book is available from the British Library.

Design by Newgen Imaging Systems (P) Ltd., Chennai, India.

First edition: February 2011

10 9 8 7 6 5 4 3 2 1

Printed in the United States of America.

Contents

Tables

Acronyms

AFL-CIO	American Federation of Labor and Congress of Industrial Organization
AIFLD	American Institute for Free Labor Development
AIDESEP	Inter-Ethnic Association for the Development of the Peruvian Rainforest
ALAI	Agencia Latinoamericana de Información
ALBA	Alianza Bolivariana para los Pueblos de América
ALCA	Free Trade Agreement of the Americas
ANIPA	Asamblea Nacional Indígena Plural por la Autonomía
ASP	Assembly for the Sovereignty of the Peoples
CAAP	Centro Andino de Acción Popular
CAOI	Coordinadora Andina de Organizaciones Indígenas
CCC	Central Campesina Cardenista
CCI	Central Campesina Independiente
CGT	Confederación General de Trabajadores
CGT	Confederación General del Trabajo de la República Argentina
CICA	Consejo Indígena de Centro América
CLOC	Congreso Latinoamericano de Organizaciones del Campo
CMS	Coordinadora de Movimientos Sociales
CNI	Congreso Nacional Indígena
CNPAMM	Confederación Nacional de Productores Agrícolas de Maíz de México
COB	Central Obrera Boliviana [Bolivia Workers' Central]
COICA	Coordinadora de Organizaciones Indígenas de la Cuenca Amazónica
CONAIE	Confederation of Indigenous Nationalities in Ecuador

CONFENAIE	Confederación de los Pueblos y Nacionalidades de la Amazonía
CSO	civil society organization
CTM	Confederación de Trabajadores de México
CTV	Confederación de Trabajadores de Venezuela
CUT	Confederación Unica de Trabajadores
DEA	Drug Enforcement Agency
ECLAC	United Nations Economic Commission for Latin America and the Caribbean
ECUARUNARI	Confederación de los Pueblos de la Nacionalidad Quichua
ELN	Ejército de Liberacion Nacional
EPR	Ejército Popular Revolucionario
ESF	Emergency Social Fund
EZLN	Ejército Zapatista de Liberación Nacional
FARC-EP	Fuerzas Armadas Revolucionarias de Colombia-Ejército del Pueblo
FDI	foreign direct investment
FEJUVE	Federación de Juntas Vecinales de El Alto [Federation of Neighbourhood Councils of El Alto]
FENCOMIN	Federacion Nacional de Cooperativas Mineras de Bolivia [Federation of Mining Cooperatives]
FLMN	Frente Farabundo Martí para la Liberación Nacional
FNC	Federacíon Nacional Campesina [National Peasant Federation]
FNCMB	Federacion Nacional de Cooperativas Mineras de Bolivia [National Labour Confederation]
FOL	Forward Operating Locations
FTAA	Free Trade Area Agreement
GATT	General Agreement on Tariffs and Trade
GDP	Gross Domestic Product
GNP	Gross National Product
ICIC	Iniciativa Civil para la Integración Centroamericana
IFI(s)	International Financial Institution(s)
IMDEC	Instituto Mexicano para el Desarrollo Comunitario
IMF	International Monetary Fund
IVAD	Venezuelan Institute of Data Analysis

MAS	Movimiento al Socialism
MST	Movimento dos Trabalhadores Rurais Sem Terra
MUPP-NP	Movimiento de Unidad Pachakutik-Nuevo País
NAFTA	North American Free Trade Agreement
NATO	North Atlantic Treaty Organization
NED	National Endowment for Democracy
NEP	New Economic Policy
NGO	nongovernmental organization
ODA	Overseas Development Assistance
OECD	Organisation for Economic Co-operation and Development
PFL	Partido da Frente Liberal [Liberal Front Party]
PMDB	Partido do Movimento Democrático Brasileiro [Brazilian Democratic Movement Party]
PRD	Partido de la Revolución Democrática [Party of the Democratic Revolution]
PRI	Partido Revolucionario Institucionalista [The Institutional Revolutionary Party
PRONAA	Programa Nacional de Asistencia Alimentaria
PSDB	Partido da Social Democracia Brasileira [Brazilian Social Democratic Party]
PSUV	Partido Socialista Unido de Venezuela [United Socialist Party of Venezuela]
PT	Partido dos Trabalhadores [The Workers Party]
RASA	Red de Alternativas Sustentables Agropecuarias
SAP	structural adjustment program
SME	Sindicato de Electricistas de México [Electrical Workers Union of Mexico]
TROLE	Law of Economic Transformation [Ecuador]
UGOCP	Unión General Obrero Campesino Popular
UNCTAD	United Nations Conference on Trade and Development
UNCTC	United Nations Centre on Transnational Corporations
USAID	United States Agency for International Development
WDR	World Development Report
WTO	World Trade Organization

Introduction

Different studies have shown that between 1982 and 1993—the first decade of capitalist development under the "new economic model" of neoliberal globalization launched in the opening gambit of a new imperialist offensive—those living in poverty increased from 78 to 150 million, in what the Economic Commission for Latin America and the Caribbean aptly termed "*la brecha de la equidad*," or the equity gap. Behind this poverty, in a decade "lost to development" (zero growth), could be found the agency and dynamics of capitalist development, including a massive diversion of financial resources into interest payments on the foreign debt and the destruction of productive forces in both agriculture and industry. Economists in the mainstream of development thinking, particularly those at the World Bank, attributed this "development" to the irresistible forces of productive and social transformation ("progress"), while many critics, including the authors of this book, see in it instead the agency of imperialist exploitation, an assault on the region's raw materials and human conditions facilitated by the neoliberal policy agenda imposed by Washington.

As for the masses of people in the popular sector of society, the working classes and the direct producers, compelled to live the conditions of this onslaught on their livelihoods and lives, they were not nearly as sanguine as the development experts. These economists were quite willing and content to believe that the pain and misery of poverty was the price of admission into the new world order—the inevitable and necessary social cost of progressive change. Unlike these economists, however, ordinary people and popular classes were quite disposed to resist these forces of capitalist development and change—to organize collectively and take action against the policies and institutions of the ruling class, including the model of neoliberal globalization used to advance the interests of the capitalist class and their imperialist backers.

If the depredations of US imperialism—what some view as "globalization from above"—created the objective conditions of deprivation or poverty, the community- and class-based organizations in the popular sector of Latin American society created and acted on the subjective conditions of widespread resistance.

Chapter 1 provides an overview of the neoliberal globalization and imperialist exploitation that have given rise to the resistance. As we see it, neoliberalism, globalization, and development are different modalities or forms of imperialism, projects first implemented in the early 1980s to advance the process of capitalist development. In this chapter we identify seven pillars of the imperialist system, constructed via (1) the repression and destruction of the class-based movements of resistance and social transformation based on organized labor and the rural poor; (2) armed force and violence—the policy of neoliberalism from the barrel of the gun; (3) debt peonage—use of the external debt as a lever of policy implementation; (4) an ideology of globalization, to mask the economic interests in play and justify a program of painful policy measures; and (5) when and where required, as in Mexico in 1997 and 2006, electoral fraud to ensure the installation of supportive regimes.

The remainder of the book is essentially an analysis of the different forms taken by the forces of resistance to neoliberalism, and the revolutionary dynamics of these forces. In effect, chapter 1 provides the context for an analysis of the changing forms taken by the resistance over three decades.

We have identified two basic types of strategic response to capitalist development and imperialist exploitation. One is to adjust or adapt, taking them as given and seeking to survive or cope with the conditions that they generate—"everyday resistance" as Scott (1985) views it. This type of response for the most part involves and is based on decisions taken by individuals, each seeking to improve their situation under the available conditions. The other is to resist the forces of capitalist development and imperialist exploitation through collective action, primarily in the form of social movements, organizations formed to mobilize the forces of radical social change.

The first part of chapter 2 focuses on the process of productive and social transformation at the center of the capitalist development process—development of the forces of production within the capitalist system. It takes as its point of departure, and subjects to relentless criticism, the conception of this process found in the World Bank's 2008 *World Development Report*. From the Bank's perspective, the forces of structural (productive and social) transformation are immutable, driven forward by forces that are difficult to manage and impossible to control. The economists at the Bank recognize that widespread poverty is the inevitable result, if not a condition, of this process. However, the conditions of this poverty can be alleviated, and the incidence of poverty in its extreme form, can and need to be made, primarily on the basis of decisions made, and actions taken, by the poor themselves with international cooperation: to migrate in search of better conditions, abandoning agriculture in favor of labor, that is, different forms of employment, which provide greater opportunities for sustainable livelihoods and improving the social condition of the family; or to change oneself from a peasant farmer into an entrepreneur, a necessary means of accessing the capital, technology, and markets needed to make farming profitable and thus sustainable.

The second part of the chapter turns to on the working class and organized labor. A major strategic response to the production crisis of the early 1970s was to change the relation of capital to labor in three ways: (1) by compressing the value of labor-power, reducing as a result the share of wages in national income and increasing the pool of available capital; (2) reducing the power of organized labor to negotiate with capital for increased wages and improved working conditions; and (3) shifting toward a new regime of accumulation based on a post-fordist regime of regulation (increased "flexibility" in the organization of the two major factors of production).

Chapter 2 reviews the efforts of the World Bank, in Latin America, to promote the "structural reforms" needed to bring about this new, more advanced form of capitalist production. The backdrop to this analysis is a radical change in the nature and structure of the working class over the course of two decades of structural reform in the region. A major consequence of this structural change, and the neoliberal policies that brought about or accelerated them, was the weakening of organized labor, a dramatic reduction not only of its organizational capacity vis-à-vis capital but also of its political capacity in mobilizing the forces of resistance. This turned out to be a major *political* development in the 1990s.

Chapter 3 turns to an analysis of the political dynamics associated with the capitalist development process in the agricultural sector of society—"agrarian transformation" in academic parlance. As already noted, capitalist development entails a process of productive and social transformation—a shift in economic activity from agriculture

to industry and the conversion of rural communities of direct producers and peasant farmers into an urban wage-earning proletariat.
There are essentially three strategies of structural transformation,
each with its own dynamics: *electoral politics* in the quest for state
power; *social mobilization* of exploited classes for social transformation through social movements; and *local development*[1] based on the
mobilization of social capital,[2] the one asset that the rural poor are
deemed to have in abundance—a strategy devised by the organizations of international cooperation as an alternative to the social movements and a means of demobilizing resistance.

Policies of neoliberal globalization in the 1980s and 1990s gave a
new impetus to the forces of capitalist development and agrarian transformation. But this time the protagonists of an ongoing scholarly and
political debate as to the fate and future of the peasantry include the
peasants themselves in the form of diverse radical social movements
as well as international organizations such as Via Campesina. The
chapter makes reference to, and departs from, an ongoing scholarly—
and political—debate on capitalist development and agrarian transformation. At issue in this debate is the fate and historic role of the
peasantry, viewed by many as a spent force, defeated by the forces
of agrarian transformation. We join the debate by suggesting—with
reference to political developments in Latin America—that, far from
disappearing into the dustbin of history, peasants once more stepped
onto the center stage of social change.

The argument advanced is that the assault on the working class took
three forms—the violent repressive actions of the state, the forces of
structural change and structural reforms reviewed in chapter 2, and
the broader cycle of neoliberal policies implemented in the 1980s and
1990s. Together, these forces and policies fatally weakened the labor
movement, decimating the forces of resistance mobilized by the working class. However, under the same conditions a semi-proletarianized
peasantry of landless or near-landless rural workers, and the mass of
landless or near-landless rural workers, took action, resisting the latest incursions of capitalism and imperialism in the countryside. Under
conditions of imperialist exploitation and neoliberal globalization
they led the resistance against neoliberalism in the 1990s.

Chapter 4 analyzes the social movements formed in the context of
this resistance to the new world order and its policies of neoliberal
globalization. These movements were mostly organized in the 1980s,
in response to a second cycle of neoliberal policies, but took action
in the 1990s against these policies in another cycle of market-friendly

"structural reforms." The most dynamic of these movements were peasant-based and -led. The chapter reviews the complex dynamics of these social movements as they unfolded in the context of a third cycle of neoliberal "structural" reform in government policy, moving from resistance to a revolutionary offensive.

This chapter places this question in the context of a broader set of theoretical issues that surround the relationship between the state and social movements. One of these issues has to do with the question of state power and the three different paths, mentioned earlier, toward achieving social change.

To elaborate, the first path to social change is electoral politics, the "parliamentary road" to state power preferred by the "political class" because it is predicated on limited political reforms to the existing system rather than mass mobilization of the forces of social transformation, the path taken by most social movements and oriented toward more fundamental and radical changes in the existing system.

The second modality of social change is associated with a postmodernist perspective on a new form of "politics" and the emergence in theory (i.e., in academic discourse) of "new social movements" (Slater, 1985; Escobar and Alvarez, 1992; Melucci, 1992). In this perspective, the way to bring about social change is not through political action in the struggle for state power but through social action involving the construction of movements advocating an "anti- or no-power" based on social relations of coexistence, solidarity, and collective action.

The third approach to social change has to do with the nongovernmental organizations (NGOs) involved in the project of international cooperation for development. The dynamics of social change associated with this approach—local development within the framework of a "new paradigm" (of "inclusive development") are explored in chapter 6. The ostensible aim and central objective of this approach to social change is to partner with governments and organizations of overseas development assistance to promote an improvement in the lives of the poor—to bring about conditions that will sustain their livelihoods and alleviate their poverty—and to do so not through a change in the structure of economic and political power, but through an empowerment of the poor. The approach is to build on the social capital of the poor themselves, seeking thereby to bring about improvements in their lives within the local spaces available within the power structure. It is predicated on partnership with like-minded organizations in a shared project (the alleviation of poverty, sustainable livelihoods). Rather than directly confronting this structure in an effort to change the existing distribution of power, the aim, in effect, is to empower the poor without having to disempower the rich.

Under conditions available across Latin America, and experienced in different ways in virtually every country, each of these three modalities of social change and associated conceptions of power have their adherents. However, in the specific conjuncture of conditions in Latin America, the postmodernist perspective on the "new social movements" has proven to be irrelevant. The most consequential and dynamic of the social movements are all directly or indirectly engaged in the struggle for state power. As for the political dynamics of the struggle the issues are diverse, but the most critical one turns on the relationship of the social movements to the state. This is the central theme of chapter 5, which elaborates on the dynamics of resistance by the social movements mounted by the rural landless workers, the proletarianized and semiproletarianized peasants, and the indigenous communities of Chiapas, Ecuador, and Bolivia.[3]

Chapter 6 reviews the development project advanced by the World Bank, the operational agencies of the United Nations, and other international organizations. The strategic albeit unstated aim of this project, implemented with the support and agency of NGOs formed and contracted to mediate between the donor (aid-giving) organizations and the "aid" recipients among the poor, is to divert the poor from taking action in the form of social movements. The primary concern of the social movements is to bring about social change by challenging economic and political power in the form of direct collective action. In this connection, the concern of the organizations that share this project is to offer the poor another option—to adopt a less confrontationalist approach to social change; to seek an improvement in their social condition within the local spaces of the power structure rather than challenging the holders of this power. The agency of "development" in this context is to empower the poor—to capacitate them to act and take advantage of the opportunities provided by the system for improving their lot.

The context for the analysis and discussion of the social movement matrix presented in chapters 3–5 was provided by the "structural adjustment program," with reference to the imperialist policy of neoliberal globalization. In chapter 6 we turn to political developments—and the strategic response of the social movements to neoliberalism—in the new, and somewhat changed if not entirely different, context of the new millennium: a generalized disenchantment with neoliberalism, the dominant target of the social movements; and, at the level of the economy, the emergence of a primary commodities boom, a period of economic growth preceded and followed by the outbreak and conditions of a systemic crisis. Under these conditions the most significant development was a turn in the political tide with the ascent of the political class on the Left to state power—the emergence of a stream of center-left political regimes. The key questions posed by this development—and taken up in chapter 6—are the significance and meaning of this phenomenon (the turn toward the Left in state power) and the relation of the center-left to the social movements in the fight against neoliberalism and imperialism.

The concern of chapter 7 is with the form taken by the resistance to neoliberalism under conditions of a global crisis as they hit Latin America in 2008, and the form assumed by the social movements under these conditions. Our argument in this respect is made in three parts: first, an examination of the social movements under conditions of the 1999–2002 crisis; second, a perspective on the social movements under conditions of the primary commodities boom from 2003 to 2008; and third, an analysis of the social movements under conditions of the global crisis that hit Latin America in 2008, putting an end to a short-lived primary commodities boom.

As for the strategic responses made to the global crisis, we distinguish between the following: (1) the response of the organizations and individuals that represent the class interests of global capital, the guardians of the neoliberal world order and capitalist system; the strategic response of most governments in Latin America, which has been to insulate the economy from the ravages of global capitalism and the financialization of production, and (2) the response of the social movements in the popular sector, which has been to question, oppose and reject the neoliberal model and imperialist policies used to guide and inform the policy of most governments in the region.

The book concludes with an appraisal of the correlation of forces ranged in support and opposition to capitalism, neoliberalism, and imperialism. As we see it, the turn to the political left in the new millennium has dampened, if not extinguished, the revolutionary spirit awakened by the popular movements in the 1990s. At the level of state power, apart from Cuba, the only regime that can be regarded as on the "Left" is that of President Chávez in Venezuela. But revolutionary forces are building in a number of countries in the region. However, they do have to contest the political space with emerging movements on the right. The prevailing situation of economic and political crisis, like all crises, is generating opportunities and forces for change, but these forces cut in both directions, left and right, and it is difficult to determine the likely or potential outcome of the existing precarious balance of class forces. However, it is incumbent on the intellectual and political Left to assess the situation and to provide support to the forces of progressive change, particularly those on the revolutionary Left. They are the best hope for genuine progress—a world beyond neoliberalism, beyond capitalism, beyond class exploitation, and beyond imperialism.

1

US Imperialism and the Neoliberal Offensive

Development... today is a strategic, economic and moral imperative—as central to advancing American interests and solving global problems as diplomacy and defence... [It is] time to elevate development as a central pillar of all that we do in foreign policy

—Hilary Clinton, Secretary of State—January, 2010.[1]

The term "development" is generally understood as a combination of improvements in the quality of people's lives marked by a reduction or alleviation of poverty, an increased capacity to meet the basic needs of society's members, and the sustainability of livelihoods. Empowerment and changes in institutionalized practices are necessary to bring about these improvements. The "idea of development" can be traced back to the eighteenth-century project of "enlightened" philosophers and social reformers as a means to bring about "progress"—a society characterized by freedom from tyranny, superstition and poverty, and social equality. However, as noted by Wolfgang Sachs and his associates in postdevelopment theory (1992), it was reinvented, as it were, in 1948, in the context of (1) a postwar world capitalist order based on the International Monetary Fund (IMF), the World Bank, and the General Agreement on Tariffs and Trade (GATT), a free trade negotiating forum; (2) an emerging east-west conflict and cold war; and (3) a national independence struggle by countries seeking to escape the yoke of European colonialism and the reach of imperial power—*Pax Britannica* in the prewar and *Pax Americana* in the new postwar context.

In this situation, an imperial(ist) project of "international cooperation" for development (foreign aid in the official parlance) and
a process of nation-building and modernization (capitalist industrialization) took shape as a means of ensuring that those countries
emerging from colonialism would not fall for the lure of communism.
The active agent of this process was the imperialist state in the form
of policies and programs designed to (1) increase the rate of savings
and productive investment [capital accumulation] (2) invest these
savings in new technology and industrial expansion [modernization
and industrialization] (3) the social redistribution of some market-
generated incomes, by means of progressive taxation, to social and
development programs; and (4) technical and financial assistance to
emerging developing countries in the south [foreign aid or "international cooperation"].

From the outset of this development process, signaled by Harry
Truman's 4-Point Program (of development assistance), to the early
1970s when the world capitalist system ran out of steam and entered
a period of prolonged crisis, this state-led form of development generated an unprecedented period of economic growth and societal transformation. In the Euro-American and a few Latin American countries
fuelled by rising wages and a rapid expansion of the domestic market as well as international trade, economic growth over these years
exceeded by a factor of two the economic growth rates of previous
decades, resulting in an incremental but steady improvement in the
physical quality of life and the social conditions of health, education,
and welfare. Some historians dubbed these advances as the "golden
age of capitalism" (Marglin and Schor, 1990).

In 1973, at the height of an apparent crisis of overproduction,
characterized by cutthroat competition, saturated markets for manufactured goods, stagflation, sluggish productivity, and falling profits, the capitalist class in the most advanced countries in the imperial
world order, including the CEOs of its capitalist enterprises and the
states in their service, abandoned the Bretton Woods system[2] that had
served them so well. To be more precise, they sought to renovate it,
to resolve the systemic crisis of capitalist production by (1) modifying
the relationship of capital to labor, advancing the former and weakening the latter; (2) incorporation of new production technologies
and a new regime of accumulation / labor regulation [postfordism];
(3) relocating overseas labor-intensive lines of industrial production,
creating a new international division of labor; and, above all (4) a
policy of structural adjustment and neoliberal globalization, in the

construction of a "new world order" in which the forces of capitalist development would be released from the regulatory constraints of the welfare-development state.

The policies that facilitated this process generated a seismic shift in international relations, an epoch-defining change in the "architecture" of global capital, and a new world order in which "the forces of freedom" (markets and elections) could prevail—with an occasional military intervention.

And Then Came Cuba: The Regional Dynamics of US Imperialism

The Second World War ended with the United States as a dominant world economic power, commanding 40 percent of the world's industrial capacity and more than half of the financial resources. However, conditions were not favorable for the unilateral exercise of its dominant military power. For one thing, the Soviet Union had emerged from the war with a loss of over twenty million citizens but with its industrial production apparatus rebuilt and the potential of constituting a major economic power and as such a major threat to the imperial interests of the United States, forcing the government to opt for the creation of a multilateral system of military alliances modeled on the North Atlantic Treaty Organization (NATO) and regional economic treaties designed to facilitate US projections of power in Europe and the Third World.

But Latin America was a different matter. It was historically within the US sphere of economic and political domination, and the state set about to ensure the compliance of governments in the hemisphere to US hegemony. First there was the overthrow of democratic socialist Cheddi Jagan in Guyana (1953) and the successful intervention in Guatemala (1954) to topple democratically elected President Arbenz. But then came Cuba (1959) with a successful socialist revolution that abrogated the rules of empire, challenging US hegemony and directly threatening US imperial interests in the country and elsewhere, forcing the US government to open up another front in the war against social revolution and the lure of "communism." The first front was established in 1948 in the form of International Cooperation for Development, a system of bilateral and multilateral support for the economic advancement of the "economically backward" countries emerging from the yoke of European colonialism pursuing national independence and economic development. The second front was established in the Western hemisphere in the form of an "Alliance for Progress," with the United States Agency for International Development (USAID) and the support of private voluntary associations within what we now term "civil society." The concern and aim here was to ensure that the workers and peasants, and the rural poor, would turn away from the path of revolutionary change staked out by Cuba.

The next major events in this imperialist offensive and class struggle against radical social democracy was the overthrow of Bosch in the Dominican Republic (1963), support for a military coup in Brazil, and the overthrow of the democratically elected nationalist Goulart regime (1964), an imperialist invasion of the Dominican Republic (1965)—and then, most significantly, the overthrow of Salvador Allende in Chile (1973).[3] As for the Dominican Republic it required a tactic that had worked in Haiti and Guatemala in the 1950s but that had failed in Cuba (in 1961, the Bay of Pigs): armed intervention in the form of direct invasion, a tactic that would not be used again until Grenada, in 1983, and Panama, in 1990, and then most recently in Haiti, in 2005, to oust a regime that was adopting independent nationalist policies.

During the 1960s and 1970s, the United States extended its imperial rule across the countryside of the region via multiple forms of "integrated rural development," to dampen the fires of revolutionary ferment, a "dirty war" against popular insurgents fought by proxy via death squads and the armed forces, and the occasional coup when needed.

The combined use of both the velvet glove (international development) and the iron fist (military force), and the mobilization of the state apparatus by its allies in the region, succeeded in establishing the sway of imperial power for the United States. But there remained one major obstacle to the advance of American economic interests. Many of the governments in the region, even some of the United States' purported allies, had taken a few mild nationalist measures to regulate the operations of US multinationals, restricting the repatriation of profits and insisting on content rules for overseas manufacturers. At the same time, with the policy advice from United Nations Conference on Trade and Development (UNCTAD) and allied agencies such as the United Nations Centre on Transnational Corporations (UNCTC) and United Nations Economic Commission for Latin America (ECLA), governments in the region embarked on a program of diversifying their economies via industrialization and promoting national development. This threat to US imperialist "interests" would require a different form of intervention, a different set of rules—indeed a new world order in which international economic relations would be governed by different rules that favored the expansion of United States and global capital.

Economic Crisis and Worker Revolts in the United States, Europe, Asia, and Latin America

The social history of the twentieth and early twenty-first century's economic crises and breakdowns is written large in working class and popular revolts on the left and elite fostered power grabs on the right. During the 1930s the combined effects of the world Depression and imperialist-colonial wars set in motion major uprisings in Spain (the civil war), France (general strikes, Popular Front government), the United States (factory occupations, industrial unionization), El Salvador, Mexico, and Chile (insurrections, national-popular regimes), and in China (communist/nationalist, anticolonial armed movements). Numerous other mass armed uprisings took place in response to the Depression in a great number of countries, far beyond the scope of this chapter.

The post-Second World War period witnessed major working-class and anticolonial movements in the aftermath of the breakdown of European empires and in response to the great human and national sacrifices caused by the imperial wars. Throughout Europe, social upheavals, mass direct actions, and resounding electoral advances of working-class parties were the norm in the face of a "broken" discredited capitalism associated with wars, fascism, and depressions. In Asia, mass socialist revolutions in China, Indo-China, and North Korea ousted colonial powers and defeated their local capitalist collaborators in a period of hyperinflation and mass unemployment.

The cycle of recession and growth from the 1960s to the early 1980s witnessed a large number of successful working class and popular struggles for greater control over their workplaces and higher living standards, and against employer-led counteroffensives. The historic highpoint in the offensive of labor against capital in the struggle for class power as well as improved wages and working conditions was in 1968 with a broad multi-front revolutionary offensive in the demand for change. However, capital struck back in 1973, both in Europe and in Latin America, where a US-sponsored military coup against the progressive, democratically elected "socialist" regime of Salvador Allende opened up a major counteroffensive of capital against popular movements and democracy in the region.

Latin America had experienced similar pattern of crises, revolts and reaction as the rest of the world had during the Great Depression and the Second World War. For example, in the 1930s and 1940s, aborted revolutionary upheavals and revolts took place in Cuba, El Salvador, Colombia, Brazil, Bolivia, and Venezuela. At the same time "popular front" alliances of Communists, Socialists, and Radicals governed in Chile, and populist-nationalist regimes took power in Brazil (Vargas), Argentina (Peron), and Mexico (Cardenas).

As in central and Eastern Europe, Latin America also witnessed the rise of right-wing movements in opposition to the center-left and populist regimes. This was the case in Mexico, Argentina, Brazil, Bolivia, and elsewhere—a recurrent phenomenon overlooked by most students of "social movements."

Latin America's history suggests—as Marx had theorized—that capitalism has an inherent propensity toward crisis, and that it is particularly endemic to agromineral export economies. Following the end of the Korean War and the launch of its global empire-building project by Washington (misleadingly termed "the cold war"), the United States engaged in a series of "hot wars" (Korea 1950–1953 and Indo-China 1955–1975); overt and clandestine coups *d'etats* (Iran and Guatemala—both in 1954); and military invasions (Dominican Republic, Panama, Grenada, and Cuba), all the while backing a series of brutal military dictatorships in Cuba (Batista), Dominican Republic (Trujillo), Haiti (Duvalier), Venezuela (Perez-Jimenez), Peru (Odria), among others.

Under the combined effect of dictatorial rule, blatant intervention, chronic stagnation, deepening inequalities, mass poverty, and the pillage of the public treasury, a series of popular uprisings, guerrilla revolts and general strikes toppled several US-backed dictatorships, culminating in a social revolution in Cuba. In Brazil (1962–1964), Bolivia (1952), Peru (1968–1974), Nicaragua (1979–1989), and elsewhere, nationalist presidents took power, nationalizing strategic economic sectors, redistributing land and challenging US dominance. Guerrilla armies of national liberation, and peasant and workers movements, spread throughout the continent in the 1960s and the early 1970s. The high point in this rebellion against economic stagnation, class rule, oppression and imperialist exploitation was the installation of a socialist government in Chile (1970–1973).

The advance of the popular movement, however, in most contexts did not lead to a definitive victory (the taking of state power). Cuba, Grenada, and Nicaragua were exceptions to the rule. US-backed or engineered military coups (Brazil 1964, Chile 1973), military invasions (Dominican Republic 1965, Grenada 1983, Panama 1990, Haiti 1994, 2005), surrogate mercenaries (Nicaragua 1980–1989), and rightwing civilian regimes (1982–2000, 2005) reversed the advance of the social movements, overthrew nationalist/populist and socialist regimes and restored the predominance of the oligarchic troika: the agromineral elite, the generals, and the multinational corporations. US corporate dominance, oligarchic political success, and the pillage of national wealth accelerated and deepened the boom-bust cycle of capitalist development. However, the savage repression that accompanied the US-led counterrevolution and the restoration of oligarchic rule ensured that few large-scale popular revolts would occur. In the 1970s and 1980s, the social movements and the armies of national liberation that had formed in the wake of the Cuban Revolution and the revolutionary ferment of 1968, with the exception of Fuerzas Armadas Revolucionarias de Colombia - Ejército del Pueblo (FARC-EP), were systematically destroyed or forced to ground.

The rural poor at the base of these movements, when not repressed directly were lured away from the social movements with USAID-financed microprojects of rural development, implemented within the framework of the Alliance for Progress with the assistance of armies of "private volunteers" that were contracted by the US government and its strategic partners (international cooperants) in the development project.

On the few occasions that a social movement achieved state power, as in Cuba and Nicaragua, the imperial state was forced to intervene, as it did regularly in the case of forces on the Left that achieved state power by democratic means. For the most part, however, deployment of the repressive apparatus of client states in the region, together with the strategy of integrated rural development financed with international cooperation, sufficed to dampen the fires of revolutionary ferment.

Dynamics of Empire-Building: The Pillars of Empire

In the postwar context of the Bretton Woods system, an incipient "cold war" and diverse movements for national independence, the

United States undertook to build an empire on the foundation of seven pillars (not in chronological order):

- Consolidation of the imperial (liberal-capitalist) world order, renovating it on neoliberal lines when conditions allowed (in the 1980s);
- A system of military bases, to provide the staging point and logistics for the projection of military power, and rule by military force, when circumstances would dictate;
- Installation of repressive military regimes to destroy by armed force and violent repression of the class-based movements, and put in place an institutional and policy framework for the new world order—to pave the road for the entry and operations of capital;
- International cooperation for development to provide financial and technical assistance to countries and regimes willing (or forced) to sign on to the Washington Consensus on correct policy, to secure thereby safe havens for US-based economic interests;
- Implementation of a neoliberal policy agenda of "structural reform" according to the Washington Consensus—to adjust policies and institutions to the requirements of a new world order in which the forces of freedom would be released from the constraints of welfare-development;
- Globalization—the integration of economies across the world into the global economy in a system designed to give maximum freedom to the operating units of the global empire and to provide an ideological cover for the advance of capitalist economic and political interests; and
- Projects of regional integration to create free trade zones in the different regions of the US empire.

Each strategy not only served as a pillar of the empire but it also provided the focal point for the projection of state power as circumstances required or permitted. Together they constituted what might be termed the imperialist system. Each element of the system was dynamic in its operations but ultimately unstable and difficult to govern or ungovernable because of the countervailing forces of resistance that they generated in the popular sector of society.

The 1990s saw the advent of a new military form of US empire building, as evidenced by a series of wars in Yugoslavia, Iraq, Afghanistan, and elsewhere. The idea of globalization, used to legitimate and justify neoliberal policies of stabilization and structural reform, had lost its commanding force—its hold over the minds of people, particularly among classes within the popular sector. As a result, the 1990s in Latin America saw the advent and workings of powerful forces of resistance to the neoliberal policy agenda and the machinations of US imperialism. To combat these forces of resistance, state officials resorted to different strategies and tactics as dictated by circumstances, generally by combining development assistance and outright repression (Petras and Veltmeyer, 2003).

How this worked in practice can be illustrated in the case of Paraguay in recent years. In 1996 the then government presided over by Nicanor Duarte decreed as legal the presence of military and paramilitary forces in the countryside because the police were unable to contain the peasant struggle. At the same time and in the same context the regime authorized the presence of American troops, giving them immunity for any violation of the country's laws that might occur in the process of their "humanitarian assistance" (counterinsurgency training) provided to the Paraguayan troops. Leaders of peasant organizations pointed out that some of the nongovernmental organizations (NGOs) operating in the area financed by USAID were also enlisted to provide assistance in controlling the population, to divert the rural poor away from the social movements, and to have them opt for local microdevelopment projects instead. In this sense, what is happening in Paraguay is in the time-honored US tradition of combining the iron fist of armed force with the velvet glove of local development on the front lines of rural poverty.

Installing the New Imperial World Order: The Policy Dynamics of Neoliberal Globalization (Phase I: 1982–1989)

The 1970s was period of transition, serving to set the stage for a new world order. It began with a serious involution in the capitalist world order, a systemic crisis of overproduction, and a major "profit crunch" that put an end to the "golden age" of capitalism. Responses to the crisis included the following: the export to the south of bank capital in the form of loans with variable interest rates, direct investments acquiring strategic lucrative enterprises at bargain basement prices. Financing served as a means of expanding the capacity of these countries to purchase goods manufactured in the north—to open up new markets for these goods. This was combined with a multifaceted assault on labor that resulted in a major change in the relation of capital to labor, and a reduced capacity of the latter to organize and mobilize any forces of resistance.

By 1980, the intense class war that had raged throughout the region, particularly in Central America, had abated and the countryside was pacified. As for labor it was on the defensive. Its leadership was decimated by the US-backed military dictatorships and replaced with trade union officials trained by The American Institute for Free Labor Development (AIFLD), the CIA-financed international arm of the American Federation of Labor and Congress of Industrial Organization (AFL-CIO). Labor's forces were in disarray and its ties to the peasant movement disarticulated. Virtually every government had to deal with a decade-long production crisis and an emerging fiscal crisis, as well as pressures to restore democracy, not so much in the authoritarian form preferred by the United States but as regimes committed to the rule of law and elected civilian administrations responsive to demands from "the people." As for the fiscal crisis, and the detritus of the systemwide production crisis, in the early 1980s it combined with conditions created by the Reagan administration's turn toward a high interest rate policy, and an unfavorable turn in the export markets, to precipitate a decade-long debt crisis and create conditions for the new world order.

Unfortunately for the Nicaraguan revolutionaries these unfavorable conditions coincided with their capture of state power in 1979, provoking the US-organized proxies to launch covert military operations against the revolutionary regime. This would not be the last military adventure of US imperialism. US collaborator regimes pursued economic policies to foment conditions for foreign investment and reactivation of the accumulation process, international cooperation for local development (to demobilize and turn the rural poor away from the social movements), and the co-opting of "civil society" in the responsibility of restoring order—"good (participatory) governance" in the lingo of the "new imperialism."[4]

The emergence of neoconservative regimes in the United States, the United Kingdom, and elsewhere facilitated the implementation of the neoliberal agenda under the Washington Consensus. At the same time the United States adjusted to a growing movement to restore "democracy" by turning away from the resort to armed force and toward the officials of the IMF and the World Bank, essential adjuncts of the imperialist state system, in the project to make Latin America safe for US capital. It would take close to a decade for this to happen. But various developments in the 1990s tell the tale: the privatization of key economic sectors and lucrative state enterprises (Petras and Veltmeyer, 2004); a major influx and reflux of capital, netting the empire, it is estimated (Saxe-Fernández and Nuñez, 2001) more than 100 billion dollars in profit over a decade of neoliberal policies.

The Contras war closed one chapter in US imperialism in Latin America, while the installation of client collaborator regimes opened another—a chapter characterized not by armed force, the projection of military power, but rather by what we might term "economic imperialism"—engineering of free market "structural reforms" in national policy, the penetration of foreign capital in the form of the multinationals, and a free trade regime. The agents of this imperialism included the IMF, the World Bank, and the World Trade Organization (WTO), as well as the host of neoconservative foreign policy advisors, neoliberal economists, and policy makers who serve the "global ruling class" as described by Pilger (2003).

The new imperial order was made possible not only by a political turn toward neoconservatism but by a new reserve of ideological power: the idea of globalization, presented as the only road to "general prosperity," the necessary condition for reactivating a growth and capital accumulation process. The idea of globalization, used to justify the neoliberal "structural adjustment program" (SAP), complemented the call for a new world order. The World Bank's 1995 World Development Report, *Workers in an Integrating World,* can be seen as one of its most important programmatic statements—a capitalist manifesto on the need to adjust to the requirements of a new world order in which the forces of freedom (big business) would be liberated from the regulatory constraints of the welfare-development state and hold sway over the global economy.

Regarding the need for political adjustments to the "new world order," the United States with its client electoral regimes firmly ensconced in power in most of Latin America declared its mission to spread democracy and free markets to make the world safe for freedom, and to support movement in diverse regions toward pro-US electoral regimes.

The stabilization measures and "structural reforms" implemented in the 1990s were unpopular to say the least, with the core opposition coming from pockets of organized labor. A few governments put up some resistance but eventually succumbed, as in Jamaica and Mexico, which were reluctant to sign up for the structural reform agenda. In most cases structural adjustment programs were introduced by presidential decree or administrative fiat. In Latin America, however, the reforms mandated by the Bank and the Fund were implemented by the civilian democratically elected regimes that came to power after the first experiments in military initiated neoliberalism, especially in Chile, crashed and burned in the early 1980s.

The combination of two factors created the conditions for a counterrevolution in development thinking and practice, and a major turn in the tide of electoral and regime politics—from *social* liberalism[5] to conservatism. This political development, represented most clearly in the regime of Ronald Reagan in the United States and Margaret Thatcher in the United Kingdom, combined with the debt crisis, created the political conditions for the new world order called for by the Pelerin Society, a neoliberal thought collective that had financed the construction of a network of politically conservative neoliberal policy forums and thinktanks. The emergence of neoconservative political regimes under conditions of a fiscal crisis in the capitalist west created conditions for a conservative counterrevolution, while the debt crisis in the south created the leverage to compel governments in the region to open up their economies to the world market freed from the regulatory constraints of the welfare-developmental state.

Most countries in the region, notably Mexico, Bolivia, and Jamaica, were brought into line on the basis of a policy consensus manufactured in Washington (Williamson, 1990). Chile—as well as Argentina and Uruguay—in fact pioneered these policy reforms in the 1970s. But in the 1980s, in a context of a generalized global production, fiscal and debt crisis, the economists at the World Bank and the IMF used their leverage over the external debt, and access to capital, to compel the new civilian governments to implement the neoliberal policy program as the price of admission into the new world order, presented and sold as the only road to "general prosperity" (World Bank, 1995).

By the end of the decade most governments in Latin America had turned toward the "new economic model" in conformity with the Washington Consensus. Those governments that had not—particularly Argentina, Peru, and Brazil—would do so in due course, in the subsequent decade, either in terms of the Washington Consensus or on the basis of a new (post-Washington) consensus on the need to bring the state back in. The aim in this post-Washington Consensus was to establish a more inclusive form of development, a more pragmatic form of neoliberalism based on a new social policy targeted at the poor, and a new development paradigm according to which the poor are to be empowered to act for themselves—to take responsibility for their own development (Ocampo, 2006, 2007).

The Golden Age of US Imperialism
(Phase II: 1990–1999)

The 1990s was a decade of major gains for US imperialism in Latin America, at a time in which it was experiencing serious competition and an erosion of economic and political power in other parts of the world. At the same time the 1990s can be viewed as a decade of major gains for the social movements in their resistance to the neoliberal agenda of governments in the region and the operations and machinations of US imperialism. Already in the 1980s, neoliberalism had generated widespread opposition and protest, which in Venezuela resulted in a major social and political crisis—the Caracazo of 1989, in which an estimated 2,000 slum dwellers protesting against the high price of food and IMF policies were massacred. More generally, the deepening of neoliberal policies generated widespread opposition and resistance. By the 1990s this resistance took form as radical movements on the social base of indigenous communities, landless workers, and peasants. The most dynamic of these movements were the Rural Landless Workers Movement in Brazil (MST) and the Confederation of Indigenous Nationalities in Ecuador (CONAIE).

Rural social movements represented the most dynamic forces seeking to reverse the policies of neoliberal globalization and US imperialism. In a number of cases, as in Ecuador, they managed to halt and even reverse the policies implemented under the neoliberal agenda (Petras and Veltmeyer, 2005). In this context it is possible to see the 1990s as the leaders of the indigenous movement saw it: as a decade of major gains for the movements.

However, neoliberalism in these conditions and at this time was not the neoliberalism of the Washington Consensus. Already by the end of the 1980s it was widely recognized by the guardians of the new world order and US imperialism that neoliberalism was economically dysfunctional and ungovernable, generating as it does forces of resistance that could be mobilized against not just the policy framework but also the entire system. The solution, from the perspective of class power and imperial rule, was a more inclusive form of neoliberalism—to give the structural adjustment process a human face via a new social policy targeted at the poor, via self-help organizations and micro politics dubbed "empowerment" (Sandbrook, Edelman, Heller, and Teichman 2007).

Under these political conditions the 1990s gave way to a major shift in the correlation of class forces mobilized for and against neoliberalism.

On the left, the political class was largely on the defensive, unable to make gains under condition of a divided and demobilized working class—and with few ties to the new, principally rural, forces of resistance mobilized by organizations such as the CONAIE. The Left at the time materialized basically in the form of social movements and, to some extent, social organizations for local development that mushroomed paradoxically in the soil of neoliberal policies (Veltmeyer, 2007).

Most political regimes at the time were still aligned with the United States. But the United States, seeking to reverse major setbacks in Asia and other parts of the world, was rapidly losing influence as well as the capacity to dictate policy and to counter the growing power of the social movements in the region. The major exception here was Colombia, where the United States continued with a major military presence, indeed expanding this presence under the pretext of fighting drug lords in the context of the armed struggle against the FARC.

Civilian Rule, Neoliberalism, Economic Stagnation, and the New Social Movements

Prolonged stagnation, popular struggles, and the willingness of civilian politicians in the 1980s to conserve the reactionary structural changes implanted by the dictatorships, hastened the retreat of the military rulers, giving way to what was widely conceived as a "(re) democratization" process. The advent of civilian rule in Uruguay, Brazil, Chile, Bolivia, and Argentina in the 1980s—a process of political liberalization—was accompanied by an extension and deepening of neoliberal "structural reforms" in macroeconomic policy under the "Washington Consensus," the price of admission exacted by the architects of the "new world order." This was spelled out in the putative "Washington Consensus" and was integral to the world order of neoliberal globalization called for by neoconservative thinktanks and foundations such as the Heritage Foundation and members of the neoliberal thought collective behind them.

Although the new neoliberal order failed to reactivate the accumulation process, it did nevertheless facilitate the pillage of thousands of public enterprises, their privatization and denationalization. At the same time the massive outflow of profits, interest payments, and royalties, and the growing exploitation and impoverishment of the working people led to the growth of new sociopolitical movements throughout the 1990s (see chapter 4). The most powerful of these movements were organized within and on the basis of indigenous communities that understood capitalism as imperialism, an uninterrupted process of more than 500 years of exploitation, oppression, and genocidal subjection in the face of their proud resistance.

In the context of a neoliberal state that had retreated from the provision of welfare and responsibility for development a new generation of "nongovernmental organizations'" expressions of an emerging "civil society," flourished. Billions of dollars flowed into the accounts of the NGOs from "private" foundations and the development associations that joined forces in a project of "international cooperation." The World Bank and US and EU overseas agencies viewed the NGOs as integral not only to their development strategy (to alleviate excessive poverty) but also to their counterinsurgency strategy—as strategic partners in the fight against international communism and the forces of social revolution.

A substantial number (by no means all) of the social activists who were embedded in the NGO-funded feminist, ecology, self-help groups, and the development NGOs, colluded with the agents of a more inclusive and sustainable form of development in opposing the demand of the social movements for structural change in the direction of "another world" of communalism and radical egalitarianism if not socialism. At issue in this collaboration is a coincidence of interest in a nonconfrontational approach to social change—to bring about a better world without the agency of class struggle and a violent confrontation with the agents of imperial power and class rule.

In this context, the NGO-connected advocates of the "new Left" referred to the forces for progressive change as the *"new social movements,"* which in theory served to press for progressive change but in practice worked to undermine the emerging class-based anti-imperialist movements of the indigenous communities, peasants, landless workers, and unemployed workers. These class-based mass movements emerged in response to the imperial pillage of their natural resources and naked land grabs by powerful elites in the agromineral export sectors with the full support of voracious neoliberal regimes.

By the end of the 1990s, neoliberal pillage throughout Latin America had reached its paroxysm. Billions of dollars were siphoned and transferred out of the region—especially Ecuador, Mexico, Venezuela, and Argentina—into overseas banks and the accounts of multinational corporations. Saxe-Fernández and Núñez (2001) estimate that the operations of the multinational banks and financial institutions resulted in a net transfer of US$100 billion from the region to the center of the imperial system. Table 1.1AB presents in tabular form some of the dynamics of this pillage.

Table 1.1A Capital inflows and outflows (net), Latin America 1985–2002 ($US billions)

	1985–90	91–92	93	94	95	96	97	98	99	00	01	02
Capital Inflows	–	105	124	126	67	99	104	109	97	97	83	50
Overseas Development Assistance (ODA)	38	10	5	6	6	6	-9	11	2	11	20	13
Private Flows	95	118	120	116	75	99	106	82	94	69	64	–
FDI[a]	43	29	17	29	32	44	66	73	88	76	69	42
Portfolio[b]	–	45	74	63	5	12	13	-2	-4	2	1	–
Loans	42	44	28	24	38	33	27	11	10	-9	-6	–
Returns to Capital	142	74	73	79	79	83	99	108	91	100	97	99
Profit on Assets	–	62	35	37	41	43	48	51	52	53	55	53
Interest payments[c]	211	76	38	35	36	35	33	46	54	35	43	42
Royalty payments[d]	5	2	1	2	2	12	2	2	2	2	2	–
Net Resource Transfer	-150	31	51	46	46	16	5	1	6	-3	-14	-49
Accumulated capital stock Debt	420	480	520	564	619	641	667	748	764	741	728	725
FDI	–	–	168	186	226	321	375	397	191	207	216	270

Sources: ECLAC, 1998; UNCTAD, 1998: 256, 267–268, 362; 2002; US Dept. of Commerce (1994); World Bank (1997). Data on FDI stock 1999–2001 is for United States only (US Census Bureau, US Direct Investment Position Abroad on a Historical Cost Basis, 2002).

[a]In 2005 and 2006 net FDI inflows were around US$73 billion, but it shot up to $106 billion in 2007, almost a third of it—($34,6 billion— accounted for by Brazil, which was almost double that of the year before) (ECLAC, 2007: 72).

[b]Data are redrawn from World Bank, Global Development Finance-2002, Statistical Appendix, Table 20.

[c]Data re "returns to capital" and drawn from World Bank, Global Development Finance-External Debt of Developing Countries, 2000, 2002. For 2003–2005 the data on capital inflows were drawn from World Bank, Global Development Finance 2006, Statistical Appendix.

[d]Data are redrawn from World Bank, World Development Indicators, 2002.

Table 1.1B   Capital inflows and outflows (net), Latin America 2003–2008 ($US billions)

	02	03	04	05	06	07	08
Capital Inflows	50	139	118	138	131	183	178
ODA	13	23	14	12	15	13	19
Private Flows	–	116	104	126	116	170	159
FDI (net)[a]	42	38	50	55	31	86	92
Portfolio[b]	–	−0.5	−0.6	12	11	30	−9.7
Loans	–	38	41	42	33	31	44
Returns to Capital	99	–	–	90	122	135	141
Profit on Assets	–	23	37	53	77	90	94
Interest payments[c]	–	54	40	41	46	48	46
Royalty payments[d]	–	–	–	2.9	3.6	4.1	4.9
Other capital movements	51	38	50	55	31	86	92
Total external debt	–	776	772	676	663	752	779
Net Resource Transfer[e]	−41	−40	−69	−81	−98	12	−39
Accumulated Debt	614	662	619	625	684	735	

Sources: ECLAC, 1998; UNCTAD, 1998: 256, 267–268, 362; 2002; US Dept. of Commerce (1994); World Bank (1997). Data on FDI stock 1999–2001 is for United States only (US Census Bureau, *US Direct Investment Position Abroad on a Historical Cost Basis*, 2002).

[a]*Source*: ECLAC (2009), "Economic Survey of LA and the Caribbean," *Briefing Paper* 2008–2009. ECLAC. Tables A.14. In 2005 and 2006 net FDI inflows were around US$73 billion, but it shot up to $106 billion in 2007, almost a third of it—($34,6 billion—accounted for by Brazil, which was almost double that of the year before) (ECLAC, 2007: 72).
[b]Data are redrawn from World Bank, *Global Development Finance- 2002, Statistical Appendix*, Table 20.
[c]Data on "returns to capital" and are drawn from World Bank, *Global Development Finance-*External Debt of Developing Countries, 2002, 2010. For 2003–2005 the data on capital inflows were drawn from World Bank, *Global Development Finance 2006, Statistical Appendix*.
[d]Data are redrawn from World Bank, *World Development Indicators*, 2010 (the thirteen major countries in the region).
[e]Data are drawn from ECLAC (2009), "Economic Survey of Latin America and the Caribbean," *Briefing Paper 2008–2009*.

The table 1.1 points to a massive hemorrhage of financial resources, and associated weak levels of economic growth and capital formation,[6] brought on by diverse forms of "official and private capital inflows" (FDI, portfolio investments, bank loans and ODA, which is often extended with higher rates of interest than commercial bank loans). Without mentioning the enormous pillage of "natural" resources associated with the operations of the empire's multinational corporations, facilitated by the neoliberal policies of the governments in the region, the pillage of financial resources documented by Saxe-Fernández for the 1990s, and by table 1.1AB for the next phase of capitalist development and imperialism (see the following text), can be traced back to the reverse flows of capital attached to the inflow of foreign investment and bank loans, and other forms of capital movements: debt repayment; repatriation of profits derived from accumulated assets; interest payments on portfolio investments; and royalty charges. Table 1.1AB documents a net financial resource outflow of US$500 billion from 2002 to 2008, in addition to the $100 billion identified by Saxe-Fernández. And these calculations do not consider the even larger outflow of capital hidden in the free trade process of unequal exchange and in what Delgado Wise and James Cypher (2005) refer to as exploitation via the "exportation of labour."

This pillage was facilitated by a Washington-engineered neoliberal policy consensus, which, to all intents and purposes is intact notwithstanding the ongoing efforts to give neoliberal structural reform (structural adjustment) a human face by incessant reference (and both a relevant academic and policy discourse) to the "post-Washington consensus." Over the course of these neoliberal "structural reforms" (privatization, deregulation, liberalization, etc.) thousands of lucrative state-owned enterprises were "privatized"—and many of them denationalized—at prices set far below their real value, handed over to, or purchased by, a select group of private US and EU-based multinational corporations and local regime cronies. Enormous fortunes were made in the process, including that of Carlos Slim, a Mexican "financier" and business tycoon who over the years has produced nothing of material value but today ranks as one of the richest men in the world. Much of the capital that flowed into Latin America over these years was unproductive in that it was not invested in new technologies to expand production but used to purchase the assets of existing lucrative privatized state enterprises.

The blatant looting and the predictable economic collapse and crisis provoked a wave of popular uprisings, which led to the overthrow of incumbent elected neoliberal officials and administrations in Ecuador (three times), Argentina (successfully three times), and Bolivia (twice). In addition, a massive popular uprising, in alliance with a constitutionalist sector of the military, restored Chávez to power in Venezuela. During this period mass movements flourished and numerous center-left politicians, claiming allegiance to these movements and denouncing "neoliberalism," achieved state power by riding the popular wave of disenchantment with neoliberalism and using the trappings of liberal "democracy."

A downturn in the economy and a repudiation of neoliberalism marked the emergence of the social movements as major players in shaping the contours of Latin American politics. These political developments included the emergence of new social actors and forces of change and the continuing decline of the trade unions as the leading protagonist of structural change.

From Crisis to Crisis: US Imperialism in the New Millennium (Phase III: 2000–2010)

The 1980s opened with a regionwide debt crisis of historic proportions—and, in Chile, a major production crisis derived directly from a decade of experimentation with neoliberalism. The Chilean economy had collapsed, recording a fall of 20 percent in national output, the doubling of an historic unemployment rate and a massive bailout of the big banks valued at 6 percent of the GDP. Over the course of the decade, within the institutional framework of a new world order of free market capitalism, the heavily indebted governments in the region were constrained by the World Bank and the IMF, acting in tandem, to channel more than 50 percent of their export earnings into debt repayment as opposed to investing them productively. The result was described as "a decade lost to development"—a decade of no growth.

According to ECLAC the 1990s fared little better, despite a massive infusion of private foreign capital. ECLAC even raised the specter of another decade, or half a decade, "lost to development." The context for this pessimistic prognosis was a persistent trend of sluggish to slow growth, punctuated by outbreaks of financial and economic crisis, first in Mexico (December 1994 and 1995), then in Brazil and Argentina (in 1998). By the new millennium, in 2001, the crisis plunged a number of countries into a political crisis as well. In Argentina, conditions of the economic and political crisis, which included an official unemployment rate of 24 percent (over 30 percent in major urban centers), led to the organized resistance of the urban unemployed workers, giving rise to a social movement of "desocupados"—*piqueteros*, so named because of the tactic of highway blockades used to force the government into negotiations (Petras and Veltmeyer, 2002).

In 2003, some of the countries beset by crisis found a new road to economic recovery in a propitious turn in the global economy—an urgent and growing demand for primary commodities fuelled by the dynamics of economic growth in Asia. Against a backdrop of two decades and a half of neoliberal reform, instability, and exceedingly sluggish growth—growth that barely averaged 0.5 percent a year from 1981 to 2002—the regional economy, according to ECLAC (2007), posted its best performance in forty years. Some countries grew at rates around 8–9 percent from 2003 to 2008 (table 1.2).

By different accounts, the economic recovery and five-year growth spurt can be attributed almost entirely to the ascension of China (and India) in the global economy.[7] Some countries, especially those dependent on the export of raw materials, agroproducts, and minerals in commodity form,[8] rode a five-year primary commodities boom fuelled by the explosive demand in China for energy, minerals, and other industrial inputs—and middle-class consumer goods. Over the course of this boom, the rate of economic growth in the region increased from an average of 0.6 percent in 1996 and barely 1 percent in 2002 to a regional average of 6.2 percent in 2004, 5.5 percent in 2005, and 5.6 percent in 2006. For the countries in South America that led the boom, the economic recovery and rate of sustained growth from 2003 to 2007 was even greater, ranging from 8.3 percent in Argentina and 8.0 in Venezuela to 6.3 in Peru, 3.9 in Bolivia—and, in a different systemic context, 9.0 in Cuba.[9]

In 2008 this primary commodities boom went bust, caught up as it was in the vortex of a financial and economic crisis of global proportions. The initial response to the crisis, at the level of the state, was to deny it—as in the case of Mexico's President Felipe Calderón,

Table 1.2 Growth rates of GDP (percent), selected countries Latin America, 1995–2007

	1995	2000	2003	2004	2005	2006	2007
Argentina	−2.1	4.8	8.8	9.0	9.2	8.5	8.6
Bolivia	4.9	2.5	2.7	4.2	4.0	4.6	3.8
Brazil	4.2	4.3	1.1	5.7	2.9	3.7	5.3
Chile	10.6	4.5	3.9	6.0	5.7	4.0	5.3
Colombia	5.2	2.9	4.6	4.7	5.7	6.8	7.0
Cuba	–	3.8	5.4	11.8	12.5	7.0	–
Ecuador	1.8	2.8	3.6	8.0	6.0	3.9	2.7
Mexico	−6.2	6.6	1.4	4.2	2.8	4.8	3.3
Peru	8.6	3.0	4.0	5.1	6.7	7.6	8.2
Venezuela	4.0	3.7	−7.8	18.3	10.3	10.3	8.5
LA	0.6	3.9	2.1	6.2	4.7	5.5	5.6

Source: ECLAC (2007: 85).

who argued (at Davos, to the assembled elite of world capitalism) that Mexico and Latin America generally were more or less insulated from this particular virus, and that it could ride out the storm. Ironically, Calderón headed the most vulnerable economy in the region vis-à-vis the epicenter of the crisis. As for Mexico itself, Calderón's public pronouncement did nothing to soothe tempers back home where economists were predicting the loss of at least 500,000 jobs in a contracting economy—at least 175,000 in the first half of 2009. By mid-March, the estimate of Mexico's GNP growth for 2009 was reduced from -1.5 percent to -3 percent.[10] By December the estimated degree of shrinkage of the economy was increased to 7.5 percent.

Other Latin American governments were not so quick to discount the effects of the crisis on the regional and local economies, even though the initial response of many, in the last quarter of 2008 and even into 2009, was the belief that their country could ride out the crisis on the basis of relatively high reserves of foreign currency and relatively healthy (reduced) levels of short-term debt. This was particularly so for those countries in South America that rode the wave of the primary commodities boom on the world market that ended in recession to the dismay of both the agro-elites and the governments who had substantially benefited from the boom in the form of higher prices, windfall profits, and increased fiscal revenues.

Uruguay at the time managed to weather the global storm, tacking with the winds of change to post a surprisingly "robust" growth rate of 11 percent over the course of the year preceding the elections that brought to power another group of center-leftist politicians. But if the economists at ECLAC (2009a) and the participants in a January 19–21, 2009, colloquium on the "Global Crisis and Latin America" in Mexico, were correct in their assessment and prognosis, the leaders of the other countries in the region had no reason to be sanguine in the face of the apparent failure of the G-8 to solve the crisis at the epicenter of the system.

According to ECLAC (2009a) the responses made by Latin American governments would not elude the crisis but would suffice to ameliorate its impact. Even those who benefited from the primary commodities boom and were careful not to overspend or to cut short-term debt on the global market and to build-up reserves of hard currency went into recession. The economists who gathered in Mexico City to analyze what the crisis might mean established that no country in the region would be safe from the maelstrom of the global crisis, notwithstanding what the *Economist* saw as Latin America's "valiant efforts" to manage the crisis. The *Economist* had put Mexico, Brazil, Argentina, and Venezuela among the nations most likely to fall, although it was the private sector, rather than the governments, in these countries that confronted the greatest challenges.[11] Governments and capitalists in the private sector, it turned out, either still had a high amount of short-term debt as a percentage of total reserves, or their bank loans as a percentage of total deposits were at risk with the impending credit squeeze.[12]

In any case, Latin America, according to the Washington Office of ECLAC, certainly felt the brunt of the crisis, primarily at the level of the market with a credit crunch, a slowdown in capital inflows and a dramatic decline in portfolio investment flows, large declines in stock price indexes (the destruction of up to $220 billion in the value of financial assets), significant currency adjustments, and an increase in debt spreads. Latin America's GDP projected growth for 2009 declined from 3.6 percent in September 2008 to 1.4 percent in December 2008 (*Financial Times,* January 9, 2009). In reality, Latin America's GDP per capita fell to –2 percent.

As a result bankruptcies increased, and state spending on social programs and services declined, pushing an estimated nine million people in the region back into poverty.[13] State credit and subsidies to big banks and businesses also increased. Unemployment expanded, especially in the agromineral and transport (automobile) export sectors. Public employees were discharged and experienced a sharp decline in wages. Latin America's external financial flows suffered the loss of billions of dollars and euros in declining remittances from overseas workers. Foreign speculators withdrew tens of billions of investment dollars to cover their losses in the United States and Europe. Foreign disinvestment replaced "new foreign investment," eliminating a major source of financing for major "joint ventures."

According to the IMF, 40 percent of Latin America's financial wealth (2,200 billion dollars) was lost in 2008 and 2009, because of the decline of the stock market and other asset markets and currency depreciation. This decline reduced domestic spending by 5 percent in 2009. Latin America's terms of trade deteriorated as commodity prices fell sharply, making imports more expensive and raising the specter of growing trade deficits.[14] The onset of the recession in Latin America was evidenced by the 6.2 percent fall in Brazil's industrial output in November 2008 and its accelerating negative momentum.[15] As a result, Latin America experienced a delayed entry into a period of profound and likely prolonged recession without, it would seem, any serious plan or program to counteract its destructive impact.

As a result of these "developments" governments in the region— regardless of ideological complexion but particularly those like Chile, Peru, and Colombia that are particularly "open" and dependent on the flow of foreign direct investment—took defensive action to protect their domestic markets and to minimize their exposure to this deadly virus by means of diverse "counter-cyclical policies to buffer the impact of the crisis."[16] But thus far this policy response has been to little avail.

Governments in the region were not the only organizations to respond strategically to the global crisis. Nor did all governments respond in the same way. Sectors of the intellectual and social Left, and popular sector organizations that bring together unions, diverse social organizations, and the social movements throughout the region, conducted their own analysis of what the global crisis means. As they saw it—and there is a virtual consensus on this (at least at this level)—although production had been "financialized," the crisis reflected the demise of neoliberalism as an ideology and as a model used to guide government policy. Further, although the crisis assumed multiple and diverse forms, it was primarily a production rather than a financial crisis, bringing with it a massive loss of jobs, the erosion of incomes and pensions wrapped up in capitalist financial institutions, the cutback of essential government services and the lack of access (affordability) to food—problems that in different contexts are reaching crisis proportions with disastrous social effects.[17]

Conclusion

US imperialism has shaped the major conditions for capitalist development or underdevelopment in Latin America, through direct military intervention and through proxies. Between and against these imperial intrusions, popular movements based on labor, peasants, and unionized public employees have succeeded in electing leftist and center-left governments, and in the case of Cuba, Nicaragua, and Grenada carrying out social revolutions.

The outcomes of these epic struggles had enormous socioeconomic and political consequences in terms of the economic models that subsequently emerged. The great alterations in income and class inequalities, concentrations to wealth and property, popular participation and representation, individual freedoms and social rights have been profoundly affected by the strength and ascendancy of these two determinant forces in Latin America's equation of power.

The rise of neoliberalism and the regressive socioeconomic patterns that dominated the region from the 1970s to the 1990s were, in the first instance, the result of the violent political triumph of the United States and its Latin allies over the working class in the great social confrontations of the 1970s. The defeat of labor laid the groundwork for the implementation of the neoliberal agenda and set the stage for the rise of rural based social movements as the motor force for social transformations.

2

Capitalist Development, Labor, and the Rural Poor: The Politics of Adjustment (Nonresistance)

The forces presumed to be operating on rural society in the 1960s and 1970s, and impoverishing them in the process, were by numerous accounts bringing about the transformation of a society of small-scale agricultural producers or peasant farmers into a working class. As noted earlier, this process was conceptualized in various ways. Marxist scholars theoretically constructed the process as "primitive accumulation" (the separation of the direct producer from the land and other means of production) proletarianization, construction of the working class working class. Non-Marxist scholars, however, operating with a theory of capitalist modernization, analyzed the same dynamics with a different language (but even so not altogether differently), by reference to a process that would see the disappearance of the peasantry as an economic agent or as a category of economic or political analysis.

In the 1970s this view of structural change, shared by both Marxists and non-Marxists in a structural form of analysis, gave way to a heated debate between "proletarianists," adherents of Marx's thesis of the "multiplication of the proletariat," and "peasantists," who argued that the forces of change were by no means immutable and that resistance by the peasants could even defuse or derail these forces, allowing the peasants to survive and sustain their rural livelihoods.[1] After a hiatus of some years, essentially a decade and a half of neoliberal reform, this debate was renewed in the study of a "new rurality" as well as of the dynamic forces of resistance against the neoliberal agenda mounted by the landless workers, the indigenous communities, and peasant or small producer organizations in the 1990s (Kay, 2008).

Although, by several accounts (e.g., ours) this wave of active resistance has subsided, the debate continues, some arguing in favor of the trend toward the inevitable disappearance of the peasantry, others the contrary.

Agriculture for Development: A Pathway out of Rural Poverty?

A recent formulation of development as capitalist modernization and the elimination of the peasantry is provided by the economists at the World Bank in its 2008 *World Development Report* (hereinafter WDR-08). It focused on "agriculture for development" and diverse "pathways out of (rural) poverty." As the economists at the bank conceive of it, "development" is a protracted but incessant process of *structural* change. At issue (in the bank's structural analysis) is a process of productive and social transformation (*modernization, capitalist development*—and *urbanization*, rather than *industrialization*, as in the earlier formulations of this modernization theory), which provides a way out of poverty.

In this view, the agency and politics of capitalist development is entirely abstracted from analysis. The destruction in the 1960s and 1970s, in Mexico and elsewhere, of the forces of production in both industry and agriculture, leading to a massive exodus from the countryside and the impoverishment of many that remained, appeared to be the result of "structural" forces beyond human control rather than the actions and agency of capital in search of profit.

Similarly, in the 1990s the unconditional opening of the Mexican economy required by the North American Free Trade Agreement (NAFTA) served not only to consolidate neoliberalism—and increase popular discontent with the structural adjustment measures—but also led to the resulting bankruptcy of the countryside and the exodus of millions of *peasants* and unemployed Mexicans to the United States, as analyzed so eloquently by Armando Bartra (2005), revealed NAFTA's "heads I win, tails you lose" deal: "export bankrupted farmers and import agricultural products." Even more seriously, the dispossession of small producers led to the massive growth of recruits for the lucrative illicit drug trafficking business, eventually penetrating the entire state apparatus. The "lumpenization" process was one route out of poverty that the World Bank failed to anticipate, although its consequences ravage Mexican society. Moreover, the issue of the transition from lumpen to lumpen as of yet has barely entered the debates on agrarian transformation.

As the WDR-08 has it—by abstracting from its analysis all issues of agency and politics, presenting capitalist development as a process advanced by structural forces—there are fundamentally only three pathways out of poverty, requiring each individual or family to adjust to (and not resist) the forces of change operating on the rural poor. These pathways are: *farming, labor, and migration.*

As for farming or agricultural activity, it evidently provides a pathway out of poverty for very few in that it requires the transformation of the small-scale "peasant" producer into a capitalist entrepreneur to access credit, markets, and technology, and to mobilize the available productive resources. The driving force behind this transformation is capitalist development of agriculture, which entails both a concentration of landholding and a technological conversion of production based on a significant increase in the rate of productive investment (in modernizing or upgrading production technology).

The pressures on farming to increase the productivity of agricultural labor via technological upgrading or modernization (increasing the capital intensity of production) are immense. However, agricultural activity under these conditions is clearly not an option for the vast majority of peasants, who are encouraged when not compelled to abandon the farm and for many also the countryside to migrate in the search of better opportunities for self-advancement or productive economic activity.

Thus there are essentially two remaining pathways out of poverty, according to the economists behind the report. One is labor—to work off-farm or in the cities for wages—a strategy that by many accounts large numbers of the rural poor have and are continuing to pursue, if the statistics on rural household incomes are any indication (more than 50 percent acquire more than half of their income from non-farming activities, i.e., off-farm wage labor).

The other pathway out of poverty is migration, a route or exit-path that by numerous accounts many of the rural poor have opted for by migrating either to the urban centers or to the cities, or further abroad. In Bolivia, it is estimated that at least 40 percent of the population now lives outside the country. And the same applies to Mexico. It is estimated that in the wake of the 1995 crisis, over five million Mexicans migrated. The theory behind this "development" (migration as a pathway out of poverty) is that the countryside is a massive reservoir of surplus labor, and that the opportunity for wage-remunerated labor in the cities would attract and pull the displaced rural proletariat into the cities, absorbing them into the labor force of an expanding capitalist nucleus of urban-based industry.

The theory behind this development took various forms but was first constructed as a model by Arthur Lewis.[2] However, research into the dynamics of this rural-to-urban migration suggests, and later studies have confirmed, that the outcome of the forces of change did not conform to this theory. In the 1980s the nucleus of capitalist industry did not expand, generating an enormous supply of migrant labor surplus to the absorptive capacity of the urban labor market, and leading instead to the growth of a burgeoning informal sector of unregulated or unstructured economic activity—not, as projected, work for wages in industrial plants, factories, mines, and offices, but labor in the form of self-employed work in the streets: microenterprises in the view of Hernando de Soto (1989).

It was estimated that in the 1980s and into the 1990s anywhere from 80 to 90 percent of new jobs and employment "opportunities" in the growing urban economies in the region were generated in the "informal sector," which in many countries absorbed and accounted for at least 40 percent of the urban economically active population. As Mike Davis (2006) documented, and analyzed on the basis of a Marxist theory of surplus labor, this new urban proletariat is associated with the growth of a "planet of slums" in the periurban areas, with a floating surplus population that has one foot in the urban economy and the other in the rural communities.

The notion that labor and migration constitute effective pathways out of rural poverty is based on the belief, deeply embedded in the modernization theory that dominated analysis and policy in the 1950s and the 1970s and evidently shared by World Bank economists even today, that

- The dominant form of agricultural production, the small-scale agricultural producer or peasant farmer, is economically backward, marginal, and unproductive;
- The peasant economy of small-scale localized production is a drag on development;
- Capital invested in urban-based industry has a considerably greater return, with much greater multiplier-effects on production and employment, than a comparable investment in agriculture;
- Development requires, and is predicated on, a modernization process of structural transformation—of agriculture into industry and the peasantry into a working class;

- Rural society and agriculture in this process serve development as a reservoir of labor surplus to the requirements of capitalist development and modernization;
- Farming opportunities for the rural poor, most of whom are engaged in relatively unproductive economic activities and are either landless or near landless, are scarce and restricted either because the limits of land reform have been reached or because of the requirements of capitalist modernization (large or increased-scale production, capital-intensive technology, external inputs, access to markets, etc.);
- Many of the rural poor who retain some access to land are compelled to turn toward wage labor as a source of livelihood and household income; and
- Because of the economic and social structure of agricultural production there are simply too many people in rural society chasing too few opportunities for productive economic activity. Thus, farming provides few "opportunities" for the rural poor to change and improve their situation—to escape or alleviate their poverty.

The combination of these ideas led many economists and sociologists—including, as it turns out, the authors and consultants behind and associated with the WDR-08—to view the peasantry by and large as an anachronism, seeking desperately, and futilely, to defend a way of life, and an economy, that is inherently not viable, entrenching them in a poverty trap. The best, if not precisely the only pathway out of this dilemma is to abandon farming and migrate in search of wage-labor employment opportunities and inclusion in government services, also more accessible in the cities and urban centers. However, not a single World Bank study has identified and explored the actual path taken by many unemployed rural youths out of poverty, who are joining the fast-growing lumpen gangs engaged in the well-paying drug trade.

The Structural and Policy Dynamics of Labor Reform

The World Bank, the Organisation for Economic Co-operation and Development (OECD), and other international organizations, policymakers, and academics in numerous reports have addressed a perceived need for labor to adjust to the requirements of the new economic order—to become more flexible.[3] The rationale for this policy agenda is that labor either adjusts to these requirements or it will confront a worsening of the problems that afflict workers—unemployment, economic insecurity, bad jobs, and low income. In this context, these and many other organizations have taken up the banner of labor and labor-market reform—of a mandated or legislated restructuring of "industrial relations" and associated labor markets, the organizations of labor (regime of labor regulation) in production.

This entire process of labor reform, we argue, together with the ideological battle of convincing labor to go along with and adjust to it (on this see the World Bank's 1995 *World Development Report*) is part of an offensive waged by capital against labor, based on an agenda that reflects the interests of capital, and thus to be opposed and resisted at all costs.

Latin American Labor in a Global Context

According to the World Bank, about 99 percent of the workers projected to join the world's labor market over the next thirty years will live and work in what it terms the "low- and middle-income" countries of Africa, Asia, the Caribbean, and Latin America (the latter currently constituting about 8.4 percent of the world's economically active population; 6.1 percent of production; and 3.9 percent of exports and 3.2 percent of imports, down from 12 and 10.1 percent in 1950).[4]

The bank claims that the shift toward globalization is irresistible but there is no discernible trend toward convergence—toward equality in the form and conditions of such integration among countries, or between the comparatively small number of relatively well-off workers and the much larger number of poor workers across the world. Indeed, the bank argues, there are serious "risks that the workers in [the] poorer countries will fall further behind," and that some national groups of workers, especially in sub-Saharan Africa but also in Latin America, could be marginalized in a global process that is leading to an increase in "the general prosperity in countries that are enjoying growth" (World Bank, 1995: 6).

The only preventative remedy—and means of participating in the projected global dynamic of rising incomes, better working conditions, and enhanced job security—is for all countries to systematically pursue the sound policies that promote labor-demanding economic growth. Such policies, the bank notes, involve "the use of markets to create opportunities," and legislation designed to create more flexible forms of labor and labor markets.

Flexibility on the part of workers means greater mobility—the capacity to relocate or migrate if necessary—and a willingness to accept whatever jobs are on offer, with possibly lower levels of remuneration; and, on the part of employers, increased capacity to participate in the production process; to hire, fire, locate, and use workers as required at the point of production; and to pay them on the basis of market conditions.

With explicit reference to this idea—of a labor market in which the forces of supply and demand can and do reach equilibrium, providing an optimum allocation of resources (returns to factors of production)—World Bank officials in the 1990s stalked the corridors of political power in the search for policymakers with the political will, and the institutional capacity, to introduce a program of legislative (and, if necessary, constitutional) labor reforms. Associated with this agenda was the notion that in general wages were too high, the result of government interference in the labor market (particularly in the legislation of minimum wages) and the excessive power of the unions. As the bank saw it—and argued with as much technical support and data it could muster—high wage rates, the excessive benefits accorded workers in the social programs introduced by earlier populist governments, and the inflexibility of workers led private sector "entrepreneurs" to withdraw from the production process, contributing toward the problems of high unemployment, informalization, and poverty.

How did Latin American policy-makers and governments respond to this pressure? First, as noted in chapter 1, governments implemented a neoliberal program of "structural reforms" that created the preconditions and an institutional framework for the proposed new labor policy, the material conditions of which were formed on the basis of an ongoing process of technological conversion and productive transformation. The governments that had not done so in the 1980s all came around in the 1990s in a third round of neoliberal reforms.

With reference to these "reforms," the entrepreneurs and employers of labor joined the financiers—and the World Bank—in demanding further labor reforms and, where required (as in Brazil), the constitutional amendments required to allow and secure greater flexibility of labor markets.

In some cases, as in Mexico and El Salvador, the new labor regime was established within the export enclave of an expanding maquiladora industry. In other cases, as in Chile, the new labor regime was introduced in a process of industrial conversion and productive transformation.[5] In each case, the process of structural adjustment and productive transformation was accompanied by a political struggle to introduce via legislative reform, executive decree, or administrative fiat a more flexible form of production and corresponding labor regime. At the time of this writing, the electrical workers of Mexico (Sindicato Mexicano de Electricistas), one of the most powerful and militant Mexican unions in the struggle against neoliberalism is engaged in a seemingly losing battle with the neoliberal PAN regime of Felipe Calderón. More than 40,000 workers were fired, and despite strikes, marches, and other peaceful protests, the government prevailed, setting the stage for another sellout of public utilities to private investors.

Labor Market Reform: Toward a New Regime of Accumulation

The basic idea advanced in the World Bank's 1995 *World Development Report*, widely diffused in various publications and numerous conferences staged and sponsored by the bank and its sister institutions, and underlying the plans for economic and social development introduced in country after country as of around 1989, is that the solution to the region's problems, particularly that of unemployment, requires a new and more flexible mode of organizing production, as well as legislative (and perhaps constitutional) reform leading to an increased flexibility of labor.

In Latin America as elsewhere, the bank argues, government regulation of labor was designed primarily as an instrument of social policy, above all to secure and protect the right to full employment, adequate and minimum wages, and secure tenure. In practice, such legislation, particularly as relates to minimum wages, rather than serving as it should, as a means of achieving an efficient allocation of resources, has produced a most inefficient and inflexible labor market in which the demand for labor has not been able to keep up with its supply, resulting in, among other things, an unmanageable and costly problem (in economic and social—as well as political—terms) of high unemployment and the increasing informalization of work arrangements and conditions.[6]

The strategic response of the bank to this problem reflects its concern that "at the world level [as well as in the region] there exists a serious [problem] with unemployment and informality"—that governments need to reform their labor codes to ensure a greater flexibility of labor (and thereby the reduction of labor costs in production and the generation of more and better employment).[7] The problem, as the bank saw and sees it, was and is twofold. On the one hand, minimum wage legislation distorted the proper functioning of the labor market, leading to the withdrawal of capital from the production process, and thus unemployment as well as informalization. On the other hand, it was necessary to reduce or suppress the monopolistic bargaining power acquired by labor through its sector-wide "representative unions" so that entrepreneurs and workers could arrive at and arrange independent agreements in accord with market conditions and requirements.[8] And one of the key requirements, the bank made clear, was that the lowering of excessive wages in the productive and public sectors of the economy, and of the associated benefits legislated by government, which inhibits the participation of capital in the production process.

The effective response to these requirements and the solution to the underlying and associated problems was labor market reform, to make labor more flexible. Such reform was placed on the political agenda of most countries in the region at the turn into the 1990s, in a third cycle of neoliberal policies. Labor reform was added to a policy of technological conversion / productive transformation, a new social policy designed by the World Bank to soften the blow of "structural reform" on the poor,[9] the decentralization of government (to create a more participatory form of community-based development),[10] and the modernization of the state apparatus (to create a more efficient and democratic system of public service and administration).[11]

The Capital-Labor Relation in the Production Process

The most distinctive feature of the World Bank economists' view of the labor reform process and of the policy measures needed to bring it about is the lack of any theoretical justification, a total inability to explain the apparent "structural" forces at play—forces generated by the very policies advocated by the bank; their apparent political innocence in pressing these policies on government officials, posing as agents of national development. We elaborate on this point below, but it is evident that the bank's labor reform policies, just as the other policies in the neoliberal package, is designed to advance a process of capital accumulation, not national development. Indeed, it is evident that these policies are designed to advance and accelerate the destruction of the forces of national production in the region, to separate the direct producers from their means of social production and proletarianize them, to generate a reservoir of surplus labor. That this process seems to have stalled in the creation of a large semi-proletariat—neither, or both, a working class and a land-connected peasantry—is not (as the World Bank economists imagine or prefer to think) due to the failure of governments in the region to proceed systematically with a policy of labor reform. It has to do, rather, with changes in the relation of labor to capital induced by these reforms under available conditions of capital accumulation.

The change in the relation of capital to labor wrought by the reform process (neoliberal policies) can be traced out on both the structural and political level. In structural terms, the change relates to (1) the organization of labor within a process of technological conversion and what ECLAC (1990) terms "productive transformation"; (2) the contribution of labor to production as measured by its productivity; (3) the rate of exploitation (extraction of surplus value) as measured by the share of profit and wages in national income and value added; and (4) the evolution of real wages relative to growth in the Gross National Product (GNP).

In regard to productive transformation, regulated by the rate of investment and the pace of technological conversion, significant advances have been made in key production sectors and industries in a number of countries, particularly Argentina, Brazil, Chile, Colombia, and Mexico (CEPAL, 1990; Boom and Mercado, 1990; Morales, 1992; and UNIDO, 1992).

The pace of advance in this transformation has been both conditioned and limited by the generally low levels of productive investment, which generally reflect relations of "dependency"—the dependency of countries in the region on foreign capital. Chile is the only country in the region that has had what would appear to be an adequate level of productive investment comparable to levels found in the expanding economies of East and Southeast Asia. Table 2.1 indicates this for some countries in the region over the first two decades of capitalist development under the neoliberal policy umbrella.

Another critical factor in the regional process of productive transformation is the relative contribution of capital and labor and the impact of what in the modern theory of growth is termed "total factor productivity."[12]

Table 2.1 Levels of capital formation—investment as a percent of GNP, 1980–2008, Selected countries

	1980	1990	2000	2008
Argentina	25.3	14.0	19.9	23
Brazil	23.3	21.9	24.5	19
Chile	16.6	23.3	29.3	19
Mexico	27.2	21.9	24.5	26
Bolivia	14.2	13.2	15.5	19
Latin America	**24.8**	**19.7**	**19.6**	22
Developing Countries	25.7	24.7	25.8	30
Least Developed Countries	17.3	16.1	15.5	24
East Asian NICs	34.4	31.3	32.1	40
South Korea	32.0	36.9	38.4	31
China	30.1	33.2	42.6	44

Source: UN (1996): 143, 156, 193, 196, 305; World Bank (1995, 1996).

It appears that the relative contributions to production of both capital and labor (the increase in output per units of capital and labor employed) has been and remains relatively low and less than the increase in "total factor productivity." Although this point needs more detailed and systematic analysis, we can postulate that the relative increase in productivity can be associated with a change in the organizations of production—increased flexibility, as well as the incorporation of the new information-rich technology and an increased orientation toward export markets, which has had the additional effect of a greater realization of the surplus value embodied in the social product.

The Relative Shares of Capital and Labor in Social Production (and Income)

As for the social distribution of the national income between capital and labor, governments in the region generally have not established any specific policy, leaving it to the market. In the 1970s the government did in fact intervene to the point of taxing all forms of income and channeling the revenues into social and development programs in the public concern for "equity"—a more equitable distribution of the social product ("growth with equity" in development parlance).

The operating theory behind this do-nothing approach, adopted in the 1980s in the context of a policy to deregulate markets and private economic activity (i.e., "capital,") is the same as used to justify the proposed policy of labor flexibility and the elimination of minimum-wage legislation: the free market is the most efficient mechanism for allocating resources on the basis of equitable returns to productive factors.[13]

In these terms the World Bank pushed for the elimination of minimum-wage legislation as an obstacle to the proper functioning of the labor market and indirectly to an efficient and equitable distribution of the social product (national income) or the economic surplus. On the same basis, the World Bank designed a Plan for Economic and Social Development, subsequently adopted by virtually every country in the region, that did not include an explicit wages policy, it being understood that the advocated liberalization of prices, together with the proposed labor market reforms, by itself would lead to an optimum level of wages and employment; and that, therefore, any minimum wages, like that of wages in general, should be negotiated directly by the parties involved under market conditions. Thus the bank put into motion its proposal to abolish minimum wage legislation, supported with the argument (or assertion, rather) that such legislation causes unemployment and interferes with the working of the market forces of supply and demand.

Another proposition of the theory underlying the bank's plans for national development is that when liberalized (freed from government interference), the labor market would automatically regulate the level of wages according to the marginal productivity of labor, at which point the supply of labor would equal the demand for it.[14] So what has been the dynamic of this relationship between wages and the marginal productivity of labor?

As for the "research" reported on by the bank at its Second Annual Conference on Latin American and Caribbean Development in Bogota,[15] the experience of Chile, Colombia, and Peru with labor market reform has been demonstrably positive: a decrease in the official rate of open unemployment and an adjustment of wage levels toward the marginal productivity of labor. However, on the issue of the marginal productivity of labor there appears to be no basis in fact.[16] If the bank were correct in its assertion one would expect to find a long-term empirical trend toward the growth of average productivity at a rate below that of real wages, which, in turn, would tend to reduce the participation of capital in the production process.

Is there any evidence of such a trend? First, it is clear enough that real wages have generally declined over the course of the neoliberal era, a trend that can be traced out in every Latin American country since at least 1982. On average, real wages dropped from 15 to 25 percent between 1985 and 1999, but in a number of cases they have dropped by as much as 50 to 86 percent.[17] In the case of Argentina, Peru, and Venezuela real wages in 1999 had not yet recovered levels achieved in 1970, while in Mexico, according to the Bank of Mexico, they had lost 71.4 percent of their 1976 value, reaching their lowest point in thirty years.[18] Given this trend, coupled with a tendency for a decrease in the number of workers in the formal sector—reflecting the destruction of the forces of production in key industrial sectors brought about by the agency of US imperialism (but presented as the inevitable result of the productive transformation process)[19]—it is difficult to imagine that the rate of growth in labor productivity could have been negative as presumed (and argued without evidence) by the bank.[20]

Given the relatively low levels of participation of both capital and labor in the regional production process, this increase in productivity can be explained in terms of factors other than labor and capital, such as the greater flexibility of labor. At one level, the decline in real wages could reflect a reduced level of labor productivity associated with the destruction of productive capacity brought about by the cut in social programs and an investment in "human capital" (the education and health of workers). Given the divergence over time between rates of productivity growth and wage rates,[21] it is evident that real wages, both on average and at minimum levels, are neither adjusted to nor determined by the marginal productivity of labor.

More generally, the brutal compression of wages in the 1980s and 1990s can better be explained in terms of structurally- or politically determined conditions of unemployment as well as, more directly, the repression of working-class organizations and the weakening of their capacity to negotiate collective agreements with capital.[22] In any case, over the long term real wages have tended to evolve to levels well below the marginal productivity of labor, creating thereby an essential condition for a process of renewed capital accumulation: the extraction of surplus value from its direct producers, the working class.

In structural terms, the contribution of labor to a process of capital accumulation is reflected in the share of wages in the income derived from the social product—and in its share of the value added in the

Table 2.2   Employee earnings as a percent of value added in manufacturing, Selected countries

	1967	1971	1975	1979	1983	1987	1989	1992
Brazil	17.3	23.6	18.9	20.7	19.7	15.1	15.0	23
Chile	25.1	22.8	12.3	18.2	17.1	16.8	16.6	18
Mexico	44.0	42.7	39.1	34.7	23.8	19.8	19.8	22
Venezuela	30.1	30.0	27.3	28.5	31.6	26.8	24.2	19

Source: World Bank, World Development Report. Various years.

process. In each case, these ratios have tended to decrease over the course of neoliberal reforms, in some cases by as much as 50 percent (CEPAL, various years). And, by the same token, the share of capital in national income (and value added to production) increased correspondingly, anywhere from around 60 to 75 percent, fueling a process of highly profitable investments even without any productivity gains.[23] However, the significant increase in the rate of exploitation (estimated by Montesino and Gochez to be in the order of 190 percent in the case of El Salvador), and in the transfer of income from labor to capital, did not translate into a process of renewed and sustained capital accumulation.

To explain this, it would seem that (1) the sharp compression of wages and reduction in the share of wages in national income has been used as a mechanism of internal adjustment,[24] but that (2) the extraordinarily high social costs of this adjustment, borne largely by workers, cannot even be justified in terms of the imperative of renewed accumulation and sustaining the process of national capitalist development. Productive investments in the region have been and remain at levels well below the level of surplus value extracted and the income transferred from labor.[25] Only in Chile has a substantial part of the income transferred from labor been converted into capital, generating a comparatively high level of productive investment in physical and social capital.[26] In most other countries a substantial part of the economic surplus generated by, and extracted from, the workers and the direct producers has been dedicated to the servicing of the external debt,[27] unproductive or speculative "investments," the purchase of the shares of privatized companies (accounting for up to 50 percent of the new wave of foreign direct investment [FDI] in the 1990s, and consumption of the wealth and income generated in the process).[28]

Exploitation in the Production Process

At issue in the World Bank's ideological approach to labor market reform in Latin America are the policies required to reduce the high levels of un- and underemployment in the region as well as the trend toward informalization and its associated conditions of low productivity and income. The evident tendency for an extension of these conditions, and a deepening of their social effects, underscores the seriousness of the issue—confronting the World Bank's conception of the problem and its remedy of labor market reform which, we have argued, is at best designed to address and solve quite a different problem (to create the conditions for a renewed and sustained process of capital accumulation). And, as we see it, the bank's proposed remedy does not correctly identify the structural sources of the problem—as experienced by labor or as perceived by capital. Thus it might be useful to review some points of our analysis and to briefly identify the key dimensions of the problem as we see it, to contribute thereby toward a better understanding of it as well as a more appropriate political response.

The aim of the World Bank's approach to labor market reform in Latin America and elsewhere is to restructure the capital-labor relation in the production process. And it is well understood by the bank and other agents and apologists of capitalism (as well as it is explained by Marx) that the essence of this capital-labor relation is the extraction of surplus value from its direct producer, the worker, in the form of the wage, which represents the value of the labor expended in the process.

The actual facts and nature of this *social relation* are well known, although it fell upon Marx over a hundred years ago to unveil its then hidden secret. As Marx noted and emphasized, the key to a sustainable process of capital accumulation is the extraction of relative surplus value on the basis of an exchange of equivalents (wages for labor-power), the value of which, as with every other commodity, is determined by the socially necessary labor-time needed to produce it. The production of relative surplus value, Marx argued, is the truly revolutionary path toward capitalist development, as opposed to the production of absolute surplus value—increasing the productivity of labor via technological conversion as opposed to the lengthening of the work-day, or reducing wages without a change in the technological and social conditions of production. The production and extraction of relative surplus is predicated on the substitution of capital for labor, the incorporation of new technologies that (1) will raise the organic composition of capital, (2) slough off surplus labor,[29] and (3) increase labor productivity.

In this process of technological conversion and productive transformation, to use contemporary language, labor is exchanged for wages at its value, which, given that this value is determined by and reflects the latest technological advances, implies that it has some connection to the resulting increases in productivity. In this process, the value of labor power is essentially a function of technology, although, as Marx emphasized, the rate of exploitation, conditioned as it is by the capacity of workers to participate in any productivity gains, by and large is shaped by the class struggle—the correlation of class forces.

In this context of developments in the region and that have unfolded worldwide as of the mid-1970s, it would seem that the balance of class forces has turned against labor, resulting in (among other things) a reduced capacity of workers to participate in the productivity gains of new technology—to adjust wages to productivity.[30] Although this development is worldwide, the situation of workers in Latin America and elsewhere on the margins of the globalized capitalist economy is worse than at the center of the system in that the conditions of relative surplus value extraction, at the heart of the accumulation process, are often and generally combined with those of absolute surplus value[31] as well as of what has been conceptualized as "super-exploitation"— the reduction of wages below the value of labor-power.[32] The detritus of this process can be seen in the deterioration in the condition of the Latin American working class since the 1970s, as well as its reduced capacity to resist the incursions of capital and the forces of productive transformation generated by these incursions.

The conditions of this super-exploitation are complex and variable but the basic mechanisms involved are easy enough to identify: the formation and operation of what Marx regarded as an "industrial reserve army," a large reservoir of surplus labor—surplus to the requirements of capital. The second mechanism is a highly developed system of state repression, which keeps the surplus labor discontent from spilling over and affecting the process of accumulation. The existence of such a reservoir of surplus labor can be identified at the global level—in, for example, the large mass of unemployed or migrating workers across the world, as well as the interstices of an emerging global labor market—but its most substantial and significant formation is found in the economies of Latin America and other countries and regions that are, as it were, "in the process," or "on the way" toward development. A characteristic feature of this process is the formation of what in the urban economies of these societies has been identified and defined as an "informal sector" of street workers and microenterprises, and, in the countryside, in the formation of a class of landless or near-landless (proletarianized or semi-proletarianized) "peasants."

Although it applies equally well to the large and growing informal sector, the conditions of a surplus population have been documented and to some extent analyzed in the context of the region's "peasant" economies of small producers. In this context, what has been emphasized has been the classic working of a surplus population as a lever of capital accumulation—allowing capitalist entrepreneurs to depress wages, and, in the process, to increase profits and maintain the competitiveness of their enterprises. However, several additional dimensions of this system have been identified for the subsistence and commercial operations of the small-scale producers linked to the peasant economy: as with the informal sector they provide wage goods at low prices, even below the cost of production, as well as a source of employment and additional income for family members. In this regard they provide a subsidy to the capitalist enterprises. Evidence of this can be found in the basic grain component of the food basket on the basis of which the Ministry of Planning and policy-makers generally estimate the minimum income requirements, and the incidence of poverty, within the urban population. What has been found is that the cost of basic grains over time tends to rise more slowly than the other components of the food basket (*ECA*, 1995: 560: 971).

Analysts also tend to agree that the small producers of these basic grains, the social base and a principal target of the bank's—and the government's—ubiquitous antipoverty programs under the post-Washington Consensus, often serve as a refuge (a source of employment) for an overabundant surplus population. In this regard, the small-producer sector of Latin America's rural society, like the urban informal sector, serves as a reservoir of surplus labor, holding at bay the labor of the semi-proletarianized *temporeros,* the rural landless workers who are forced to migrate for wage-work seasonally in the agroexport industries that dominate the rural economies of so many Latin American societies.[33] In addition, in the border and northern and central states of Mexico such as Zacatecas, the small producer sector provides a source of cheap surplus labor for the low-wage service industries and the agricultural sector of the US economy. In both cases, the rural society of small producers assumes some of the reproductive costs of the labor subsumed directly or indirectly by the capitalist enterprises in the maquilla sector and in the industries that have been subject to the process of technological conversion and productive transformation.[34] We view this as superexploitation.

These developments and conditions can be found all across Latin America. Not only do they underlie the problems targeted by the "development community" (un- and underemployment, marginalization, and social exclusion and poverty). But they are connected to the identified problem of a relatively limited unsustainable process of capitalist development in the region.[35] The major problem in this regard is the failure of the capitalists and policy-makers in the region to convert the surplus value extracted from the workers (and the disproportionate share of national income that they have appropriated) into capital. The problem is that most profit-driven capitalists divert their earnings into overseas accounts, speculative investments, the stock market, real estate and rental investments, conspicuous consumption, and unproductive mergers and acquisitions. When they do invest locally they focus on capital intensive technologically advance agromineral export activity that absorbs few workers but displaces many small producers. Another problem is that these capitalists also rely on a strategy of cheap labor for enterprises and entire industries oriented toward exports on the world market.[36] In this regard, the cost of labor in the production process in many cases has been lowered to a level of 20 percent and lower—10 percent in the case of Mexico.[37] Even so, capitalist enterprises in the region cannot compete with capitalist enterprises in China.

In terms of an export-growth strategy capital has little or no interest in maintaining the purchasing power of wages and dynamizing the local and regional markets on which the process of capitalist development depends.[38] Nor does it have a particular interest in taking what Marx regarded as the revolutionary path toward capitalist development—productive investment and capital accumulation on the basis of relative surplus value.[39] In this context, the World Bank's proposed labor market reforms, even when designed to facilitate the process of technological conversion and productive transformation, is condemned to failure.

They will also not prevent either capital or labor, which will undoubtedly be forced to bear the social costs of adjustment, from being marginalized in the globalization process identified by the bank: "the general prosperity of countries that are enjoying growth."

Capitalist State and Parastate Violence, and the Decline of Resistance and the Labor Movement

One of the striking features of the decline in the resistance to capitalist development over the past three decades is the extraordinary intensity of state violence against the labor movement. In the preceding phase of capitalist development organized labor was a major factor, if not the decisive force, in shaping state social policy. But the onset of neoliberalism was preceded and accompanied by unprecedented levels of capitalist state violence. Thirty thousand, mostly workers, movement leaders, and militants, were murdered in Argentina, and hundreds of thousands were jailed, tortured, exiled, fired, and blacklisted. In Chile at least four thousand workers, peasant, and community leaders and activists were murdered; tens of thousands were fired, exiled, and blacklisted. In Bolivia, Uruguay, Peru, and Brazil lesser levels of repression weakened the labor movements. In Central America and the Caribbean over 300,000 peasants, workers, and indigenous activists were slaughtered. In Guatemala, over 200,000 workers; in El Salvador the slaughter of 70,000 workers, peasants, and teachers including leaders and militants during the 1980s was the key to the decline of labor resistance to neoliberal policies in the 1990–1999 period.

The quiescence of the labor movement as of the 1980s can be explained easily enough by reference to the extraordinary level of violence in the repression of the movement. This repression is part and parcel of the global class war launched by capital against labor in the early 1970s, in retaliation for the gains that it had made in two decades of struggle that culminated in the revolutionary offensive of 1968.

By different accounts organized labor lost many, if not most, of the battles in this war, leaving the movement seriously weakened, its forces of resistance disarticulated. It is also possible to explain the organizational and political weakness of organized labor, its lack of political dynamism in recent decades, in "structural" as opposed to political terms, that is, as the result of structural forces operating on labor, as described earlier. Not that these structural forces operate in a vacuum, or without apparent agency. As argued earlier, the forces of change operating on workers, both rural and urban, responded to the agency of organizations such as the World Bank that sought to advance the process of capitalist development by means of a policy agenda of

"structural reform" that created the conditions not only of immisera-
tion and poverty but what appeared as "structural change"—forces
beyond anyone's control—the very forces that decimated the working
class and its organizational—and political—capacity. In effect, the
working class in its organizational form was the effective target of a
strategy and actions that combined structural force and violent state
and parastate repression. In some contexts, an additional factor in
the weakening of organized labor was the cooptation of the leadership, as was the case, for example, with the CTM (Confederación de
Trabajadores de México) in Mexico and the CTV (Confederación de
Trabajadores de Venezuela) in Venezuela.

Under conditions of this onslaught in the class war, it is not difficult to explain the relative quiescence of the labor moment in recent
years, and its reduced role in the class struggle. We just need to point
toward the resistance of the metalworkers and Confederación Unica
de Trabajadores (CUT) in Brazil in the 1979–1980 strike and onward,
or organized resistance of public sector workers in Peru and elsewhere.
And in Mexico, in the current context of neoliberal globalization,
the movement of electrical workers—the Sindicato de Electricistas de
México (SME)—was leading the fight against neoliberalism with the
broadest, deepest, and most unified resistance, until its most recent
setbacks, suggesting that without a political instrument movement
struggles are incapable of defeating the neoliberal onslaught.

3

Dynamics of Agrarian
Transformation and Resistance

Capitalist development entails a process of productive and social transformation (proletarianization), dispossession of small and medium producers, and conversion of family farmland producing food for local markets into plantations producing staples for export. In some cases this has been characterized as "primitive accumulation"—the dispossession of direct producers from their means of production. However, the structural and political dynamics of this process is only one side. On the other side are the dynamics of resistance against this development—a class struggle against the concentration and centralization of capitalist development—and a struggle for social transformation via agrarian reform. On this side are diverse class- and community-based political organizations formed in the popular sector, but none as important as the peasantry and landless rural workers who have led the fight—the long class war—against the most recent incursion of capitalism in the countryside, defending an economy of small scale agricultural production and demanding the redistribution of land from the ravages of capitalist development.

Over the course of the twentieth century, the virulence of the capitalist land concentration have led generations of analysts to argue that there is no defense—that the forces of capitalist concentration are so strong as to extinguish alternative modes of production and bring about the demise of the peasantry as a socioeconomic and political reality. This argument has waxed and waned over the years, with a high point in the 1970s and then again in the last few years as another cycle in the process of capitalist concentration subjected the peasantry to the new world order of global capitalism. Once again the "disappearance of the peasantry" is on the agenda of scholarly debate and politics.

The policies of neoliberal globalization have given a new impetus to the forces of capitalist development and agrarian transformation. But this time the protagonists of an ongoing scholarly and political debate about the fate of the peasantry include the peasants themselves in the form of radical social movements as well as international organizations such as *Via Campesina*, formed for the purpose of confronting the dominant neoliberal model and constructing a new agrarian order based on cooperatives, family farms, and self managed agroindustrial complexes.

This chapter argues that far from disappearing into the dustbin of history, peasants once more stepped onto the center stage of societal transformation. Our argument is that the repressive policies of imperial-backed neoliberal states weakened labor, decimating the forces of resistance within the working class. However, under the same conditions the peasantry, and the mass of landless or near-landless rural workers, a rural semi-proletariat, managed to resist the latest incursions of capitalism and imperialism in the countryside and in some cases went on the offensive to topple the most egregious neoliberal regimes. In the 1990s they led the resistance against neoliberalism and even succeeded in overthrowing several important client regimes of the empire.

The peasant struggle for land and rural livelihoods continues and has imposed limits on the capitalist transformation of rural society. The strategic response of the peasantry—both indigenous and nonindigenous—to the latest onslaught of capitalism is a strategy of direct action and the mobilization for land occupations and state supported land reform (see chapter 4 on the dynamics of this resistance).

An important part of this strategy is the links forged between the peasant movements and the urban-based social organizations in the popular sector and the middle-class organizations of so-called civil society. Not that these rural-urban links, which have both structural and political dimension, are entirely benign. In fact, they constitute a double-edged sword, working as much to demobilize the popular movement as to advance it. Chapter 5 elaborates on this point.

The "Great Transformation" and the Strategic Response of the Peasantry

At the center of the process of capitalist development outlined in chapter 1—represented theoretically in the historical narratives of industrialization, modernization, and capitalist development—is the conversion of the direct producers on the land—"peasants"—into a mass of rural landless and migrant workers, an urban proletariat of informal workers, a rural semiproletariat of small-scale producers forced to combine direct production with wage labor, and a "lumpen proletariat" affiliated to the burgeoning narcotics sector as producers, traders, and security enforcers.

Under current conditions of this "great transition"—that is, within the new world order of imperial centered neoliberal globalization—peasants are "on the move" in three senses. One is at the level of spatial relocation—migration from diverse rural localities and communities to the city. The dynamics of this response to the forces of capitalist concentration, centralization, dispossession, and proletarianization are everywhere in evidence, manifest in the uprooting and displacement of huge numbers of landless producers and their families from the countryside. The vast majority of these rural migrants are absorbed into the urban economy at the level of work or economic activity as a mass of informal workers, working "on their own account" on the streets, rather than for wages in industrial plants and factories, in private and public sector offices or in transportation or construction. Within the "informal" sector, the most dynamic and lucrative growth area is in the narco-economy, which is, according to 60 percent of Mexican poor youth (in a recent official survey), the "most viable economic activity" for them in the country (*La Jornada*, March 2010). These rural migrants and landless workers are incorporated into the urban economy in the burgeoning growth of barrio organizations linked to competing popular and elite patronage networks.

Migration is one response of the rural proletariat to the forces of social change generated in the capitalist development process. Another is labor—to exchange labor-power for a living wage. Responses along this line, a matter of individual decision rather than collective action, are reflected in the resulting process of social transformation, which for peasants has meant entering into a relation of labor under whatever conditions are available. This response has resulted in the formation of a semiproletariat with links to both the land and the wage-labor, allowing "peasants" to secure the livelihood of their households, and, at a different level, to constitute what Marx in a different context termed an "industrial reserve army" of workers whose labor is held in reserve without capital having to assume the costs of its reproduction.

A third response of peasants assumes a "political" rather than "structural" form (the outcome of economic decisions made by countless individuals), which is to join the social movements as a means of organizing and mobilizing the resistance against the processes of primitive accumulation and proletarianization—against forced migration and the subsumption of labor, the loss of livelihood, the policies of the neoliberal state and its governing body. We review and analyze some of the dynamics of this response in chapter 5, with reference to social movements formed in the 1980s and dominating the political landscape in the 1990s, and in chapters 3 and 8, with particular reference to the politics and emerging movements of unemployed youth, gangsters, and landless peasants in Mexico and elsewhere in the context of a rapidly expanding narco-economy.

The Dynamics of Social Transformation

This process of structural change and productive transformation over the years can be traced out easily enough in the ebb and flow of academic debate between those who argue that the incessant trend toward proletarianization will bring about the disappearance of the peasantry, and those who argue the contrary, that the peasantry, albeit reduced in number, rather than disappearing is being reproduced in different forms. This issue was at the center of a debate between "peasantists" such as Gustavo Esteva (1983) and "proletarianists" such as Roger Bartra (1976) in the 1970s (Nugent, 1994). After a lapse of some years as political sociologists turned their attention and lens to the "new social movements" of the 1980s, the peasantist-proletarianist debate has resumed in an era of neoliberal globalization in which the forces of modernization, industrialization, and capitalist development have worked to accelerate a process of agrarian transformation.

The brutal effects and painful consequences of this process are reflected in the detritus of grinding poverty left behind in the countryside. In a sense, both sides of the argument regarding the process of the capitalist development and agrarian transformation are supported by some of the "facts" and thus able to explain some of the changes taking place across the Latin American countryside. This is because, under conditions of what some have conceptualized as "peripheral capitalism," the peasantry is being transformed but not completely so, converted and reproduced in different form in a process that we might conceptualize as "semiproletarianization."

Rather than the "disappearance of the peasantry" we have its reproduction in diverse but identifiable and, in some contexts, sustainable forms. Peasants under these conditions appear as a rural proletariat of landless workers forced to combine direct production on the land with wage-labor—working off-farm to secure the livelihood of their households and families; and an urban proletariat in the informal sector of the urban economy to work "on their own account" and live in a "planet of slums."

There is nothing particularly "new" here. The process can be traced out in the dynamics of productive and social transformation all over the world in different spatial and historical contexts. What is perhaps different or distinctive about this agrarian transformation in the current context of neoliberal globalization is that the process, has been "stalled" in the formation of a semiproletariat of rural landless workers forced into seasonal or irregular forms of wage-labor. Under these conditions, and considering the politics of resistance in the 1990s, there is no question of the peasantry disappearing into the dustbins of history.

Social Change and the Land Question

The forces of social change associated with the process of agrarian transformation have always been resisted by organized groups on the receiving end of these forces—primarily direct producers on the land, that is, "peasants" as viewed in the academic literature (Otero, 1999) and by peasants themselves. Nowhere is this more evident than in Latin America.

In Latin America the tendency for different categories of "peasant" to engage the struggle for land and social change was evident as early as the first twentieth-century agrarian revolution—in Mexico. In this historic struggle, peasants—a good number located in marginalized indigenous communities—not only won the rights to large tracts of expropriated land but they also constituted a watershed in peasant-state relations. In the wake of the Mexican Revolution, and then again in Cuba some forty years on, the state, under pressure for revolutionary change, tolerated partial land reform as a means of keeping the social peace and taming, if not settling, the class struggle for land. Under similar conditions but changed circumstances peasant movements emerged in the 1930s in El Salvador, Nicaragua, Colombia, Brazil, and Peru.[1] In the Caribbean, rural workers, particularly sugar workers in Cuba, the Dominican Republic, Puerto Rico, Guyana, and elsewhere, also took up the struggle. In each case, with the exception of Mexico under Cardenas, repressive measures were taken by the state to suppress or destroy these rural "rebellions." In Mexico, agrarian reform was extended to hundreds of thousands of poor rural families (Katz, 1988).

In Nicaragua, the Dominican Republic, and Cuba, armed forces of the US imperial state and its anointed tyrant-presidents—Somoza, Trujillo, and Batista—slaughtered thousands, decimating the peasant and rural workers' movement. In Brazil, the state defeated Prestes's rural-based guerrilla army while pursuing a strategy of national industrialization. As for Chile, a Popular Front of radicals, socialists, and communists encouraged—and then abandoned—the peasant struggle, together with demands for agrarian reform, in exchange for national state-sponsored industrialization in a political agreement with the center-left Radical Party.

In the most successful cases, peasant-based revolts or rebellions were able to secure institutional reforms in the agrarian sector. But these reforms usually followed a process of active mobilization and de facto land occupations. The government, in effect, was compelled to legalize the status quo as well as dampen pressures for more radical land redistribution. In Mexico, this process began in the early 1900s and reached its high point in the 1930s.

Subsequently, in the 1960s and 1970s, some government in the region used the repressive power of the state to alter the distribution of land for different categories of producers and households, and to redefine the right to land for those given "improved access" in the process. This was no matter the ideological or political complexion of the regime. In 1952, for example, a revolution of miners and peasants in Bolivia led to a sweeping agrarian reform that resulted in the expropriation of many large estates. At the end of the decade, in Cuba, the victory of the 26th of July movement resulted in the confiscation of most of the American and Cuban-owned plantations, the land subsequently collectivized or distributed to smallholders (McEwan, 1981).

Land reforms also took place in Peru from 1958 to 1974, in Brazil from 1962 to 1964, in Chile from 1966 to 1973, in Ecuador from 1964 to 1967, in Guatemala between 1952 and 1954 (and again after the civil war following the peace accords), Honduras in 1973, and Nicaragua, under different political conditions (a short-lived "socialist" regime) from 1979 to 1986.[2] These reforms were led by the state, regardless of its form (authoritarian, military, liberal reformist, populist, socialist). They were undertaken in response to mass peasant mobilizations and a general threat of "social revolution" (Petras and La Porte, 1971; De Janvry, Gordillo, and Sadoulet, 1998).

These state-led land reforms were undertaken in tandem with a strategy of rural development that was designed as a means of appeasing the landless or near-landless rural poor and to dampen the fires of revolutionary ferment (the soft-glove of development) and a strategy of outright repression (the hard fist of armed force) against the rural poor who had taken up arms and joined the armed struggle. As for the strategy of rural development, pursued within the framework of the Alliance for Progress, the operational agency (or "actor") was the "private voluntary association," a middle-class form of nongovernmental organization (NGO) contracted in large numbers to prosecute the war against rural poverty on the front line of this war within the localities and communities of the landless and near-landless rural poor. On this front, divisions of PVOs (NGOs as they would later be termed) worked in tandem with *Acción Católica*, an agency set up by the Vatican to the same purpose: to provide an alternative to the growing pressures for radical change and revolutionary transformation in the countryside—to prevent another Cuba.

The 1980s brought about entirely new conditions for the class struggle both in the countryside and in the cities. In the cities the labor movement was severely weakened and in some cases entirely destroyed by military regimes that launched a process of structural adjustment to the new world order. Under these circumstances at first the urban poor took up the struggle against the authoritarian (nonelected) capitalist state and a cycle of "structural reforms" initiated under the aegis of an emerging neoliberal state (Leiva and Petras, 1994). Under similar circumstances, neoliberal policies of administrative decentralization and "democratization" (privatization of the responsibility for social welfare and economic development) gave rise to a new generation of NGOs within the middle-class sector of an emergent "civil society," and with it a "new" type of social movement concerned with a broad range of non-class issues ranging from protecting the environment and the violation of human rights to advancing the status of women (Escobar and Alvarez, 1992; Melucci, 1992; Slater, 1985).

A new generation of scholars, armed with a postmodern political imaginary and a new sensibility regarding various emerging "subjectivities" (Brass, 1991) conceptualized this "development" as the emergence of "new social movements" that managed to elude the iron cage of Latin America's class structure.

In the countryside the strategy of globalization—integration into a new world order in which the forces of economic freedom are released from the regulatory constraints of the development state—had a rather different outcome. In the countryside the forces of neoliberal globalization and capitalist development accelerated the historic process of primitive accumulation—the dispossession of the direct producers, converting many peasants into a landless or near-landless proletariat, forced to migrate to the cities in search of new opportunities or resort to wage-labor to sustain the livelihood of their households. However, as noted, not all "peasants" responded in this way. The response of many peasants was to join a social movement of resistance to the neoliberal state and its policies of structural adjustment to the new world order—to the exceedingly high social costs of this adjustment, that the direct producers, as well as the working class more generally, were expected to (and did) bear.

Destruction of the Labor Movement

Peasants and workers have been the chief target of neoliberal globalization—of the forces of change and transformation released in the process. But it is evident that the working class and the peasants have responded in very different ways, the former more passively in an adjustment to these forces, the latter more actively in a movement of resistance and opposition. In the 1960s and 1970s the industrial proletariat, in the limited form that it took on the periphery of world capitalism, as well as public-sector workers in the form of a labor movement, led the resistance.

But in the 1980s the labor movement collapsed as workers succumbed to the forces of change ranged against them. Under the working of these forces, the organizational and mobilizational capacity of labor was drastically reduced, in some contexts destroyed. But in the countryside conditions were very different. For whatever reason, the peasantry in its diverse forms was able to more actively respond to the policy conditions of neoliberal globalization and structural adjustment, creating for itself space for a politics of active resistance against the forces of agrarian transformation and the reaction of the democratized neoliberal state.

The earlier liberal-capitalist development state in its offensive against the forces of resistance in the countryside had pursued a twofold strategy of land reform and rural development, adding to it as circumstances demanded a strategy and tactics of accommodation, cooptation, and repression. This strategy worked—more or less—as the wave of revolutionary change subsided and the remnants of defeated movements in the armed struggle either dispersed or went to ground as in Chiapas and Guerrero in Mexico. But in the 1980s as the state turned against the working class the rural poor of landless and near-landless peasants regrouped and began to reorganize, constructing in the process social movements that would come to represent the most dynamic forces of resistance in the class struggle.

The state's response to the pressures for revolutionary change exerted by the peasants in the wake of the Cuban Revolution ranged from rural development to outright repression with violence. But the preferred approach was to combine a strategy of rural development based on international cooperation with a program of state-led land reform. As noted earlier, in response to the Cuban Revolution most governments in the region enacted legislation in support of a land reform programs designed to return the "land to the tiller"—turning over to the restless and rebellious peasants and the rural poor land that was surplus to the production requirements (not in productive use) of the landed aristocracy—the big proprietors who over the years by one means or the other had acquired ownership of most and the best arable land.

Notwithstanding the state-led land reforms of the 1960s, and despite continuing pressures on governments to adopt legal reform measures, with the exception of Cuba there was no fundamental change in the structure of land tenure. Many categories of rural households remained—and remain to this day—landless or near-landless. Close to 90 percent of all arable land in Latin America are concentrated in holdings owned by only 26 percent of rural proprietors. Despite the state-led land reform programs of the 1960s and two decades of grassroots land reform (direct action in the form of "occupations"), up to two-thirds of arable land in Brazil remains in the hands of an exceedingly small class of proprietors who account for barely 3 percent of all landowners, while close to 5 million families remain landless. In Argentina, not Latin America's worst case of an inequitable land tenure system, 43 percent of the productive land is owned by fewer than 4,000 landowners, representing less than 1.5 percent (1.3 percent) of agricultural producers. At the other extreme 83 percent of small landholders and producers own and work 13.3 percent of the land. And these figures are typical for Latin America, a region that has the most unequal and inequitable distributions of land (and other wealth-generating assets) in the world despite several decades of state-led reform in the twentieth Century.

Moreover, over the two decades of "pro-growth" (= neoliberal) policy measures (= "structural reform") the degree of concentration in land ownership, and the disparity in accessing means of production in the rural areas, if anything has increased. In Argentina, this has meant the expulsion or forced out-migration of more than 200,000 smallholding producers over the past decade and a half. In Brazil, it is estimated that it has involved an exodus over 5 million rural inhabitants over the course of the last two decades of neoliberal reform.[3] In addition—and this is true for many countries in other parts of the world—the majority of those who have retained some access to the land are barely able to subsist let alone make a commercially viable living. They are forced into a relation of wage-labor under conditions of precarious forms of employment, miserable working conditions, and poverty. At least one-half of all agricultural production units in Latin America are deemed to be economically marginal and are expected to disappear. There is no room for them in the neoliberal model.[4]

In response to this situation, euphemistically described as "social exclusion,"[5] vast numbers of a dispossessed rural proletariat are forced to migrate to the cities or abroad, resulting in one of the major upheavals and social transformations in "modern times": capitalist development of urban-based economic activity and an associated makeover of a rural population—much of it peasant in one form or the other—into an heterogeneous labor force of low paid service workers (domestics), peddlers, day-laborers ,wage-workers and, increasingly, narco-workers. Neoliberal policies led to the massive closure of mines, for example, in Bolivia in the mid-1980s, under the direction of Jeffrey Sachs and the International Monetary Fund (IMF), leading to outmigration to the cities and to the countryside, mainly to the coca growing fields of Chapare. The miners brought with them their organizing and class solidarity, creating the leading peasant movement in all of Bolivia.

One consequence of this transformation is that the land struggle, hitherto confined to agrarian society, moved from rural areas to the periphery of the cities. The process was well under way in the 1960s and 1970s, when up to a quarter of the rural population migrated to the urban centers in search of wage employment and housing. Most of these dwellings were constructed on a self-help basis by communities of rural migrants who invaded and "settled"—illegally occupied and squatted on—unused areas of urban land, creating in the process the *pueblos jovenes* of Lima, the *favelas* of Rio de Janeiro, the *rancherias* of Caracas, and *callampas* of Santiago, Chile. Because of this urbanization process, up to 60 percent of the nonrural population is in exceeding precarious housing and miserable living conditions (Guimarães, 1997: 191).

As a result of these and such developments, land occupations and the struggle for social change materialized in a new urban context, replicating some of the dynamics of the struggle for rural land but in a different form: land invasion, squatting, negotiations with the municipal government for services and legal title to their "property," and, through grassroots organizational efforts ("local development"), upgrading these neighborhoods into working-class *barrios*. The social dynamics of this process are complex, with diverse dimensions that include the break up of many families, with the women staying behind in rural areas to tend subsistence plots of land, and the men involved in seasonal out-migration in search of urban employment (Portes, Castells, and Benton, 1989).

Under these conditions, many landless rural workers were and are unable or unwilling to break their connection to agrarian society and their subjectivity as peasants, even without any access to the land. Despite this, the structure of landholding continues to reproduce the conditions of widespread rural poverty and to fuel an exodus of large numbers of marginal producers, dispossessed "peasants," and "landless rural workers." The exception is rural labor that succeeds in organizing, occupying large uncultivated estates, and establishing cooperatives or family farms or both.

On the Receiving End: Peasants and Indigenous Communities

The social structure of agricultural production can be defined in terms of size of landholding and income distribution. In these terms the basic structure includes three categories of landholders: large, middle, and small—the relative proportions of which vary by context. In Brazil, for example, smallholders constitute somewhat over 90 percent of the total number of peasant producers, a proportion that has not substantially changed over the course of the neoliberal macroeconomic policy regime since its institution in the early 1990s. Large and medium–sized landholders in the same context have also been reproduced within this structure, the former more so than the latter for whatever largely unstudied reason (see table 3.1).

Table 3.1   Peasants by size [hectares] of landholding and percentage of total, Brazil 1992–2003

	1992		1998		2003	
Large [2000–100,00+]	19,077	0.6	27,556	0.8	33,104	0.8
Medium [200–2000]	204,753	7.0	259,654	7.2	286,172	6.6
Small [<1– 200]	2,700,374	92.3	3,299,315	92.0	3,971,255	92.6
	2,924,204	100.0	3,586,525	100.0	4,290,531	100.0

Source: Nera, *Dataluta, Relatorio Preliminar 2004*, Tabala 13, p.20. (Small = Peasant).

Table 3.2   Percentage share of land acreage by category of peasant, Brazil 1992–2003

	1992	1998	2003
Big	40	43	45
Medium	34	33	37
Small	26	24	28
Total Acreage	310,030,972	415,548,885	418,483,332

Source: Nera, *Dataluta, Relatorio Preliminar 2004*, Tabala 13, p.20. (Small = Peasant).

Table 3.2 provides for Brazil data on changes in the distribution of land acreage owned by the three categories of peasants. It shows a surprisingly strong trend toward divergence in the share of total land owned by the big holders on one extreme and smallholder on the other. The trend toward land ownership clearly reflects on the relative dynamism of the capitalist development process vis-à-vis the land struggle of the rural landless workers. Considering the large number of families of rural landless rural workers settled (asentados) on the land over this period as the direct result of actions taken by the MST, the figures also point toward the correlation of class forces in the land struggle. Table 3.3 provides a graphic representation of this correlation in the ratio of total acreage share to the share of total number of producers for each category of peasant. Again, the striking feature of this dynamic pattern is divergence at the extremes of land distribution. The big landowners increased their share of landholding over or despite fifteen years of land struggle by the MST, eight years of state-led reform and four years of market-assisted land reform.

Table 3.3   Ratio of total acreage share to share of
total no. producers, by peasant category

	1992	1998	2003
Big	56.7	50.0	61.3
Medium	4.9	4.6	5.6
Small	0.4	0.3	0.2

Source: Nera, *Dataluta, Relatorio Preliminar 2004*, Tabala 13, p.20. (Small = Peasant).

As for the income generated by economic activity in the form of agricultural production, many if not all of the big landholders can be classified as "rich," some rich enough to accumulate capital and to be transformed out of the peasant economy into rural and/or urban capitalists, by investing their income productively in different ways in different sectors. At the bottom of the land size/income hierarchy, a sizeable proportion—in many contexts, the vast majority—are income poor and subject to forces of expulsion or primitive accumulation. Many of the smallholder peasants under these conditions—making up the bulk of landholders—are rendered landless or near-landless, virtually all of them impoverished and forced to either migrate to the cities or work off-farm for wages, converting them—at least over 50 percent in many contexts—into a vast rural semiproletariat.

As for the patterns of change in the social structure it is difficult to determine in most cases for lack of data and analysis. Dynamic studies of size distribution of landholdings—to measure the distribution of landholding by size at different points of time—have been conducted in some contexts but the resulting data are difficult to determine in terms of the inner social dynamics of the process of change. Thus, it is likely that in each size category some conditions tend to both reproduce producers in that size category while other induce either downward or upward mobility. In the big landholder or income rich category, a small proportion is able to save and thus accumulate capital, and to be converted out of the peasantry into capitalists.

But does this diminish the number and proportion of landholders in this size category of producers? Table 3.1 suggests that it does not. Relevant studies in other contexts show that it depends on demographic and other social processes, including the likelihood that a number of middle-size/income producers are elevated into large/high income category and the possibility that some peasants in this category will experience downward mobility. Also some unknown percentage of middle-sized landholders are likely to be converted into a class of family farmers (*agricultures familiares*), losing not their connection to the land but rather their status and self-identification as "peasants."

Under these conditions, the question is whether the middle size/income category of peasant is growing in proportion; that is, in relation to the large/rich and small/poor peasant as Chayanov found to be the case for Russia in the 1920s? Alternatively is there a tendency toward size/income differentiation, a relative hollowing out of the middle and increasing growth at the extremes—as Lenin had argued in his classic study of social differentiation and the transformation of the Russian peasantry? Tables 3.1–3.3 suggest that the trend identified by Lenin is closer to reality for Brazil in the most recent phase of capitalist development. If this is the case, what are the social dimensions of this process of land concentration and social polarization? What are the dimensions of this apparent social dualism: wealth and capital accumulation at one extreme of the social structure, poverty, and proletarianization at the other?

As indicated, more study of these dynamics need to be undertaken to establish a national or regional pattern (of conditions of reproduction and transformation in each landholding/producer category). The one dynamic trend that can be definitively established is that of out migration and proletarianization vis-à-vis the small landholder category of peasant. Undoubtedly, some elements of the middle size category are also led to migrate and abandon agriculture, and a larger number are evidently converted into a non-peasant category of agricultural producer—family farming based on simple commodity production—losing thereby not their connection to the land but to their identity as peasants. It is even possible, although not likely, that some middle-sized peasants can increase their handholding by resorting to the market-mechanism to buy land and become larger if not rich. However, it is for the largest category of peasant, the smallholder that a clear pattern has emerged, even with only a cursory examination of the available data and without a systemic dynamic analysis of trends by landholding size and income and associated social and political processes. The pattern is for a significant and increasing proportion of peasants in this category to be proletarianized, fueling a well-established process of outmigration and resulting in the impoverishment and proletarianization of a large (and seemingly growing) proportion of smallholder peasants.

Peasants Take Action and the Neoliberal State Responds

In 1978 David Lehman, among others, declared the era of state-led land reforms to be over, having exhausted its political limits, and the state itself beating a retreat from the counter-offensive launched by the big proprietors (and capital) against these reforms. The first step toward this counter-revolution was taken in Latin America in the form of the coup launched against the democratically elected regime of Salvador Allende. But within a decade, the State was everywhere in retreat, giving way to the "new world order" in a process of structural adjustment and neoliberal globalization. State-led land reform was a casualty of the process.

In the cities a major structural response to these developments was the emergence of a "civil society"—a broad spectrum of social organizations spanning the space between the family and the state. Within the middle class sector of this "civil society" there emerged a broad array of NGOs, associational in form and concerned to assume responsibilities abdicated by the state. In 1970 by at least one account there were only some 250 of such organizations. But by the end of the 1990s, this sector of "civil society" had grown to an estimated 25,000 to 40,000, including at least 10,000 of what the World Bank (the lead agency in the war against global poverty) regard as "operational" agencies or strategic partners in the field of "development"—"developmental NGOs" in the lingo of the "development."

However, in the countryside the organizational—and political—form of resistance to the forces of capitalist development was entirely different. It was to organize opposition to government policies, to change the government if not its policies. The forces of this resistance were rooted in the popular sector of what was subsequently termed "civil society"—in the class-based or community-based organizations of rural and agrarian society. By the end of the decade class- or community-based social movements were constructed in the countryside of Bolivia, Brazil, Ecuador, Mexico, and elsewhere, and in the 1990s a number of these movements initiated a programs of direct action and social mobilization against the neoliberal state and its policies.

The response of the state and the guardians of the new world order (neoliberal globalization) to these mobilizations were predictable. This strategic response can be placed into three categories: (1) redesign of the "new economic model," moving beyond the "Washington Consensus" by adding to the neoliberal programs of "pro-growth" structural reforms in macroeconomic policy a "new social policy" as well as specific measures to protect the most vulnerable groups in society—to give the entire process of "productive transformation" a human face;[6] (2) a decentralized local development process targeted at the localities and communities of the rural poor, and designed to open up a local front on the renewed war against rural poverty; and (3) a market-assisted land reform program.

Market-Assisted Land Reforms

In the 1960s and 1970s, the state in Latin America initiated land reform programs ostensibly to correct a serious imbalance between property ownership and agricultural production but in fact to appease the popular demand for land. These programs were in part a response to the Cuban Revolution and in large part to growing pressures for revolutionary change exerted by the social movements of the peasantry.[7] In the 1980s, however, sweeping changes and a neoliberal program of structural reform in national policy generated conditions for an alternative path toward "agrarian transformation" (Kay, 2000).

Another factor was the institution of a community-based form of alternative development designed by its theorists to secure the sustainability of rural livelihoods (Amalric, 1998; Brockett, 1988; Chambers and Conway, 1998; Helmore and Singh, 2001). This and several other forms of local or community-based development, predicated on the accumulation of social capital rather than the politically messy process of improving access to the land and other wealth-generating "assets," had the effect of reducing, if not removing entirely, the pressure on governments to expropriate large landholdings and redistribute them to the landless or near-landless, a large and rapidly growing segment of the rural population.

In these circumstances state-sponsored programs of redistributive growth and land reform came to an end, signaled by the recognition in academic and policy-making circles that "land reform is dead" However, under the same conditions two alternative forms of land reform emerged, one initiated from within the popular sector of an emerging "civil society" (see the discussion below on the politics of revolutionary change), the other constructed by economists at the World Bank: a market-assisted approach toward land and agrarian reform (Deininger, 1998).

This market-led and-assisted approach dominated government policy in the 1990s but it evolved in stages. The first was the formulation and implementation, in the early 1990s for the most (Mexico, Ecuador, etc.), of an agrarian modernization law designed to commodify land—to create or strengthen the functioning of a land market. In countries such as Mexico with a system of collective or community ownership (the *ejido*) modernization entailed the institution of individual over collective rights.

The second stage involved the market mechanism of land titling—giving the direct producers secure legal title to the land so as to allow for its sale. With an opening of local economies to the world market, and under conditions of a production crisis that pushed many peasant farmers and independent small and medium-sized producers into debt, the agrarian modernization law had the predictable result of increasing the concentration of land ownership, adding to the other "push" factors working on the peasantry, accentuating ongoing processes of dispossession, proletarianization and urbanization.

A third and highly contested stage in the process of market-assisted land reforms entails a policy of instituting land banks (World Bank 1996, 1997). In regard to this policy, the World Bank instituted pilot projects in Brazil, Colombia, and the Philippines. The aim of the policy, and the institution of this particular market mechanism, was not only to promote and improve the functioning of the land market but, at least in the case of Brazil, to counteract the tactic of land occupations used by the movement of rural landless workers. That is, the aim was to stimulate use of "the market mechanism" in lieu of what the leaders of this movement take to be "the broader class struggle" (Stedile, 1998).

In 1998, with an initial injection of $25 million of capital, the World Bank launched the Land Bank in Brazil, searching at the same time for a way of securing support for this strategy in the small landholding sector. One of these ways was to rally support from within the non-peasant elements of this sector—more democratically minded small-scale family farmers, effectively dividing the movement of rural landless workers on political lines. The dynamics of this process are still unfolding and need a closer look and more study.

Very few Latin American countries with a significant agricultural sector have escaped this drive to create a land market and other forms of a market-assisted approach to land reform. In the 1990s, country after country instituted an agrarian "modernisation" or "reform" law in one form or another. In Mexico and Ecuador this meant the abolition of constitutional protection of indigenous communal lands, a policy successfully instituted in the case of Mexico (1992), where the dominant peasant federation was under control of the government. In Ecuador, however, this policy hit a political snag in the form of an "indigenous uprising." More generally, governments closed down their land redistribution programs and turned toward the market mechanisms of land titling and land banks in improving the access of the rural poor, and peasant farmers, to the land and the resources needed to convert themselves into productive producers.

Between 1991 and 1994, at the behest of the World Bank and within the framework of its neoliberal agenda, the governments of Mexico, Ecuador, Bolivia, Peru, and a number of other countries in South and Central America, turned toward a market-assisted approach to agrarian reform. This approach was based on legislation that included the abolition of the constitutional or legal protection of communal property and legal entitlement to land worked by smallholders, increasing their capacity to sell their land and, in the process, to build a land market, as well as, supposedly, increasing the "efficiency" of production.[8] However, combined with the elimination of subsidies to local producers, the commercialization of credit, the reduction of protective tariffs, and in many cases an overvalued currency, these measures (land titling, *etc.*), rather than resolving the agricultural crisis, have created what analysts have termed a "difficult environment" for various categories of producers of tradable products, especially "small scale peasant producers" (Crabtree, 2003: 144). The latter, as Crabtree points out concerning Peru (but which can be generalized), have been "extremely vulnerable to the inflow of cheap agricultural products." Not only has this "development" destroyed local economies, forcing large numbers of local producers into bankruptcy or poverty, or to migrate, it has either brought about or accelerated a fundamental change in production and consumption patterns away from traditional subsistence and commercial crops, especially grains like quinua, kiwicha, coca, alluco, beans, and potatoes. The full impact of this change, and its implications, has not been evaluated.

In the not atypical case of Peru, the abolition of a number of government marketing boards and agricultural price support institutions liberalized the national market in rice, removing organizations that had maintained price stability for the benefit of local producers. Some of the functions of these marketing boards were taken over by the Programa Nacional de Asistencia Alimentaria (PRONAA),[9] a government-subsidized food programs for the poor that bought directly from small-scale producers. However, such an institutional change had relatively little impact on the poorest farmers, many of who had never benefited from government programs of any sort (Crabtree 2003: 147).

As for the producers who managed to integrate themselves into the competitive local urban markets, the disappearance of *Banco Agrario* meant that they were forced to rely on various agro-industrial firms for commercial credit. This credit was extended to the same producers only under the most onerous terms, with rates that in the case of Brazil under Cardoso reached 20 percent a month, given the level of presumed "risk" assumed by creditors. These creditors are extremely reluctant to lend, even to larger-scale, more prosperous landowners with privileged market access. When they do lend, interest rates charged reflect the perception of risk involved in lending to small-scale peasant producers. Their appetite for lending is also reduced by the incidence of bankruptcies in sectors such as asparagus that had briefly seemed to offer endless possibilities (Crabtree 2003: 145–47).

In Mexico and Peru these and other such institutional reforms and recourse to "the market mechanism" resulted in a drastic deterioration in the life-situation of the smallholders and their relation to the market, compelling them to sell the product of their labor at prices well below the costs of production, and pushing many of them into debt, poverty and bankruptcy. In Mexico, this situation generated one of the largest mass movements in the country's long history of land struggle—an organization of indebted "independent" (non-peasant) farmers (*El Barzón*).

As for the peasant economy in Ecuador, Mexico, Central America, and elsewhere in the region, it has been devastated, forcing large numbers to flee the countryside in the search of wage employment in the cities and urban centers. The only nonpolitical alternative to this route was—and remains—rural poverty.

Urban-Rural Links among and with the Peasant Movements

The wave of rural activism that emerged in the 1980s and unfolded in the 1990s had specific conditions, including, paradoxically, a growing democratization process and repression of the forces mobilized in the process. Under these conditions, the peasant and indigenous organizations in the countryside responded by mounting a resistance movement that has cut across the rural-urban divide, forming an extensive, if shifting, complex of strategic and tactical alliances with other civil and political organizations, mostly urban, involved in the popular struggle.

These alliances and linkages can be put into three categories, each with its own dynamics: (1) horizontal linkages among networks of NGOs and grassroots movements such as *Sem Techos* in the urban areas: (2) intra-and inter-sectoral linkages with class- abased organizations and sociopolitical movements in a national context; and (3) international networks with organizations that constitute what has been termed "global civil society."

As for the NGO networks they were located within the "middle strata" of the urban centers, and formed primarily to the purpose of providing support to, and solidarity with, the struggles and social movements of grassroots organizations in the popular sector. These linkages bring together a broad range of concerns, from the protection and enhancement of political and human rights, diverse environmental issues of concern to neighborhood groups, women or minority groups of various sorts, to shared concern with the impact of government policies in the context of the processes of globalization and structural adjustment. In regard to this latter concern, and in solidarity with the struggle of class-based organizations and movements as relates to shared resistance against government policies or concern with organization-specific issues, these urban middle-class social organizations also participate in the complex of intra- and inter-sectoral alliances that characterize the organization and politics of these class-based organizations, In this connection, all of the major sociopolitical movements such as the MST, for the purpose of soliciting support for their campaigns to influence public opinion and pressure governments have tended to form linkages with international advocacy groups as well as all manner of civil and nongovernmental organizations.

As for the development agency and role of the NGOs, many have positioned themselves to mediate between grassroots or community-based organizations and the international cooperation for development (Carroll, 1992; Landim, 1988). The development-oriented NGOs entered into a partnership with both bilateral and multilateral development associations, and the local governments or municipalities that have been assigned or have assumed for themselves, the responsibility for advancing the development process within the institutional framework of the new model (Blair, 1995). In the process, as executing agents of the project of international cooperation, NGOs play an ambiguous role that has not been exempt from criticisms by many grassroots organizations and a few academics (Marcos, 1996; Harriss, 2001). The thrust of these criticisms is that often NGOs have wittingly or unwittingly served as a Trojan Horse for the forces of neoliberal globalization, advancing the interests of external agents rather than those of the communities and grassroots organizations (Wallace, 2003).[10]

It is argued that in accepting the funding and conforming to the programmatic principles and requirements of the multilateral and bilateral development associations the NGOs have contributed to the disarticulation and disempowerment of grassroots organizations in terms of their capacity to confront the power structure on the issue of improving access to land other productive resources—"asset redistribution," in the lingo of development.[11] In exchange for giving up a confrontational politics and the search for radical structural change in the structure of production and decision-making, the grassroots organizations have been empowered to participate in decisions that are strictly local in their scope and effects (Marcos, 1996).

More precisely, in the context of the partnership strategy pursued by international development agencies and the neoliberal state, community-based or grassroots organizations have been empowered to participate in the identification of their basic needs and decisions as to how, where and on what to spend the poverty alleviation funds that might come their way under the "new social policy" of "human sustainable development." From the perspective of grassroots and community-based organizations, particularly those concerned with more fundamental change in the direction of radical egalitarianism or socialism, this has been a *Faustian* bargain at best.

In this connection,[12] the 1990s was characterized by the construction of inter-sectoral alliances and transnational activist networks. These alliances and networks in many cases and diverse contexts (Brazil, Ecuador, Mexico...) were formed or joined by federations of peasant producer organizations, producer coops, indigenous organizations and labor unions. In the 1980s a number of such alliances were formed by organizations that were otherwise careful to retain their autonomy vis-à-vis political parties and some distance from the NGOs that were sprouting all over the region in the hospitable soil of neoliberalism.[13]

In the 1990s, linkages and strategic alliances among these organizations were broadly extended in the form of regional and international associations of diverse national organizations. In Latin America ASOCODE, formed in Tegucicalpa in 1991, is an example of this trend. Other examples include Iniciativa Civil para la Integración Centroamericana (ICIC), a lobbying group formed by a network of cooperatives, NGOs, labor organizations, community groups, and diverse organizations of small enterprise operators and agricultural producers; and *Via Campesino*, formed in 1993 as an transnational network of fifty-five peasant organizations from thirty-six countries in the Americas, Asia, and Africa.

Although there are few studies on the workings and outcomes of these regional associations and transnational networks, there is little question about their positive role in raising awareness of common problems, establishment of shared principles, and, in some contexts, the concertation of action and in others the formation of a common front or solidarity actions to improve the capacity of local grassroots organizations to influence the policies of governments in the region.

However, the formation of alliances with nonagricultural groups, a rejection of political party ties and the building of transnational networks coincided with, or has led to, a more pluralist and less confrontational approach to politics—a turning away from the strategy of "peasant wars" and the tactic of armed struggle. In the case of the Confederation of Indigenous Nationalities of Ecuador (CONAIE), the leading although battered and weakened force in Ecuador's popular movement, the weekly *Boletin ICCI "RIMAY"* provides a documented report on the changing dynamics of struggle waged by the indigenous movement.

As for intersectoral linkages, they were initially formed between peasant and indigenous organizations and labor unions and workers' *centrales* on the other. However, in many cases these strategic alliances broke down or were ineffective, leading a number of organizations in the agrarian and indigenous movement to turn toward associational-type social organizations in the cities and urban center. In some cases, these linkages are mediated by political parties in the pursuit of state power, but for the most part they relate to strategic alliances around critical issues affecting both urban and rural organizations in the popular movement In some contexts (i.e., Bolivia) shared concerns and actions were concerted and pursued within the framework of a common organization, designed to the purpose of broadening the social base of a common struggle against the neoliberal state and its policies. More generally, however, the diverse interests of class-based social groups were brought together not organizationally but in a strategic alliance between diverse federations of peasants, indigenous peoples, and organized workers. This has been the case, for example, in the struggles waged by the MST, the Zapatistas and CONAIE.

In this connection, the MST is an organization of landless or near-landless rural "workers" while CONAIE and the Ejército Zapatista de Liberación Nacional (EZLN) are organizations of indigenous peasants and their communities, the economies of which are based on a peasant household mode of production. The Revolutionary Armed Forces of Colombia (FARC), in a very different context, and under conditions that are to an extent shared yet unique to Colombia, also has its social basis in the peasantry broadly defined. In each case the noted dynamism of the social movements, in terms of the mobilized forces of popular resistance, can be attributed, at least to some extent, to the system of class and inter-sectoral alliances involved. This is why the political landscape of the Central and South American countryside in the 1990s is littered by so many cross-sectoral organizations.[14] By the same token, the relative failure of these organizations of peasant farmers, indigenous peoples and rural workers to create a sustained popular movement against neoliberalism, and to advance an alternative project, can be similarly explained.

The mid-1990s seems to have been a turning point in the popular movement in terms of both the strategy of inter-sectoral linkages and resort to the mechanism of democratic elections as a way of bringing about social change *with* state power. To that point the indigenous and peasant movements had relied primarily on a strategy of social mobilization and the tactics of direct action. However, in the mid-1990s, the major organizations in these movements, such as the MST and CONAIE (also the cocaleros in Bolivia and the Zapatistas in Chiapas) in some cases opted for the parliamentary road to state-power (to use of the electoral mechanism in their politics) but in all cases turned toward "civil society" for political support and assistance—for a "no power" approach to social change, to bring about change in government policy without resort to political confrontation and direct action. In effect, the popular movement was divided as to what road it might take to social change: (1) social mobilization and direct action—in the form of a social movement; (2) democracy—use of the electoral mechanism in their local and national politics; and/or (3) local development—to seek improvements in socioeconomic conditions and social change in the local spaces of the power structure rather than challenging it.

The divisive effect on the popular movement of the decision to take the "parliamentary road" to social change is clearly illustrated in subsequent political developments in Bolivia and Ecuador. In the case of Bolivia the resort to the electoral apparatus of liberal democracy and the election of Evo Morales did bring legal, cultural and political rights to the indigenous communities, but it also led to the cooption of the movement by the state. Cultural gains were at the expense of organizational and political unity, and with extremely limited socio-economic benefits (absolutely no change in the structure of landhold-ing despite the revolutionary rhetoric). In the case of Ecuador, resort to the parliamentary road to social change almost destroyed CONAIE as a social movement.

As for the MST, the largest and most dynamic of Latin America's peasant movements, it did not resort to the electoral mechanism, choosing instead to combine a strategy of social mobilization and direct action, as a means of improving access of movement members to the land (if not a fundamental change in the structure of owner-ship), with a strategy of alliances with "civil society" in Brazil itself and abroad—in what might be termed "global civil society." The out-comes of this strategy vis-à-vis global civil society need more study but they do seem to include limited positive benefits such as enhanced access to financial resources and a level of organizational support that could be used as form of political capital, a potential lever of change in public policy. However, in regard to the partnerships forged with the NGOs in Brazil's civil society, the outcomes thus far are mixed to say the least, and negative to say more.

The problem, one also discovered by the Zapatistas, is that regard-less of the professed ideological concern with neoliberalism the NGOs are after all agents of the neoliberal state, funded and contracted in order to bring the peasants into line with the new world order, to adjust the best way they can to its dynamics. In this connection, vir-tually all of the developmental NGOs that operate in Brazil—and the same is true for Chile, Ecuador, Peru and Colombia—are financed either by the intergovernmental "overseas development associations" or, increasingly, by the state itself. As a result, the peasant and indig-enous movements are expected, as a funding condition, to moderate their politics and to channel and transmute their demand for social change into an acceptable form within the limits allowed by the system of democratic politics. Indeed, the effect of this political adjustment on the politics of the MST has been noted by a number of observers, who point toward evidence of ideological moderation in the stance and politics of the leadership, a change that can be attributed directly to the strategy of links to Brazil's civil society. Indeed, the MST itself, in seeking to move beyond the politics of land occupation to the politics of production on the land, to an extent has been converted into an NGO, with the inevitable consequence of an implicit agreement to abide by the rules of the game decreed by the political class.

Conclusion

It is possible to identify across Latin America a growing trend toward linkages among diverse organizations involved in the popular struggle.[15] The most important of these linkages brought together peasants, indigenous communities and workers—both urban and rural—within the same organization (e.g., the CMS—Coordinadora de Movimientos Sociales in Ecuador) but more often bringing them together in the limited non-organizational form of a strategic or tactical alliance.

The importance of multiclass alliances to the popular struggle cannot be overemphasized. The dynamics of these alliances are critical to an understanding the nature and scope of political responses to neoliberal capitalist development in the region, and for gauging the forces unleashed in the process of popular struggle against these conditions. For one thing, horizontal links and alliances among organizations in the popular movement provide conditions for coordinating and directing the accumulated and mobilized forces for change—for moving beyond resistance and opposition to constructive revolutionary change and development. The agency for this cannot be found in the state and certainly not the market, whether regulated or free or in business associations. They have to be sought within the popular movement itself as well as civil society.[16] The question is whether alliances should be sought and constructed with the associational type of NGO in the middle-class sector of this society or with class-based organizations—with a reconstituted labor movement.

To this extent, the strategic turn of the popular movement toward civil society is not necessarily misplaced. The problem consists in the fact that for the NGOs this turn toward strategic partnerships with "civil society" conforms to a strategy pursued by the guardians of the neoliberal world order, anxious to control and limit any dissent from its policy prescriptions, to preserve capitalism from its opponents and enemies. A turn to class society for allies relates to conditions that are real enough, the identification of a possible agency for change, and an assessment of the social forces that can be mobilized for resistance and a democratic socialist transformation.

Neoliberalism and the Social Movements: Mobilizing the Resistance

The imposition of the neoliberal imperial order in the early 1980s polarized society and sharpened the contradictions between regions, classes, and ethnic groups. This chapter focuses on the dynamic growth of social movements that organized to recover political space and reverse the regressive market-friendly capitalist "reforms" imposed from above with the blessing and backing of Washington. This chapter analyzes the revival and build up of the new class-based movements and the ensuing class and ethnic struggles that culminated in the new millennium in the overthrow of client neoliberal regimes. From the smoldering embers and the ashes of the Washington Consensus, there emerged a new more pragmatic neoliberal order based on a perceived need to retreat from an unregulated form of free market capitalism and establish a more inclusive form of development.

We noted in chapter 1 that the neoliberal agenda of "structural reform" in macroeconomic policy was widely implemented in the 1980s via the agency of the World Bank and the International Monetary Fund (IMF) as extensions of the imperial state system, in the context of a call for a new world order, a region-wide debt crisis, and the defeat and destruction of both urban-centered labor movements and the rural movements for land reform and national liberation. However, these neoliberal policies in their turn generated forces of resistance.

At the time the state was in partial retreat, having shed its responsibility for social welfare and economic development, turning it over to the "private sector" (the multinational corporations and financial institutions of global capital) and civil society in an alliance with the overseas development associations formed under the umbrella of international cooperation. As for the popular movement for national liberation and social change, in the dual form of organized labor and the land struggle, for the most part they had been defeated, decapitated, or brought to ground in a process of integrated rural development and the deployment of the repressive apparatus of the client states, backed up by imperial power.

In the vortex of these political developments, and with the dual and combined agency of the World bank and the IMF, Latin America entered a period "lost to development" in terms of productive investment of capital, and the destruction of the productive forces in both industry and agriculture, with a resulting regression in living standards and a deterioration in the social conditions of most people in the popular sector.

In response to the forces and the policies that generated these conditions a variety of new social movements were organized. Some of them were class-based, focused on a concern with issues of land reform and the rights of labor. But others were focused on issues that were not directly connected to the class struggle, giving rise to all sorts of postmodernist misconceptions.

In the working class barrio movements were formed to defend members of the community from the ravages of free market capitalist development (soup kitchens, self-defense organizations etc.), to demand an end to military rule and to protest the new wave of neoliberal policies (Petras and Leiva, with Veltmeyer 1994). This movement, as well as a growing cycle of spontaneous protests against "IMF reforms"—culminated in the *Caracazo* of 1989, were class-based. However, the attention and concern of many academics at the time, armed with a postmodernist political "imaginary" and ensconced in their offices, was with a wave of "new social movements" formed in conditions of an emerging "civil society" composed of a myriad of social organizations rooted in the urban middle class. These organizations, and the associated "new social movements," were concerned with issues such as the protection of human rights and the environment and the advancement of gender and other forms of social equality, issues that to a new generation of postmodernist scholars attuned to cyberspace rather than the real world appeared to have no class basis or any connection with the workings of capitalism.

As for the neoliberal policies foisted on the governments in the region under these conditions, opposition and resistance was marked by sporadic protest—IMF riots, as they were termed, with reference to the perceived agency behind neoliberal policies. But at the time there was little organized resistance to these policies—only sporadic outbreaks of protest, allowing a new generation of postmodern intellectuals to advance their theory of "new [non-class] social movements." But with the emergence of new sociopolitical movements mounted by rural landless workers, peasants, and in some contexts, indigenous communities, this would change soon enough. These class-based movements would come to dominate the political landscape in the 1990s, rendering irrelevant the postmodernist theory of "new," non-class social movements.

The Resurgence of the Latin American Left

The Left in Latin America, both in its political parties and in the form of labor movements in the cities and the movements for land and national liberation in the countryside, appeared in retreat, defeated by the forces of reaction mobilized by the imperialist state and its lackeys in Latin America. However, all was not as it seemed. The neoliberal model itself was already under serious question, surrounded by periodic outbreaks of protest in the urban centers and besieged by opposition and resistance, even from within the ramparts of empire—by those concerned that the advance of "economic freedom" (and economic stabilization) came at an excessively high social cost that was likely to translate into political instability.

Although most publicists, journalists, academics, and government and World Bank officials celebrated the advent of "neoliberalism," opposition, which in time could lead to a challenge to the whole free-market power structure, was growing. As yet only loosely associated—in forums, seminars, and international gatherings—this new oppositional force had solid roots in a number of countries and was extending its support from specific regions and classes to the construction of several national counterhegemonic blocs. The Left was staging a comeback.

To write about the Left in this context may be somewhat misleading because there was more than one: there were the older parties that remained, weakened but active, and the new sociopolitical movements. What many casual observers, and not a few journalists and academics, referred to as "the Left" included "referents" who had long ago abandoned the class struggle and in large part had been assimilated into the liberal political establishment or its nongovernmental organization (NGO) periphery. What may explain the confusion is the manner in which this conversion was staged: many former leftists at the time resorted to intellectual posturing in which they labeled their own earlier positions—and that of an emerging revolutionary left, concerned to mobilize the forces of resistance against neoliberalism—as "outmoded" or "orthodox," presenting themselves as more up-to-date, renovated, modernized, post-something, or other—a social democratic Left.

To come to terms with these political developments at the beginning of the last decade of the old millennium, we need first to identify the different waves of social movements that had emerged and were emerging on the Left and to differentiate them; second, to identify their social base, style of political action, and political perspective; and third, to document the growth, internal contradictions, and political challenges that confronted the burgeoning sociopolitical movements on the Left.

Form and Substance of the Resurgence on the Left

The stronghold for the resurgence of the Left at the turn into the 1990s was in the countryside. In a number of countries, the period was characterized by massive land occupation movements of landless rural workers, a semiproletarianized peasantry. The most important of these was the Landless Rural Workers Movement (MST) in Brazil. With hundreds of peasant organizers and hundreds of thousands of active supporters in the countryside, it forced the renewal of a national debate among all the political parties on the issue of agrarian reform.[1] Most observers of Brazilian politics at the time agreed that the MST was the most dynamic, best organized, and effective social movement in Brazil, if not in Latin America. In Bolivia, the closing of most of the tin mines, and the heavy influx of cheap imports and government-condoned contraband had weakened the mining and industrial unions. In their place the peasant confederations, particularly the coca farmers, led major confrontations with the state and their American patrons, blocking highways and spearheading general strikes that paralyzed the country (Contreras Baspineiro, 1994). In Paraguay, the National Peasant Federation was at the core of the political mobilization that blocked the return of the military, forcing agrarian issues into the center of a national debate. Together with other peasant organizations, they led 50,000 peasants through the streets of Asunción to the Presidential Palace and National Congress (*Informativo Campesino* [Asunción], No. 91, April 1996). In Mexico, major popular struggles took place in the countryside. Guerrero, Chiapas, and Oaxaca saw large-scale confrontations between indigenous peasants and the state (*La Jornada*, August 10, 1996, p. 3). In Ecuador, Colombia, and El Salvador, similar processes of peasant mobilizations redefined the national political agenda.

Not all the instances of left resurgence were located in the countryside. There was also a renewal of civic, peasant and labor movements as well as growing guerrilla groups in Colombia, a growing influence of the Chilean Communist Party in the trade unions, urban movements in Venezuela and Argentina, the emergence of an independent, "class oriented" trade unionism in Mexico City and in the north among auto workers; dissident and combative sectors of the National Labour Confederation (CUT) in Brazil; and militant teachers' unions led by Marxists in Bolivia, Paraguay, Chile, Mexico, and Brazil. Nevertheless, while organized, urban, working-class movements were not absent from the struggle, and in some instances took center-stage, the truly revolutionary action and the most dynamic movements in this resurgence of the Left were rural.

Many commentators and analysts, even those as distinguished as Eric Hobsbawm (1994: 8, 289), wrote of the political eclipse of the peasantry. The obituaries, however, proved premature. There are a number of reasons why demographic arguments about the shrinking size of the rural labor force do not necessarily translate into political analysis for Latin American countries. First, notwithstanding the forces of productive and social transformation, shrinking numbers do not nullify the fact that tens of millions of families continued to live in the countryside. Second, given the crises affecting urban areas then and now, particularly growing unemployment and poverty, the cities no longer were seen as sites of "opportunity" for young peasants seeking a more secure livelihood and better living conditions for their families. Third, when and where land occupations were on the agenda, there was even a movement from provincial towns and cities back to the countryside—a "re-peasantization" effect. Fourth, neoliberal policies had battered small producers, driving down prices of staples and increasing indebtedness, creating family and social bonds between the mostly young landless sons and daughters involved in the land invasions. Fifth, "structural" considerations apart, a new generation of (primary or secondary school) "educated" peasant leaders, with strong organizational capabilities, a sophisticated understanding of national and international politics, and a profound commitment to creating a politically educated set of cadres, had emerged.

Local leaders of both genders intervened in regions of conflict, transforming previously spontaneous and easily defeated occupations into well-planned and executed mass political actions. The combination of structural conditions and the growth of a new political leadership built around the principle that "every member is an organizer" were instrumental in the rise of the peasant movements.

It should be noted, though, that these were neither peasant movements traditionally nor were the rural cultivators who comprised them divorced from urban life or activities. In some instances, the new peasants were former workers, particularly, in the case of Bolivia, miners, displaced because of plant or mine closures, or they had been peasants a generation earlier.[2] In other cases, they are the "excess" sons and daughters of peasants who entered religious institutions, became involved in the rural struggles, and abandoned the church to lead the struggle for land reform.[3] In many cases, they were daughters of small peasants with a primary or secondary education who joined and sometimes led land occupations rather than migrate to the cities to work as domestic servants.[4]

The "new peasantry," especially those who led the struggle, traveled to the cities, participated in seminars and leadership training schools, and engaged in political debates. In short, even as they were rooted in the rural struggle, lived in land settlements, and engaged in agricultural cultivation, they had a cosmopolitan vision. The quantity and quality of these "peasant intellectuals" have varied from country to country depending on the resources and maturity of the movement. In Brazil, the MST was well known for its heavy investment in leadership training, with hundreds of its members passing each year through different levels of sociopolitical and technical education (MST Dirección Nacional, 1991). Other movements such as those in Paraguay and Bolivia still relied on a small number of well-informed leaders.

Another point regarding the "new peasantry" was that it was generally autonomous of any electoral and/or sectarian left parties, even the most radical. It was largely engaged in direct action rather than the electoral process. The MST in Brazil had, and still has, "fraternal" relations with the Workers' Party (PT), generally supporting their candidates and occasionally presenting its own within the Party.[5] But the main strength of the MST was its extra-parliamentary struggle, including land invasions, the blocking of highways, and sit-ins at the Agrarian Reform Institutes. MST tactics, strategy, and ideological debates are also decided within the movement and are not subordinated to the PT or its parliamentary representatives. On the contrary, the MST's actions shaped the commitment of the PT leadership to the agrarian struggle at the time, before Lula's advent to state power.

Similarly in Bolivia, the militant peasant organizations broke with the nationalist parties and socialist sects on the parliamentary Left, and engaged in internal debates about forming their own political movement (MAS, the Movement towards Socialism, as it turned out). In Paraguay, many leaders of the National Federation of Peasants who sought to provide a national focus for the peasantry launched a new revolutionary socialist movement.

In discussion with the leaders of CUT, the major Confederation of Brazilian Workers, it was clear that the MST was on the frontlines and at the cutting edge of the popular struggle for land and against neoliberalism. Most trade union leaders readily admitted that the MST was far more cohesive and organized for confrontation than the urban industrial unions, which, as elsewhere in Latin America, had lost both their radical edge and their capacity to wage political struggle. Posters plastered on the walls of downtown Rio condemning a major massacre of MST militants in Pará made it clear that the rural struggle had became a major "cause" for militant sectors of the CUT. Hitherto, the labor movement based on organized labor tended to marginalize if not totally neglect the struggle in the countryside.[6]

Furthermore, the new peasant movements were strongly influenced by a blend of classical Marxism and, in differing contexts, by ethnic, gender, and ecological considerations. In Paraguay, and particularly in Bolivia, the questions of social liberation and rural struggle are strongly infused with a revindication of ethnic, linguistic, cultural, and even national claims.[7] In Brazil and Bolivia, organized groups of peasant women pressured these movements for greater influence and representation.[8]

The new peasant movements were linked together in a Latin American regional organization, the Congreso Latinoamericano de Organizaciones del Campo (CLOC), and they were increasingly involved in the international formation Via Campesino set up to advance the struggle for land and rural livelihoods, and against the neoliberal model of capitalist development and agrarian change. Through these links and others, an emerging "internationalist" consciousness and practice emerged. For example, the militants of the Brazilian MST began to work across national borders with their counterparts in Paraguay and, to a lesser degree, Argentina, Bolivia, and Uruguay.

In summary, the resurgence of the peasant movements in the 1990s was not a simple replay of the movements of the 1960s. In many cases the successes and failures of the earlier movements had been studied and debated within the movement. While there was a certain continuity because of the presence of a handful of older militants in the new movements, and some of the leaders were the children of the past generation of activists, a series of important differences at the tactical, strategic, political, and organizational levels indicated that the indigenous, landless rural workers and peasant-led movements of the 1990s were to some (or a considerable) extent "new"—not "new" in the sense ascribed by Holloway (2002) to the Zapatista movement in Chiapas, but nevertheless a promising and creative political force.

The Political Context for the Resurgence of a Popular Movement

The resurgence of the popular movement in the 1990s took place in a complex and changing political context, some elements of which were described in chapter 1. In the first place, the policies of the neoliberal regimes negatively affected a vast array of social groups and classes, including segments of the bourgeoisie—operators of small and some medium-level "enterprises," farms and ranches—many of which were forced into bankruptcy or bank indebtedness.[9] Since the late 1980s, the urban movements and trade unions were in decline in most countries, their organizational and political capacity seriously diminished. In this situation, the rise of the indigenous and peasant movements was looked upon favorably by social groups adversely affected by the neoliberal policies pursued by virtually every government. They were regarded as a political mechanism to delegitimize or weaken the application of neoliberal policies—hence the favorable press and media accounts that appeared on occasion, particularly in Brazil. Support for the MST by sectors of the bourgeoisie was graphically illustrated while the authors were in Brazil in May 1996, when a group of entrepreneurs organized a luncheon for the MST to express their support for agrarian reform.[10]

The peasant movements in resistance and opposing neoliberalism filled the political space abandoned by electoral coalitions on the center-left. The center-Left at the time either failed to win elections or turned toward assimilating liberal politics, in some cases joining neo-liberal regimes. This ebbing in the tide of electoral center-left oppo-sitional politics was accompanied in many cases by the weakening of the trade unions, partly as a result of antilabor legislation, mass firings, and high unemployment, and partly because of the accom-modating attitudes of the trade union leadership. And, as argued in chapter 2, there were also "structural" forces at work in weaken-ing the organizational and political capacity of organized labor. The working class of the 1990s was very different from that of the 1970s. The makings of an industrial proletariat were entirely replaced by the formation of a new class of street workers—the vaunted (and often misconceived) "informal sector." Under these conditions, the erup-tion of class warfare in the countryside was a "spark" that served to ignite public debate and call into question the overall political project of the neoliberal regime everywhere in power.

The Left Social Movements: Mobilizing the Anti-Neoliberal Resistance and Social Revolution

Over the last three decades of neoliberal rule, what we might describe as the "social movement Left" emerged in three district waves. To understand the significance and nature of those sociopolitical move-ments, it is important to place them in the context of conditions at the time and to distinguish them from their predecessors.

The first wave took place as the import substitution phase went into crisis and led to the confrontation between socialist popular movements and what became the neoliberal restoration and military-led regimes. The first wave of the contemporary Left began in the 1960s and continued into the mid-1970s. It included mass social movements, guerrilla armies, and electoral parties. Sometimes class and military activities merged.[11] Sometimes electoral and trade union politics were combined.[12]

This was the period of the so-called New Left—movements and parties that challenged the dominance of the pro-Moscow communist parties. There were Maoists, Fidelistas, those influenced by Trotskyist ideas, and others who grew out of the Christian and Populist move-ments. As mentioned earlier, the national security regimes or dictator-ships that dominated the political landscape at the time decimated this wave. Hundreds of thousands of activists were killed, jailed, or forced into exile. As a result of the repression, and overseas relations with social democratic foundations, the great majority who returned to politics did so as social democrats, and sometimes as neoliberals. This connects with the first wave of anti-neoliberal social movements.

The second wave of leftists emerged in the dictatorial period and the years following—first in opposition to the authoritarian regimes and later to the "neoliberal agenda." This wave found expression in the Foro of São Paulo and included the FLMN (Frente Farabundo Martí para la Liberación Nacional) in El Salvador, the Sandinistas in Nicaragua, the Workers' Party of Brazil, the Broad Front of Uruguay, Venezuela's Causa R, the Revolutionary Democratic Party of Mexico, and the Frente Grande in Argentina.[13] These parties, coalitions and ex-guerrilla movements, however, were sucked into the electoral politics trap and began to accommodate to neoliberal policies on privatization, "globalization" and other issues. In time, they lost a good part of their identity as parties of the Left and became more and more divorced from the popular struggles in the shantytowns, countryside, and factories. Some were assimilated into the NGO framework, working in the niches of the World Bank's free-market and antistatist politics. In most of these parties or movements there remain leftist and activist currents, but they are marginalized in the interests of respectability.

The third wave of the movement to some extent overlapped with the second group but demonstrated greater force and resilience. Its leaders tended to be young, in their early twenties to mid thirties, and were drawn from the peasantry, provincial trade unions, and school teachers. These activists differed significantly from their predecessors.[14] First, many were not from the university—in fact, the intellectuals were still largely oriented to the center-left electoral machines or to their professional careers. Second, the new movements had few financial resources but tremendous élan and "mystique." Their leaders traveled to meetings by bus (sometimes thirty or forty hours), lived on their wages or farm income and had rather Spartan offices. There were very few full-time paid officials and virtually no bureaucracy. There were no privileges—no cars, office equipment, or staff. The leaders (e.g., Evo Morales) were "moral persons," honest and scrupulous in their financial affairs and personal relations. Very few were "personalist," concerned with their own mystique. Rather, they debated in assemblies and were part of a collective leadership. The idea of the new organizations was that each member would be an organizer. To a greater or lesser extent, these leaders were highly critical of the opportunism of the electoral Left and NGO intellectuals who they experienced as manipulative outsiders serving external patrons.

Those who were previously part of guerrilla struggles were highly critical of the vertical style leadership in those organizations. They generally rejected the call to become cogs in the electoral machines of the "political class" on the Left, choosing instead to deepen ties to their social base. Even so, while this third wave represents intransigent opposition to the imposition of neoliberalism, it has never offered a fully articulated plan for the seizure of power or for an alternative form of national development, such as constructed by Bolivia's current social movement regime since Evo Morales assumed state power in 2006.

A Third Wave of Anti-neoliberal Movements

The most dynamic of the third wave of anti-neoliberal social movements, for the most part organized in the 1980s, grew massively and escalated their activity in the 1990s. They were invariably based on an organization of rural landless workers, peasants and, in some contexts, indigenous communities. Here we will provide more details about the dynamics of the most important of the movements formed in Brazil, Ecuador, Bolivia, Paraguay, Argentina, and Mexico.

The Rural Landless Workers of Brazil Take Center-Stage

The MST is not a revolutionary organization, and it has never been concerned with the seizure of state power as such. Rather, it has worked toward an effective implementation of the constitution, which stipulated that uncultivated land could be expropriated for social use. Thus, it has been both "legalist" and oriented toward direct action. The politics of direct action were inserted into the gap between democratic ideology (and the progressive clauses of the constitution) and the socioeconomic ties of the liberal regime with the ruling class. The resurgence of the Left in Brazil took place in distinct settings and is not easily pigeonholed. The MST, for example, grew from a regional movement that was based largely in the south-central region into a national movement with organizers increasingly active in the north, northeast, and western regions of the country (*A Luta pela Terra No Brazil*, pp. 23–39). Their struggle over the course of the 1990s increasingly drew support from the cities among trade unions and sectors of the church. They were viewed with respect and sympathy by the bulk of the *favelados* (slum dwellers) of Rio and São Paulo. Midway into the decade they shifted toward organizing large-scale land occupations near provincial cities, both to facilitate the gathering of mass support and to form urban alliances.[15] As they moved into the inner heartland of large uncultivated estates, however, they faced increasing violence and in some cases were forced to set up self-defense committees to confront marauding *pistoleros* (gunmen) hired by the landowners to drive out the settlers.

Over the course of the decade they organized over 139,000 families into productive cooperatives, some of them even engaged in export agriculture. They "expropriated" a total of 7.2 million hectares of land and organized 55 rural cooperatives in 12 states. They established 880 schools with 38,000 pupils.[16] Successful cooperatives usually freed activists to participate in the support of landless peasants making new occupations, and they contributed food to land occupants waiting for government expropriation and credits. The MST Congress in July 1995 drew more than 5,000 delegates representing several hundred thousand peasants (*Jornal dos Trabalhadores Rurais Sem Terra*, São Paulo, August 1995). Each state hired buses and brought their own food and bedding. The leadership training school in Santa Catarina houses approximately 80 persons in bunk beds. There was bread, cheese, and coffee for breakfast, cold showers, and rudimentary classrooms. But it all came together.

The countryside in Brazil in the mid-1990s was a tinderbox. The problem was not organizing land occupations; hundreds of thousands of hungry families were ready to respond—and usually did—to an MST appeal. The problem was organizing to win. For that, there needed to be political support before any occupation, political organization to resist displacement, and logistical support—food, supplies, and so forth—while the movement negotiated with the government to finance production. For the most part, the MST was able to generate the needed level of public and popular support to conduct its "occupations" and campaign. In 1995, for example, the MST led 92 land occupations and by June 1996 another 120 land occupations, resulting in a total of 168 *campamentos* (land settlements) with 40,000 families awaiting government expropriation (*Sem Terra*, July 1996, p. 8). However, the rightward shift of the PT in 1995 following its defeat in the presidential elections by Fernando Henrique Cardoso (it would take another two national elections before Ignacio [Lula] Da Silva would assume state power in the name of the PT), set the stage for another major land occupation offensive.

This offensive in part was in response to the recognition that Cardoso, the former Marxist sociologist and advocate of "dependency theory," was closely tied to the parties of the right-wing agro-export landed elite (the PFL [Partido da Frente Liberal] and PMDB [Partido do Movimento Democrático Brasileiro]) as well as the reactionary sectors of his own party (the PSDB [Partido da Social Democracia Brasileira]). Cardoso's links with the World Bank and overseas multinational corporations deepened his commitment to privatize strategic industries, promote agro-export sectors, and encourage large-scale foreign investment in Brazil under favorable "rules of the game." Another reason for the offensive was growing pressure from a number of MST militants for a more aggressive policy outside of and independent of the PT, which was correctly perceived as being an electoral party in which sectors were moving beyond classical social democratic politics toward "social liberal" policies.[17]

Finally, it was recognized that "objective" conditions and "subjective" factors in the countryside were increasingly "maturing" for an offensive. The initial response to the first occupations was extremely positive in the areas adjoining them. Spontaneous land occupations materialized. The MST decided to provide organizational leadership and conscious organization to turn these spontaneous local activities into a national movement.

Toward the end of 1995 and in early 1996 land invasions became everyday affairs all over the country in regions that had previously been bulwarks of the Right. Cardoso responded by threatening to use force and by offering empty promises to settle squatters in exchange for a moratorium on new occupations. The MST negotiated but pointedly refused to stop the land occupations—knowing that a truce would eliminate its main negotiating card, weaken its appeal to the landless and demobilize hundreds of its young leaders and activists ("Sem-terra nao aceitan a trégua dos ruralistas," *Jornal do Brasil*, June 4, 1996, p. 1). So the struggle deepened and was extended into the most dangerous regions.

In retrospect, it is evident that from mid-decade of the 1990s to 2002 was a watershed in MST politics. At one level it sought to develop an effective counterhegemonic strategy and a powerful political bloc that could integrate the city and countryside. At another level, however, the MST was forging links and alliances with diverse groups and NGOs in an emerging "civil society" in both Brazil's cities and globally, to broaden the social base of political and financial support for its struggle and to transform a politics of land occupation and settlements into a strategy for cooperative social production.

To understand the direction, dynamics, and particular forms of this struggle, we need to make reference to the analysis provided by MST leader and strategist João Pedro Stedile. There have been diverse attempts to analyze and assess the ideological orientation and the class nature of the MST as a social movement—whether the movement has a socialist character (anti-neoliberal, anti-capitalist, and oriented toward socialist transformation) or whether its fundamental aim is limited to maximizing gains for its members within the capitalist system. In this connection, it appears (by different, if not all, accounts) that the MST leadership is Marxist, with a clear anti-capitalist, anti-neoliberal socialist orientation. On the other hand, it is evident that the members of the MST over the years have been mobilized not on the basis of this ideology but by an appeal to class interest. The political practice of the MST from the beginning and since has been confined to advancing the land struggle within the political limits of the existing economic and political system: mobilizing land occupations rather than mobilizing against the government's neoliberal policies. Within these limits, the MST has cultivated a dense network of ties with all sorts of organizations in the antiglobalization movement and has helped form a dense global network of organizations concerned with bringing about "another world," an alternative to neoliberal globalization. However, at the level of national politics the MST's approach has been pragmatic rather than ideological—directed by what is possible in diverse conjunctures of the class struggle.

Stedile's own position vis-à-vis what he sees as the broader class struggle (beyond the politics of mobilization for land) is fairly clear, enunciated in different documents and discussions. In 1996 (June 22), in an interview and discussions with the authors and movement militants, he identified three moments in the recent history to that date of this struggle: (1) the final stages in the struggle against the military dictatorship in the late 1970s and early 1980s; (2) the mass struggle to impeach former President Collor; and (3) the current phase in which Cardoso was actively implementing the neoliberal agenda. In each period, he noted, important sectors of the bourgeoisie and their allies in the mass media and the major political parties were interested in weakening the incumbent power-holders, in effect giving "conjunctural support" to the MST. However, after they accomplished their mission and achieved their goal (to advance their immediate, medium- and long-term economic interests) they withdrew that support.

Thus, as Stedile saw it, points of internal division within the ruling bloc provide propitious moments for the MST to launch activities that at least had the tacit backing of sectors of the elite and the press. On the other hand, the strategic and tactical moves made by the MST in subsequent conjunctures of the class struggle, especially under the more opportunistic neoliberal regime established by Da Silva ("Lula"), suggests that the correlation of class forces have not been too favorable to the MST. Not only has the pace of rural mobilization been on the decline, in large part because of its "critical support" of the Lula regime but it also appears that the MST has lost some of the active support of the broad public it once had before Lula's election. Rather than advancing the anti-neoliberal forces of socialist transformation, the MST seems to have settled for advancing the land struggle within the existing system.

CONAIE: A Decade of Class Struggle and Major Gains for the Indigenous Movement in Ecuador

A number of analysts of the indigenous movement look at the 1990s as a decade of not only class struggle but also significant "gains" for the movement—attributed to its capacity for, and strategy of, mass mobilization. The major agency of this political development in Ecuador, and in the 1990s the most powerful indigenous movement in Latin America, was the Confederation of Indigenous Nationalities of Ecuador (CONAIE), a nationwide amalgam of indigenous nationalities in the highlands, the coastal areas and Amazonia.

The history of CONAIE as a social movement in the 1990s can be traced via a succession of political conjunctures that began and ended with a major uprising. The first of these conjunctures was in 1988, two years after CONAIE's formation as a social movement and almost a decade before the formation of Pachakutik, a political formation that allowed some members of CONAIE to participate in the system of electoral politics and use elections rather than social mobilization in their politics of change. At this conjuncture, the main concern for CONAIE was to raise awareness within the movement about precisely "who the enemy was," namely "the rich, a dominant class that has the power to dictate laws against another class, the poor, who have no power and suffer the consequences of these laws" ("Antecedentes al surgimiento de Pachakutik," *Riccarshun*, December 1988; ECUARUNARI, 1998: 255).

The ultimate aim of CONAIE was to remove the "oligarchs," the "enemy of the people" who caused "the poverty and misery of millions of Ecuadorians" from their position of state power ("*derribarles del poder del estado*"). The adopted means for doing so was a campaign to elect a popular constituent assembly that would see through a political project of securing social justice for Ecuador's indigenous peoples within a new plurinational state. To this end CONAIE's base were mobilized against the government, with particular reference to its policies and the underlying neoliberal model of free-market capitalist development. Each of CONAIE's constituent organizations "actively participated" in this process, "consolidating the new political space with a proposal for an alliance with other social sectors of the popular movement, seeking to overcome problems of internal disunity, particularly as regards the 'Amazon Question'—a matter of an urgent, and as it turns out persisting, political crisis" (ECUARUNARI, 1998: 257).

The next critical conjuncture in the indigenous movement was in 1990 in the context of, and in direct response to (1) the government's implementation of neoliberal economic reforms and austerity measures designed in Washington and mandated by the IMF; (2) heightened class conflicts over land; and (3) a number of broad political demands, including abandoning the neoliberal economic model and implementing a program of alternative legal and constitutional reforms pressed upon the government in the form of direct actions initiated with the takeover of the Santo Domingo church in Quito but followed by similar actions in the altiplano. These actions, it turned out, "sparked the flame that lit the straw" of a conflagration that consumed the whole country. With the supportive and coordinated actions of diverse groups and organizations in the urban sector, especially the church-based communities in popular barrios, the mobilization by CONAIE was transformed into an uprising of historic significance, an important reference point for subsequent surges of the movement over the decade, culminating in the January 21, 2000 uprising. In effect, the decade began and ended with a major uprising of the indigenous movement.

Major achievements of the 1990 uprising included the emergence of the indigenous movement as a new actor on the stage of national politics and the unity of the majority of indigenous nationalities organized by CONAIE, particularly in terms of the "contradiction" between not only the movement in the highlands and Amazonia, but also the two discrete dimensions of the movement, namely the "land question" and the struggle for cultural and political identity. In the heat of the first uprising these two dimensions of the movement were combined into one.

The next major conjuncture in the movement, in 1993, included a referendum on the government's proposal to privatize the social security system and continuing class struggle over land. As for the government's political campaign in support of its privatization agenda, it was a total failure. The year was marked by a mass mobilization against the government's privatization agenda orchestrated by the National Federation of Indigenous Social Security, and joined by CONAIE and other popular sector organizations on the political left. But the defeat of the government's agenda, put to the test in a referendum, did not deter the government from proceeding with other parts of its neoliberal agenda. Nor did it slow the rhythm of class struggle and violent confrontations over the land question. Both the Chamber of Agriculture and CONAIE presented the government with alternative legislative projects related to this question, and CONAIE stepped up its tactic of mass mobilization.

To force the government to negotiate the demands of the indigenous movement and engage in a process of dialogue, indigenous communities and peasant organizations across the country mobilized a series of direct actions including protest marches and *"cortas de ruta"*—the blocking of highways, a tactic used with considerable political effect by indigenous peasants throughout the 1990s, and later by the movement of unemployed workers in Argentina. The press saw these direct actions as the radicalized form of another possible "uprising." Although this did not materialize, it was clear to everyone, including the official press, that the antagonism between the big and medium-sized landowners on the one hand and the *minifundista* peasants and landless workers on the other constituted an explosive mix that could produce a very grave "revolutionary" situation in the future if not resolved within "a framework of dialogue and social justice" (*El Tiempo*, June 16, 1993).

In December 2003 the government introduced a state modernization law eliminating price controls and soon thereafter a law (March 2004) that liberalized the domestic market, and then another law (April 2004) designed to "modernize" the agricultural sector—a law that was regarded by CONAIE as a "death sentence" for indigenous peoples, something similar to what North American Free Trade Agreement (NAFTA) represented to the indigenous peoples of Chiapas.

The 1994 Agrarian Development Law had been intended to put an end to the state-led Land Reform program initiated in 1964 in the form of transfers of land to the tillers (peasants/indigenous communities), but in the immediate context of 1994 it resulted in a heightened level of class conflict over land. The year 1995 had seen another turning point in the popular movement mobilized and led by CONAIE but orchestrated via the formation of the Coordinadora de Movimientos Sociales (CMS), a loose coalition of thirty-four labor and social organizations as well as indigenous groups and organizations that included FENOCIN, a leftist grouping of indigenous peasant communities and blacks from the coast that had led the indigenous struggle in the 1970s, as well as CONAIE.

The advance in the popular movement, as well as a shift in emphasis from the land question to the issue of indigenous "rights" and state reform, and a sharper focus on broader national issues (opposition to neoliberalism, protection of the country's "strategic resources," etc.), took place in a situation of deepening economic and political crisis. On the one hand, the country's economic problems, which most analysts attribute to the government's neoliberal policies, which exacerbated rather than attenuated conditions of widespread poverty, had assumed crisis proportions in 1995, a situation that reached its peak in 1999.

Under these conditions of economic contraction and social decline, the political system entered another period of instability, which led to Vice President Alberto Dahik being forcibly removed, and that subsequently forced two presidents to leave office. In this situation of impending economic and political crisis, the indigenous movement, led by CONAIE, engaged its dual political project of strategic alliance with urban social organizations and the formation of the Movimiento de Unidad Pachakutik-Nuevo País (MUPP-NP or Pachakutik), a political organization or movement designed to allow the indigenous communities to participate directly in the system of electoral politics, to contest national and local elections.

In the 1980s the indigenous movement had participated in this political system but for lack of a political instrument of their own, they had to work through the party structure of the Ecuadorian left. During the 1990 uprising, the government claimed that the upswell was orchestrated by the political opposition, forcing CONAIE to turn away from any participation in the electoral system. In any case, the CONAIE leadership was of the view that the critical political dynamics of social change were to be found outside this system. Pachakutik, just as the CMS, was conceived in 1995, but it was not until 1997 that it was given a solid organic structure with a national executive committee, provincial coordinating bodies, diverse commissions, and so on.

This structure allowed CONAIE to advance its own candidates for government office, without having to support the candidacy of other politicians, even those who had very broad support of social organizations in the popular movement. The formation of Pachakutik also undercut clientelism, a structural feature—and seemingly unavoidable feature—of electoral politics.

Notwithstanding this consolidation of an indigenous political movement the major political event of 1997—namely the ousting, in February, of Abdal Bucaram's four-month old government—was brought about not by electoral means but by mass mobilization. The ousting of Bucaram can be compared to the similar event in January 2000 when the governing regime was overthrown temporarily (for a few hours) and replaced by a triumvirate that included Antonio Vargas, CONAIE's president at the time, as well as Lucio Gutiérrez, a leading representative of a group of young army officers who had moved against the government.

The ousting in December 2001 of two presidents in Argentina and the overthrow and forced exile (to the United States, of course) of Bolivia's De Lozada, in October 2003, provided similar lessons to the popular movement: that mass mobilization provides popular sector organizations with a more effective means of regime change than the system of electoral politics, which, from the perspective of long experience, has proven to be full of traps and pitfalls designed by the "political class" as "rules of the game."

The populist politician Abdal Bucaram was a tragicomic figure in the convoluted history of Ecuadorian class politics. He represented the coastal (Guayaquil) commercial bourgeoisie in its longstanding factional dispute over national politics with the Sierra's landed oligarchy, represented by the traditional parties that have tended to dominate both the legislative and executive branches of the government. The push to remove him from office was precipitated by his efforts to extend the package of neoliberal reforms and austerity measures introduced by Léon Febres Cordero in 1984–88, continued in the subsequent social democratic regime of Rodrigo Borja (1988–1992), and further extended by Sixto Durán Ballén in his regime from 1992 to 1996. Febres Cordero had turned Ecuador's national economy toward a neoliberal model of capitalist development with the adoption of an IMF-mandated stabilization program of austerity measures and a process of structural adjustment in the form of financial and trade liberalization. Borja, in response to the Washington Consensus as to the required package of economic reform measures, sought to insert Ecuador into the recently announced and heralded process of "globalization" via policies of trade liberalization and labor market reform, to create thereby a more flexible regulatory regime vis-à-vis the labor process—"*la flexibilización laboral*." The contributions of Durán Ballén in this regard was to both deepen the IMF's program of austerity measures and extend the neoliberal "modernization" reform program via a policy of privatization, turning over strategic areas of the economy (oil, electric generation) to the private sector. Because of the offensive launched by Durán Ballén against labor and the labor movement at the very beginning of his regime, the privatization of public sector enterprises became the central issue of class conflict and remained so until 1998.

The public sector in 1992 included the most powerful unions and the country's biggest enterprises—Petroecuador, Inecel, and Emetel. According to the Centro Andino de Acción Popular (CAAP), which monitors the level of social conflict, of 1,000 significant social "conflicts" from 1996 to 1998, 30 percent originated in the public sector and revolved around the issue of privatization (Equipo de Coyuntura del CAAP, 1998). This was more or less the same share of total social conflicts as Sánchez Parga (1993) found for the labor movement in the 1980s in the heyday of Ecuador's labor movement. Thus, it is not surprising that one of the major means proposed and used by the government (in its 1998 constitutional reform program) to secure "*gobernabilidad*" (governability, good governance) was to take away the right (and thus the capacity) of workers in the public sector to paralyze vital services to the public.

When Bucaram assumed the presidency in August 1996, Ecuador was well down the neoliberal path and in the throes of a protracted economic crisis, which had generated a mounting level of social discontent with conditions of poverty that afflicted 31 percent of the population in 1988, 56 percent in 1995 (76 percent in the rural areas) and, after the adoption of dollarization (an extreme form of neoliberal development) in 2000, 68.8 percent (Larrea, 2004: 50).

Policies pursued by a succession of neoliberal regimes had drastically reduced the share of workers (wages) in national income from 31.9 percent in 1980 to less than 13.6 percent in 1990 and less since, one of the lowest in Latin America (Vicuña, 2000: 76). The purchasing power of the miserable (below-poverty) level of income or wages received by the majority of Ecuadorians experienced a 22 percent fall from 1988 to 1992 and another 73.6 percent from 1995 to 1999 (Vicuña, 2000: 126–27), a situation exacerbated by a general decline in the level (and coverage) of government expenditures on social programs.[18]

In addition, government policies in the 1990s brought about a dramatic weakening of the labor movement vis-à-vis the capacity to negotiate collective contracts for higher wages and improved working conditions (SAPRIN Ecuador, 2004: 69–75). The same policies also generated a huge out-migration—up to 700,000, it has been estimated, since 1998 alone (Vicuña, 2000: 27). Today, remittances from these migrants constitute the second largest source of national revenues after the earnings generated by the export of oil.

Bucaram took over the government in a situation of incipient and occasionally disruptive social conflict in reaction to the government's neoliberal policies. But in retrospect it would seem that the most critical factor in his government's downfall was not so much the parlous state of the economy and the conditions of a broad and deep class struggle as the internal political conflicts within the ruling class, elements of which possibly helped engineer the heightened level of political conflict that shook the Bucaram regime and certainly took advantage of the popular mobilization against the government (Vicuña, 2000: 116).

The move against Bucaram was apparently triggered by a general strike orchestrated by CUT and a coordinated coalition of social organizations. However, it did little to change the policy orientation of the government, which continued on the same neoliberal path, with the implementation of the Law of Economic Transformation ("TROLE" I–II), an omnibus program of diverse measures designed to achieve structural adjustment of the Ecuadorian economy to the requirements of the global economy—and, it can be said, to benefit small groups of economic and social power within the country as well as the guardians of foreign capital. In regard to the latter, the government from 1997 to 2000 paid over $25 billion in interest alone, triple the export earnings over the period and representing up to 45 percent of central government expenditures and 10 percent of GNP (Larrea, 2004: 83; Vicuña, 2000: 1, 16). In making these payments the government not only shortchanged its system of social and development programs but cut back any plans for productive investment, mortgaging any hopes for the country's future and for escaping the economic crisis. In addition to these direct economic and social costs, the series of agreements made with the IMF to bear these costs included a commitment to implement policies that were bound to make things worse—and did.

The economic and social costs of this "adjustment" process were exceedingly high by any measure as the economy spiraled into its worst crisis to date and the "poor," some 8 million according to the

World Bank (half of this population "indigent," i.e., with "earnings" of less than $1 a day), were compensated with *"bonos de la pobreza"* (welfare payments) of $6 a month, recently adjusted to $10.50 (Vicuña, 2000: 176). Per capita production declined by some 30 percent from 1998 to 2000, with a corresponding decline in per capita income (Vicuña, 2000: 174). Under conditions of massive decapitalization and the destruction of capital invested and deployed in diverse sectors of the economy, thousands of small and medium-sized firms went bankrupt or disappeared. Unemployment soared to record heights (from 8 to 17 percent), as did underemployment (up to 60 percent), while the population living and working in conditions of poverty doubled from 1988 to 2000 (Fundación José Peralta, 2003).

This policy, together with the conditions of the TROLE (law of economic transformation) I and II, two omnibus packages of stabilization and adjustment measures, in turn sparked a broad insurrectionary social movement, an uprising that brought down the government on January 21.

The conditions that combined to produce the uprising and overthrow of the government, marked by six days of active resistance and heated struggle, have been subject to considerable analysis, mostly retrospective. Piecing together diverse accounts of these and related developments (see, in particular, *Bulletin ICCI*, various monthly issues, February 1998 to December 2000) is not easy, but it seems that in addition to the objective conditions generated by the neoliberal policy measures associated with TROLE, there were at least three other factors. First, there was serious discontent within the armed forces, with a group of disgruntled officers upset about salary and institutional integrity issues. In this situation a group of middle-ranking officers, headed by "Lucio" (Colonel Gutiérrez), entered into negotiations with Antonio Vargas, the president of CONAIE, and the MCS. Second, the ruling class was seriously divided, unable to constitute a dominant bloc and formulate a coherent government program, with an important faction of "the (highland) oligarchy" engaged in political machinations against "the (coastal) bourgeoisie" that created a favorable condition for insurrectionary action (Delgado Jara, 2000). Another and indisputably critical factor in the uprising was the existence of a highly mobilized indigenous peasantry in alliance with a broad coalition of urban-based popular sector organizations against the government's neoliberal agenda. In many ways the run-up to the year 2000–2001 was the highpoint of popular power, especially as regards CONAIE.

Bolivia: A Triangle of Popular Power

The upsurge, in the 1990s, of organized resistance to the neoliberal agenda of governments in the region could also be seen in Bolivia. There the dialectic of capitalist exploitation and restructuring confronted a labor force that resisted, was displaced, and then reorganized to become a formidable opposition to imperialism and its local apologists. In Bolivia at the time there were at least three distinct centers of popular mobilization: the peasant movements in the south, the mining regions, and the trade unions in La Paz, each formally coordinated by the COB (The Bolivian Workers' Central). In the past, the miners were both strategically and organizationally the decisive force. This was expressed in the statutes of the COB, which declared that the first secretary had to be a mining leader. The COB, unlike other labor confederations, was not, strictly speaking, a wage workers' organization: it included street vendors, professionals, students, as well as indigenous or proletarianized peasants and small producers, women and ecologists, each group allotted a proportion of delegates (*Los Tiempos* [Cochabamba], May 12, 1996).

The peasants at the time struggled for greater recognition and influence within the COB as a leading, if not hegemonic, force. This was evident in the COB Congress in June 1996 where the challenge to the miners' dominance was forcefully raised. In the Bolivian Revolution of 1952, armed worker and peasant militias had expropriated the mines, lands, and factories under the government of the Revolutionary Nationalist Movement. By 1996 every revolutionary change had been reversed or was at least under challenge. The decisive turning point was 1985 when the government of Jaime Paz Zamora under IMF tutelage decided to close most of the state tin mines, firing 30,000 miners and effectively undermining the traditional centers of trade union power. As a result, the miners' unions, particularly in the state sector, declined precipitously—over 50,000 miners were fired under the restructuring project designed by the IMF, the World Bank, and American academic advisers. Despite their reduced size—approximately 15,000—now mostly employed by foreign-owned multinationals, the miners still generated nearly 75 percent of legal foreign exchange (Tabera Soliz, 1996: d8, 9). Thus, they still held sway over a highly strategic sector of the economy.

When the miners receded, the peasants, including a contingent of over 30,000 former miners, emerged as the most dynamic and influential sector in direct confrontation with the regime. One can distinguish two sectors here: the coca farmers, made up of peasants who are ex-miners, and traditional peasant producers. The break of the peasants with the traditional nationalist parties was partly a product of the shift by the center-Left toward neoliberal policies and outright subordination to us policy-makers, particularly the military, the Drug Enforcement Agency (DEA), and the Embassy. The political independence of the peasant movement was strengthened by the influx of former miners, led by Filomen Escobar, who brought a high degree of organization and political experience to the movement. Young leaders such as Evo Morales and Alejo Velez Lazo brought new ideas and political projects from the countryside to the larger Bolivian public.

The fusion of two distinct political cultures created a movement that combines organizational forms, tactics, and strategies of confrontation from the advanced sectors of the working class with demands for land, cultural autonomy, and respect for traditional spiritual values rooted in indigenous peasant communities. The peasant movements, particularly the coca farmers, engaged in the largest and most sustained struggle with the neoliberal regime and its US overseers. The result was a heightening of national consciousness in which the concept of a nation (and state) of indigenous nationalities became common currency (Mansilla and Zegada, 1996).

Similar to the Mexican Zapatistas, the "new peasant movement" harnessed the struggle for land and cultural autonomy to the problem of US military and political incursions. Unlike Mexico, however, the public spokespeople were the Indian peasant leaders themselves: sophisticated, self-taught, militant intellectuals who shared the hardships of the rank and file. As in Brazil, their offices were rudimentary: a few old chairs, battered desks, and posters of past mobilizations and revolutionary leaders.

Important sectors of the peasant movement also took a serious step toward combining direct action with electoral politics through independent political organization. This opened a debate about the relation between social movements and parties, throwing into doubt the old position that they were distinct elements in social and political struggles. The peasant movement, frustrated by the actions of nationalist and leftist parties, launched a new political formation, the Assembly for the Sovereignty of the Peoples (ASP), and won a dozen local elections in the coca-growing regions. The *cocaleros* proposed the ASP as a national alternative, hoping to give the peasantry a decisive voice in shaping class politics at the national level. The politics of the coca growers involved harnessing ancestral spiritual beliefs to modern forms of class and anti-imperial struggle—Marxist class analysis linked to pre-European values. The cosmology of the past, an indigenous cosmovision, was evoked in support of earning a living in the interstices of a world dominated by multinational capital and overseas banks.[19]

While the land issue continues to be important for the many coca growers who owned land, the main struggle shifted to free trade against the US-directed attempts to eradicate coca production. The traditional defense of coca was based on the revindication of the historical indigenous nation, a concept that subsumes class and nation (Contreras Baspineiro, 1994; Lohman et al., 1994).

The indigenous-peasant movements faced a dual challenge: the use of not only the Bolivian military against coca production but also the neoliberal regime's "culturalist" strategies that pay lip-service to Indian demands. These were largely symbolic gratifications focusing on token representation—the vice president was an "Indio"—and bilingual education. Although the Cocaleros made cogent critiques of class-reductionist leftist parties, the rejection of cultural manipulation was based more on "empirical factors": the vice president, they told us, was not really an Indian since he served the neoliberal elite.[20]

The conversion of miners into coca farmers shifted the axis of social power not only back to the countryside but also toward a quite different type of peasantry: small-scale producers linked to the mining struggles, clearly differentiated from the traditional peasantry. Though distinctive in background, class-conscious miners turned peasants have been able to disseminate an ideology and form of leadership among the wider peasantry that provided a qualitatively different perspective to the struggle. At the same time, the settlement of the miners in peasant areas, in particular in indigenous coca-growing communities, was accompanied by their acculturation into the traditional spiritual discourses and practices associated with the coca leaf and the demands for greater indigenous autonomy.

The coca farmers of Chapare—over 90,000 family farmers led by Evo Morales—were one of the principal political opponents of President Sanchez de Lozada's neoliberal regime. The regime's free-market ("pro-growth") policies led to cheap food imports, lowering the price of traditional crops such as corn below the level at which farmers could subsist. As a result, many of the former miners—and also former factory workers—turned to cultivating the coca leaf that provided income for an adequate diet, clothes, and basic family needs.

The US government, because of its close ties to the banking and financial elites which launder most of the drug profits, chose to press its antidrug campaign most heavily against the peasant cultivators of a legal crop—coca. Under the operational leadership of the DEA, the Bolivian government periodically launched eradication campaigns against the peasant producers, jailing hundreds and killing or injuring scores during marches, general strikes, and highway blockades. According to peasant leaders, the much vaunted US funding at the time for alternative crops, estimated at $15 million, ended up in the pockets of government officials.[21]

In May 1996 the government announced a plan to totally eradicate coca production in excess of that intended for medicinal use. The Bolivian Rural Workers Confederation responded by calling the eradication plan "crazy" and "irrational" and warned the government that if the plan was put into practice the peasants would rise up in arms "in defence of our families, our lives and our survival" (*Los Tiempos* [Cochabamba], June 13, 1996, pp. a–1, a–9). Evo Morales warned that "Chapare will be a new version of the Mexican state of Chiapas in the heart of South America." The coca farmers are determined to avoid the eradication of coca, which would also mean, as they put it, the eradication of their families.

The deepening involvement of the US military advisors and DEA agents in basic political decisions that adversely affected the coca farmers—through a nominally Bolivian president who spoke Spanish with an Ivy League accent—has deepened the nationalist, anti-imperialist nature of the struggle. "Coca cultivators versus the Empire" was not a far cry from the reality of Bolivian politics. As the COB became entwined in internal conflicts and its leaders in government negotiations, the initiative for political action passed to sectoral movements and more specifically the militant peasant movement.[22] But the prognosis was that the space for political negotiation would shrink as the United States increased its pressure for immediate eradication. And armed confrontation was not excluded.

Paraguay: Recovering the Past to Change the Future

In Paraguay the transition from the Stroessner dictatorship to a conservative electoral regime was accompanied by a growing mobilization of peasants and workers.[23] In the immediate aftermath of the overthrow of the dictator, a wave of peasant land invasions was followed by a counterattack from the landlord class; paramilitary forces and then the army intervened to dislodge many families.[24] This pattern of invasions and dislodgement continued under the Wasmosy regime. Nevertheless, the cumulative effect of peasant pressure on the land had a positive outcome: some permanent settlements of occupying families and a growing sympathy for the peasant struggle in Asunción. The center of the counterhegemonic bloc was located in the peasant movement, which demonstrated a capacity for sustained confrontation.

Major demonstrations against government policy were led first and foremost by peasant groups, and the blunt-speaking peasants leaders were in no mood to be put off. In a meeting with President Wasmosy at which the authors were present, Albert Areco began the interview in the following fashion: "Three months ago you told us that you would immediately deal with the issue of agrarian reform. Nothing has happened. Either you are a liar or incompetent."[25] Wasmosy flushed. Entangling himself in the telephone cord, he tipped the phone off the desk as he walked out, and only returned ten minutes later.

As in the rest of Latin America, any electoral transition was premised on the continuation in power of the economic elite, the impunity of the military, the deepening of economic liberalization, and the repression of social mobilization. A key support for the transition was the US Embassy with its five-block-long installations, the size of a military base. When Wasmosy was threatened by a military coup, even though thousands of Paraguayan pro-democracy demonstrators filled the streets, his first reaction was to run to the US Embassy. The US strategy was to both maintain the civilian regime and the right-wing military to promote and protect the deepening of liberalization from trade union and peasant movement opposition.

Rapid military intervention reflected the symbiosis between the generals and the landowners: not infrequently, fallow land occupied by peasants had been appropriated—often illegally—by high-ranking military officers. In a land squatter settlement visited by the authors in eastern Paraguay, the peasants had sought an out-of-the-way plot of land in the "*monte.*" They did not know that a general had illegally acquired title to the land. First private gunmen and bulldozers were sent in, but they were successfully repulsed by the peasant community.

The peasant movement had its roots in the 1970s when blossoming peasant leagues were crushed by military repression (Campos Ruis et al., *Las Organizaciones Campesinas*). The activists who survived began the slow process of clandestine organizing throughout the early

1980s, and by the end of the decade regional organizations had been formed that coordinated activities.[26]

The peasant movement at the time developed on two fronts: through the formation of local and regional organizations, and their growing affiliation with national federated structures. The National Peasant Federation is currently made up of thirty regional groups, loosely associated and without formal "membership cards," a practice common throughout Latin America. The leaders were themselves working peasants. Again, there were no "full-time" paid functionaries, no vehicles (they travel by bus), and few if any professional advisors. Yet they are growing. Once again, the secret was the "virtuous" nature of the leaders: they organize, discuss, and share with their followers both struggles and jails.

In Paraguay, as in Brazil and Bolivia, there was a deep estrangement between intellectuals and peasant activists. The intellectuals were increasingly tied to NGOs and to projects that are responsive to overseas donors. The peasants are increasingly suspicious of, if not hostile to, organizational competition and manipulation by the NGOs—"who use the movement to secure overseas funding," as one Paraguayan peasant leader put it. The Marxist revolutionary outlook of the peasant militants is in direct conflict with the varieties of "post-Marxism" embraced by the intellectuals. Very few intellectuals were willing and able to serve as subordinates to the peasant movements. Although the peasant leaders were eager and deeply interested in working with committed intellectuals, they rejected working together through the "institutes" of the intellectuals.

Apart from the land issue, three discernible strands are embedded in the appeal and growth of the peasant movement. First, there was the incorporation of indigenous traditions. In the countryside, there was a fusion of indigenous and peasant styles of cultivation—community-based farming and "market" activity. The cohesion, urban orientation, and political sophistication of the peasant leaders were combined with a desire to farm in the "*monte*," to be left to themselves close to nature, and to produce primarily for self-consumption and secondarily for the market. Second, among some peasant leaders, socialism had become an important political tendency. Theirs was a socialism rooted in common opposition to capitalist depredation and embedded in traditional peasant communalism. Third, nationalism in the countryside was based on the opposition between Guarani-speaking small cultivators and landless workers and the wealthy European settlers who owned vast tracts of fertile land.

During the March days throughout the threatened military coup, while Wasmosy was shamefully hiding in the US Embassy, the peasants paralyzed highways and mobilized to march on the capital. Although students received most of the publicity, it was largely young workers and peasants who stood ready to paralyze the country if the military made its move. A few days after the threat had dissipated, Paraguay experienced the most powerful general strike in over a half century, shutting down all major activity. Tens of thousands of peasants filled the streets, highlighting not only struggle over the land but also the government's neoliberal policies.

Argentina: Between Stagnation and Rebellion

Political struggles in Argentina have been cyclical. There was widespread mobilization in the transition from the military regime—following the Malvinas defeat—and during the subsequent attempted military coups. There were six general strikes against the Radical Party government in the mid- to late 1980s. In the 1990s there were widespread provincial riots, and in August 1996 the first successful general strike against the faltering Menem regime was symptomatic of a new cycle of class conflict.

The crucial issue in Argentina was not the periodic outbursts of mass popular protest but their dissociation from any alternative political project. Where politics was joined to the social struggle, as in the general strikes of the Confederación General de Trabajadores (CGT) in the 1980s and the urban protests of the early 1990s, it was channeled into political projects assimilated to the neoliberal project.[27] The CGT, for example, helped bring down Alfonsin only to become a vehicle for the ultraliberal policies of the Menem regime. The dissident trade unionists (CTA) of the early 1990s were instrumental in the creation of the Frente Grande, which later supported neoliberal stabilization policies. The organized social movements were not able to create a political instrument expressive of their own social base.

On the surface, the Left was divided between the center-left electoral front in Buenos Aires and the provincial movements involved in direct action. In practice, these differences are subject to severe qualification. The human rights group, the Madres de la Plaza de Mayo, had become an important reference point for popular mobilization of young people, dissident trade unionists, and neighborhood organizations, as well as nuclei of university students and academics. Hebe Bonafini, the principal spokesperson, told of her concept of building an inclusive national movement, independent of the existing center-left coalitions.[28] There is no question that the Madres had an important political presence due to their intransigent insistence on bringing to justice the military personnel responsible for the deaths of 30,000 people. Beyond that, they were able to mobilize militant demonstrations of over 50,000 people, mostly the young. The problem of moving from protest to politics, however, was not resolved.

The Marxist Left was very small, internally divided and socially isolated, although individual militants could be found in some of the major trade unions. What was lacking was a left-wing movement that had political credibility among participants in the urban social struggles. Electoral politics only had meaning as part of a growing political identity that came out of the social struggles and polarizations of the direct action movements. In the meantime, as in Mexico, the social decomposition of the corrupt and inept Menem regime was accompanied by a growing militarization of politics (Lopez and Minujin, 1994). During the August general strike, the military packed the streets, blocking public protests.

The general strike of August had an ambiguous character. On the one hand, it was important in defining the further decline of support for Menem and a growing pressure on the CGT bureaucracy. On the other hand, the trade union officials saw it as an escape valve to deflect internal opposition and had no intention of deepening the struggle. In other words, the Argentine Left stood between the stagnation of the official Left of the Frente Grande and the CGT, and the promising politicization of provincial rebellion as a source of political renewal.

Mexico and the EZLN: The Revolutionary Spirit Raises Its Head

In Mexico, the internationally famous Zapatista movement and its leader, "Subcommandante Marcos," is only one of several important peasant movements that have emerged or been formed in Guerrero, Oaxaca, and other regions. What has been important about the Zapatista movement is its blend of Marxist analysis and indigenous practice, the linkage of national and international strategic thinking and local community-based support. Some analysts have gone so far as to view it as an entirely new type of social movement—the "first postmodern social movement in history" (Burbach, 2004). Equally important, however, since the center-left party—the PRD (Party of the Democratic Revolution)—continues to be marginalized from any legislative role in the state apparatus, it is the peasant movement, and in particular the Ejército Zapatista de Liberación Nacional (EZLN), which has established the basis for a national political debate on the issues of NAFTA, democratization, land reform, and social justice. Like its more powerful and numerous counterparts in Latin America, the EZLN has combined social struggle with efforts to forge a political instrument of social transformation.

In discussing the perspectives for substantive revolutionary change in Mexico, it would be a mistake to focus exclusively on the EZLN, particularly since it is no longer a major actor on the political stage, and it is confined to micro-regions and to popular struggles for local changes. In the second half of the 1990s, however, the potential for radical change and revolutionary ferment in the countryside could not be disputed. Not only was the EZLN active in pushing for change, but there was a specter of the possible emergence of other guerrilla groups that, like the Zapatistas, had "gone to ground" in the 1980s. In addition, there was the growth and proliferation across the country of diverse local and regional peasant movements, the PRD with its radical social base, and the emergence of significant splits in the official trade unions, parallel to the emergence of autonomous "class-oriented" unions such as "Ruta 100."

To expand on this point it was clear that the EPR (Ejército Popular Revolucionario), which, unlike the EZLN, is still committed to seizing state power, continued to have substantial support among some peasant communities in Guerrero (Hernandez Montoya, 1996: 1, 8, 17, 25). The radical social activists in the peasant struggle were also part of the left-wing of the PRD. These movements did not respond to the political space opened by President Zedillo's "electoral reform." On the contrary, they created their own political space despite the growing militarization of the country. Mexico's political rulers are the product of a marriage between Mexican trustees for Wall Street, narco-capitalists and viceroys from the World Bank and IMF. The growth of the popular movement is in part the result of a transition from an authoritarian form of state-capitalism to a police-state kleptocracy, which styles its economic practice as "free-market liberalism" and describes its electoral reforms—and the assassination of opponents—as a "transition to democracy."

But the fundamental point about the extension and deepening of radical opposition, however, was that it lacked a clearly defined political axis. The popular movement's diverse and local character attracted a substantial following in search of immediate solutions, but it inhibited the creation of a national movement capable of challenging the party-state. Even so, it was clear that the decomposition of the PRI (The Institutional Revolutionary Party) and its internal intrigues, power struggles, and violent vendettas resulted in a loosening of its tentacles on both the popular classes and the civil society. At the electoral level, the main beneficiary was the right-wing PAN, which nearly doubled its electoral base to almost 15 million voters. The PRD was torn between its leftist social base, which was pressuring for more active intervention, and its parliamentary leaders who wanted to make of PRD an electoral machine that catered to middle-class voters of the large cities in the north. With the election of Obregon Lopez to the presidency of the Party, the PRD attempted the difficult and, as it turned out, futile exercise of riding both horses.

The growth of revolutionary politics in Mexico should not be any surprise to students of revolution. Vice President Gore compared NAFTA to the nineteenth-century Louisiana Purchase. As John Saxe Fernandez pointed out, it is easy to speak of US policy in the late-twentieth century as the "Mexico Purchase." With the financial squeeze of the banks on indebted farmers and business operators, 40-cent-an-hour wages, and the massive displacement of peasants by agribusiness, there was a revolution to be made. This is where the Zapatistas came in, erupting on the political stage on January 1, 1994, the very day that NAFTA came into effect.

As for the EZLN it captured the imagination, sympathy, and support of a substantial part of the Left in Mexico—and throughout the world. This was evident in the *Conference for Humanity and against Neoliberalism* organized by the Zapatistas (July 27–August 3, 1996) in which over 3,000 participants from 41 countries gathered in the jungle redoubt of Chiapas to pay homage to the movement and debate strategy. From interviews and discussions, including a session with Marcos, a complex picture emerged of the evolution of EZLN and the situation at the time.

Since the initial uprising in 1994, the EZLN had already gone through several substantial shifts in political perspective. It is important to note that these changes and the policies of the Zapatistas had significance well beyond the twenty-five communities in Chiapas influenced by or connected to the EZLN. From conversations with Marcos and other EZLN leaders, as well as from published speeches, communiqués and interviews, it was clear, first, that the EZLN has had to narrow its goals. From the broad focus on basic socioeconomic transformation at the beginning (in which Zapatista militants even spoke of a socialist transformation), the overwhelming emphasis had shifted toward "democratization," "demilitarization," and "political transition." This was in part because of the tightening military encirclement. The intransigence of the government and its "salami tactics"—isolating, starving, and bribing indigenous communities to break with the EZLN—heightened the prospects for a direct military assault on the remaining communities.

For the EZLN to transform itself under these conditions, and in this context, from a military to a political structure and to establish corresponding democratic systems of accountability would have posed many problems. First and foremost there was the immediate military threat; army forces were positioned less than a kilometer from some Zapatista communities. To have prematurely put assembly-type structures at the center of decision making would have been to ignore the lesson of the lightning invasion of February 1995 and to increase the vulnerability of the leadership who supported democratic values.

The communalist culture of reciprocal exchange and social solidarity was a necessary prerequisite for the construction of democracy. The continuance in present circumstances of the Zapatista Army was one guarantee. Marcos, of course, was all too aware of the centralist tendency in guerrilla formations and anguished over the issue. But the tension between military defense and democracy could not be resolved by simply issuing democratic directives—it could only be dealt with in the concrete context of an occupied Chiapas, with helicopters hovering overhead and special airborne troops awaiting orders to strike. In the event of a government attack, the EZLN would have been separated from its social base, and the public image projected by the media would have shifted from a struggle between indigenous communities and the one-party state to a military conflict between guerrillas and the armed forces. Such a polarization would have substantially weakened the support from the urban middle-class progressives and "civil society" on which the EZLN has counted in its strategy to convert itself into a national movement.

The question of war or peace could not be resolved by unilateral concessions from Marcos. Any war would be decided within the larger political struggle in which forces outside Chiapas would play a major role. Could the Mexican regime wage a multifront struggle against guerrillas in Guerrero, a peasant mobilization in Oaxaca, and growing trade union discontent—over 300,000 marched on May Day 1996 in Mexico City—a precipitous decline in voter support in the north, and an economy heavily dependent on liquid capital ready to flee at the least sign of instability? This was the critical political question. In June, elections were scheduled for the mayorship of Mexico City, and there was a serious possibility that the PRD candidate, Cuauhtémoc Cárdenas, would win. This prospect may well have induced both the government and the EZLN to act cautiously.

The narrowing of its goals was accompanied by the broadening of international support. The indecision of the EZLN leadership resulted in each group reading into the EZLN its own political concerns. For example, some French intellectuals praised the Zapatistas as the reincarnation of nineteenth-century republicanism. Spanish anarchists saw them in terms of Durrutti's peasant armies. And, of course, left-leaning or progressive intellectuals and activists in the antiglobalization movement in the North portrayed the Zapatistas as the vanguard of a global movement against neoliberalism in search of "another world."

But while the lack of political definition as a movement had its advantages, it also had limitations for building a coherent national movement beyond Chiapas. Moreover, it was not clear if the narrowing of goals was not a reflection of an internal shift among the political currents that made up the EZLN.[29]

The second shift in the EZLN approach was away from diffuse appeals to "civil society"—which did not lead to "self-organization"—toward increasing collaboration and coordination with specific groups in Mexico that had a demonstrated capacity to oppose the government and resist its policies. In June and July 1996, the debtors' organization Barzon, which claimed 1 million affiliates, held a national conference in Zapatista territory and established links with the EZLN. Shortly thereafter a number of national and regional indigenous organizations met in the same terrain. In the same period, the EZLN leadership participated in a week-long seminar with Mexican intellectuals about reform of the state. These ties with organized groups held greater promise for building a national political alternative and served notice to the government that the encirclement strategy was not working. More important, it began to give substance to the social character of the movement that Marcos envisioned.

The third shift in the Zapatista policy was the preponderant if not exclusive emphasis on a political solution and the qualified renunciation of armed struggle. In his speech to the 1996 "Encuentro," Marcos placed the armed struggle in the context of an early "phase" in the struggle—as a means of achieving recognition, opening a political dialogue with the regime and advancing toward a political solution.

This was highlighted by the overtures to liberal-democratic public opinion and the distant, if not hostile, relation to the new guerrilla movement in Guerrero (EPR) that emerged in June 1996.

In our interview with Marcos he articulated the dilemma of choice between the military and political struggle. While he was intent on moving toward legal political activity, the regime was tightening the military circle, increasing the repression of peasants in Chiapas by its support for paramilitary groups, and offering no concessions in ending the stranglehold that the PRI-State had over all aspects of political and social life. The real political conditions in Mexico were highly repressive; an average of two PRD leaders or activists were killed every week—over 250 since the election of President Zedillo. One could imagine what would happen to the Zapatistas if they came out of the jungles and began serious organizing. Marcos emphasized that agrarian reform and cultural autonomy were essential to any peace settlement.

For Marcos and the EZLN the issue of land distribution was linked to the self-government of the indigenous communities. The Mexican government, like its counterparts in Bolivia, Guatemala, and Ecuador at the time, attempted to disassociate indigenous cultural issues from socioeconomic change and autonomous political power—*la autonomía*. In any case, the government negotiators did not place any meaningful concessions on the table, hoping (correctly, as it turned out) through time and a war of attrition to tire outside supporters, wear down the communities through deprivation and then deal a quick military blow.

The Rift between the Old and New Left

In Latin America as a whole, what was striking in the political situation in the late 1990s, on the eve of a new millennium, was the minimal influence that the former leftists of the 1960s had on the third-wave revolutionaries of the 1990s. The "halo" effect of the past no longer held. The eruption of peasant land occupations, the politics of direct action created tension between the legalist, electoralist politics of the second wave and their pragmatic center-left coalitions. The new revolutionaries called on the center-Left to support their struggles, to pass progressive legislation, to resign from repressive regimes even as they developed the strategy of building autonomous centers of popular power in communities, cooperatives, and provincial municipalities.

It appeared to be only a question of time until the right-leaning electoral coalitions and the left-moving new sociopolitical movements would part ways. Popular disenchantment with center-Left governments was provoked by their endemic corruption, and by their resort to austerity, repression, and privatization. Thus, formerly revolutionary or leftist politicians, associated with the governments in, for example, Chile, Venezuela, Bolivia, and Nicaragua, all brought discredit upon themselves and the "Left." The insurgent politicians of the 1980s who failed to win power nationally were undermined in a different way. Their electoral bids were defeated, and they lost whatever mystique they might have had. With some local exceptions, they failed to use electoral interventions as a way of building movements and propagating a long-term program of social transformation.

Even the PT in Brazil and the PRD in Mexico lacked a clear program for tackling the crises in their countries, having been outflanked by agile new forces on the Right (Cardoso and PAN) and new extra-parliamentary movements on the Left. They risked being seen as pure politicos awaiting their turn. Nevertheless, if Cárdenas were to win election as mayor of Mexico City, activists hoped that a PRD administration would clip the wings of the repressive forces and use municipal initiatives to strengthen popular movements.

As for Marcos, he was keenly aware of the pitfalls of the peace accords in Central America and the limited nature of "democratization" under the auspices of the military and the IMF in much of the rest of Latin America. Even where the Left advanced electorally, strategic retreats were hidden. In El Salvador the peace accords of 1992 allowed for electoral advances by the FLMN, with the Left winning control of the capital, San Salvador, for the first time in March 1997. The peasant activists of the Asociación Democratico Campesino naturally welcomed the end of the death squad's reign of terror and the advent of a local administration that was more likely to be open to pressure. But government policies had hit poor peasants and rural laborers hard while the FLMN's orientation toward "productive capitalism" led to a reduced concern for their interests. In these last elections abstentions ran at 60 percent, with many poorer or rural voters staying at home. Although landlord and employer intimidation was much reduced, nevertheless, four activists were killed during the election period.

Politics and Revolutionary Ethics

As the Owl of Minerva spread its wings over the decade, the twentieth century and the old millennium, Marcos offered a new type of social movement leadership. For whatever it meant, the differences between Marcos and the other peasant leaders were obvious: Marcos was an intellectual of urban origins with a literary flair unmatched among his counterparts in Latin America. Yet Marcos was equally concerned with the cultural, subjective, and historical dimensions of social revolution. While thinking "globally," Marcos and the new leadership were grounded in "national" and regional realities with a sensibility for the nuances of local customs, traditions, and norms. None of the social movement leaders at the time followed a "model" extrapolated from other countries, past or present. Most leaders were conscious of the need to avoid personality cults and to be responsive to the rank and file. While the new leaders were excellent organizers and effective leaders, they were not charismatic spellbinders or apparatchiks. They ruled, as Marcos liked to repeat, by obeying (at least to some degree) and did not force their ideas on the militants through emotional fervor; they sought instead to convince through discussion.

The resurgence of the new peasant and urban movements of the 1990s resulted from the fact that they were defending vital interests and that no one questioned the personal integrity of their leaders. If they lost these qualities, the movements would dissolve or become fragmented into electoral clienteles. Such groups were not simply "new social movements." They retained and developed Marxism in new circumstances and adapted to new class actors engaged in novel types of struggle with the clear perspective of changing the national, if not international, structure of political and economic power. Former miners became coca cultivators, indigenous communities linked to urban intellectuals became guerrilla leaders, rural landless workers built antiliberal power blocs, and Guarani-speaking peasants challenged the hegemony of drug and contraband "capitalists." It would appear that Marxism could be a creative tool in coming to terms with these new protagonists of social change.

An encouraging feature of the new movements was that, confronting an environmentally rapacious socioeconomic system, their resistance was often infused with a strong commitment to the defense of a sustainable ecology. The indigenous people's identification with their native earth remains a powerful strand of rural radicalism. And since women so often bear the brunt of popular survival strategies, the new movements only thrived when they displayed a concern for women's issues and gender equality. While most of the nationally known leaders are still men, there were increasing numbers of women taking the lead at the community level. Where water supplies were polluted or traditional cultivation plots taken over by developers, it was very often the women in the forefront of the resulting popular struggles.[30]

Also, many of the new leaders had a "religious background," either directly or through their association with their members. The Zapatistas, for example, drew heavily on the consciousness-raising of the progressive Catholics of Chiapas, particularly Bishop Samuel Ruiz. Most of the original organizers of the MST came out of seminaries and rural pastoral movements. Some of the Paraguayan peasant leaders are sons and daughters of earlier militants organized in the Ligas Campesinas promoted by progressive church people; the Bolivian leadership drew on the spiritual traditions of the indigenous communities. Thus, popular religiosity fused with Marxism in a syncretic fashion. However, we should take care in not simply carrying over 1980s stereotypes. Catholic liberation theology remained a socially radical force, but in many countries its strength had waned, partly because of the Vatican's hostility and partly because of its partial recuperation in the NGO culture. Protestant and Pentecostal groups were also a dynamic and growing presence in many parts of Latin America, with a special appeal to the rural and urban poor, to women and to Indian and black populations—indeed, it is said that in Latin America there are now more Protestants than Catholics. In this connection Latin American Protestantism should be seen as the Left's keenest rival for the allegiance of the poor, channeling popular hostility toward the political establishment into other-worldly directions and stimulating a culture of self-help and self-reform among the most deprived. Although the established Left parties failed to respond to this challenge, the practical, extra-electoral orientation of the new movements equipped them well to do so.

Conclusion

Empire-building is about the extraction of interest payments, the pillage of natural resources, and the large-scale transfer of public property to multinationals. Together, these forces in the 1990s, along with the machinations of neoliberal policies, put tremendous pressure on the Latin American social system. Since the "local power structure" is located in the central cities, in this process of extraction and appropriation, the "provinces" and the rural areas have been especially hard hit.

The logic of the expansion of the new peasant movements in the 1990s was intimately related to the internal transformations of the peasantry—politically, culturally, and economically—as well as a dialectical resistance to the extension of neoliberalism and the encroachment of imperialism. The displacement of educated peasants linked to modern urban centers created a new peasantry with modern organizational and media skills that linked agricultural activities to urban class struggle.

Notwithstanding the ebbing of the revolutionary tide of the peasant movement in the conditions of new millennium, it would be a serious mistake to dismiss the peasant movements of the 1990s as the last gasp of anti-neoliberal resistance and rebellion. In the 1990s, the empire in Latin America flourished as never before, but at the same time the activism of the social movements slowed down or halted implementation of the neoliberal agenda, placing its advocates on the defensive and providing substantive gains to diverse populations engaged in the resistance and the struggle for survival and resistance.

The empire struck and tore as under the economic, cultural, and political fabric of Latin American societies. It assimilated a few and exploited many. But as the Left struck back—in the villages of Paraguay and Bolivia, in the rural squatter settlements of Brazil, and in the jungles of Mexico—a new movement that developed its own theory and wrote its own history took hold.

5

Turning the Social Movements:
Civil Society to the Rescue

The term "civil society" denotes all manner and types of social organizations found between the family at one pole and the state at the other.[1] The idea of *civil society* has achieved prominence in liberal and conservative political and development discourse over the past two decades, particularly in connection with successive waves of "political transitions," beginning in Eastern Europe and Latin America (in the 1990s) and spreading across the developing world. In normative and organizational terms, "civil society" is described by liberal and conservative advocates as a crucial agent for limiting authoritarian government and empowering individuals, reducing the socially atomizing and unsettling effects of market forces, enforcing political accountability, and improving the quality and inclusiveness of *governance*, a term that denotes a particular set of interactions between civil society and the state.[2]

Reconsideration of the limits of government intervention in economic affairs, and a related neoconservative attack on the welfare-and-developmental state, also led to the notion and an increased awareness of the potential role of civic organizations in the provision of public goods and social services, either separately or in some kind of "synergistic" relationship with state institutions such as the government. Indeed it is possible to view the turn toward civil society in the provision of hitherto public goods and services as a form of *privatization*: turning over the responsibility for economic development (capital accumulation and growth of output) to the "private sector" (profit-oriented capitalist enterprises) and the responsibility for economic and political development to "civil society."

Recourse to the notion of civil society, and the elaboration of a *civil society discourse*, have taken different forms. In fact there are three different traditions in the use of the term, each associated with a particular conception of civil society (in regard to which organizations are included and excluded), a particular analytical use, and an *ideology*. One of these traditions, associated with a mainstream form of political science and economics in which politics and economics are treated as analytically distinct systems, can be labeled "liberal." It is fundamentally concerned with what we might term "political development," establishing a *participatory* form of politics and "good" (i.e., "democratic") governance. Here civil society is conceived of in essentially political terms, rooted in the Anglo-American tradition of liberal-democratic theory that identifies civic institutions and political activity as an essential component of political society based on the principles of citizenship, rights, democratic representation, and the rule of law. On the ideological spectrum (left, center, right) liberals see civil society as a countervailing force against an unresponsive, corrupt state and exploitative corporations that disregard environmental issues and human rights abuses (Kamat, 2003).

The second tradition, rooted in a more sociological view of the state-society relation and the ideas of Antonio Gramsci, is similarly concerned with the form of politics but sees civil society as a repository of diverse forms of popular resistance to government policies, and the basis of a "counterhegemonic" bloc of social forces engaged in a process of contesting state and other forms of class power. It is based on what might be termed a radical ideology, a shared belief in the need for radical change. Civil society here is seen as a repository of the forces of resistance and opposition, forces that can be mobilized into a counterhegemonic bloc (Morton, 2004).

The third tradition is associated with the project of international cooperation for development. In this tradition "civil society" is viewed as an array of social organizations representing "stakeholders" in a process of economic development, a strategic partner in the war against global poverty waged by the World Bank and other international development associations and agencies. In this ideological context, civil society is viewed as an agency for bringing about a *participatory* and *empowering* form of *development*, an organizational means of transforming the new *development paradigm* into practice.[3] Proponents of this conception of civil society generally share a liberal ideology in terms seeing in civil society the beneficial effects of globalization for the development of democracy and economic progress.

Conservatives in this context tend to view nongovernmental organizations (NGOs) as "false saviors of international development" (Kamat, 2003).

The aim of this chapter is to deconstruct elements of this civil society discourse, as it relates to the neoimperialist project of international development ("international cooperation") to turn Latin America's social movements away from a politics of confrontation (with political and economic power) and active resistance (against neoliberalism, capitalism, and imperialism) and derail efforts to create a new, more egalitarian social order.

Our critical discussion of the prevailing *civil society discourse* is guided by the following propositions:

- The concept of *civil society* covers over the profound class divisions within civil society, and it is designed to do so.
- It postulates a division between the state and society without confronting the profound linkages between imperial and ruling class and public authorities.
- Class exploitation, imperial pillage, and financial speculation are ignored as the parameters for devising micropolitics.
- Ideologues of a *civil society* perspective deflect or attempt to deflect social movements or their potential popular constituencies toward collaboration with their exploiters based on an implicit conception of a universal "harmony of interests."
- The advocates of *civil society*, via NGOs, have dependent financial relations with imperial states and the international financial institutions that benefit from the non-conflictual micropolitics of *civil society* organizations.
- The claims to democracy of civil society advocates, and their presumption that class-based social movements in their confrontational politics are nondemocratic, are false (for one thing, social movements tend to be more democratic than NGOs; for another, NGOs tend to use donor funds to impose their agenda).

Setting the Stage for Democracy and the Entry of Civil Society

Social change can be analyzed in terms of three dynamic factors: *agency* (the strategies pursued and actions taken by diverse organizations and individuals), *structure* (the institutionalized practices that shape or limit action), and *context* (the specific "situation" or historic conjuncture of objectively given and subjectively experienced "conditions" of social or political action). Regarding the emergence, growth, and strengthening of civil society in the 1980s there are at least five contextual elements. Each of these elements takes the form of a variable but persistent trend that can be analyzed in three critical dimensions: (1) the actions or policies that provide the driving forces of the social change process; (2) the social, economic, and political effects of these actions and policies; and (3) the strategic and political responses to these impacts by different social groups and classes, according to their location in the social structure and the broader system of global capitalism.

Globalization

The process of integration through subordination of countries across the world into a new imperial world order in which the forces of economic and political "freedom" (free trade, the market, the private sector, democracy, etc.) are able and allowed to flourish has had an ambiguous influence on civil society organizations. First, we need to distinguish between two types of change agents: the NGOs that seek to mediate between the donor organizations and the rural poor in their localities and communities but that in reality are themselves major beneficiaries of "foreign aid"; and the organizations and radical social movements that originate in the grassroots of these societies and are more often than not impeded by the NGOs. On the one hand, like other domestic agencies such as the state and private business, the invasive pressures of global markets often compromise the autonomy of civil society organizations. On the other hand, globalization in terms of freer flows of information and communication across national boundaries has fostered the spread of a *global civil society* concerned to channel the forces of change in a "democratic" direction, that is, to challenge the forces of revolutionary change.

Democratization/Political Liberalization

The spread of "freedom and democracy"—the "forces of freedom" in George W. Bush Jr.'s 2002 *National Security Report*—in recent years of ideological warfare has defined a political and institutional environment in which "civil society organizations" (CSOs) are supposed (and allowed) to operate. In some cases, civil society has been the locus of active opposition to authoritarian governments, providing a breeding ground for alternative, participatory, or "democratic" forms of political organization and governance. In other cases civil society is marginalized or weakened through state repression or withdrawal from active engagement in politics. Civil society in this context may constitute the locus in which civic values and norms of democratic engagement are nurtured, although greater political freedom can be exploited by self-interested groups to advance narrow, self-interested agendas that can so exacerbate political conflict as to undermine "good"—that is, "democratic"— governance.

Reform of Political Structures/Political Liberalization

Democracy, or more precisely *democratization*, entails the reform of existing political structures (democratizing the relation between the state and the society) or the creation of new, more democratic structures. This can involve constitutional redesign, the devolution of power to local governments (*decentralization*), and formal arrangements to widen public access to policy-making and/or ensuring greater accountability and transparency. These political developments can provide space for civil society organizations to engage in new activities, strengthen their interaction with politicians and public officials, and involve larger number of people in active politics and government affairs.

Institutional Rebalancing in the Interest of "Good Governance"

Challenges to the fiscal capacity of the state, and doubts about their institutional efficacy and political character, have led to efforts to create a "better balance between the market and the state" (Ocampo, 2007). This has meant that CSOs have taken on responsibilities for providing social goods and public services to their own constituencies and wider communities, requiring a rethinking of their organizational structures, financial base, and relations with the state. More generally it has meant a reduced role of governments in maintaining political order and an enlarged role of civil society in this regard.

Privatization

The rapid economic growth experienced by many developing countries in the 1950s, 1960s, and 1970s in large measure was fuelled by expansion of the state and growth of the public sector, and a policy of nationalization—taking over from the "private sector" (i.e., the multinationals) and buying out firms in the strategic sectors of the economy (e.g., oil production). In the 1980s this policy was reversed under the Washington Consensus on "correct policy" (privatization): turning over state enterprises to private enterprise under the guise of a presumed "efficiency." This new policy allowed capitalist corporations in multinational form and foreign-owned to acquire these enterprises at a bargain, greatly enriching their new owners (Petras and Veltmeyer, 2009).

Decentralization

Until 1980 or so, political scientists (and economists, for that matter) in both liberal and conservative traditions generally subscribed to the notion that democracy was not necessarily or particularly conducive to economic development—that authoritarian regimes provided a better agency in this regard. In the 1980s, however, there was a sea change in this idea, leading to the contrary notion that economic liberalization would lead to political liberalism or vice versa. This idea, together with the ideology of a minimalist state, led to widespread calls for "democracy" and "good governance" in the form of a more participatory form of politics and development.

To establish the required institutional framework for this "development" (and, at the same time, to reduce fiscal pressures on governments) the World Bank, on the basis of lessons drawn from Chile, argued the need for a policy of administrative decentralization, with a partnership approach to both local governments and civil society (Blair, 1995; Rondinelli, McCullough, and Johnson, 1989; UNDP, 1996; World Bank, 1994).

Financial and Trade Liberalism

The major improvement in socioeconomic conditions characteristic of the 1950s and 1960s was based on the active agency of governments in redistributing for the common benefit market-generated wealth and incomes. In the developing countries of the global south, it was also based on protectionism, a policy designed to protect fledgling industries from the forces of the world market, to give domestic companies a chance to grow by placing restrictions on foreign investment and the operations of multinational corporations in their countries. Under the "new economic model" of free-market capitalism and neoliberal globalization this policy was reversed.

Economic liberalization has had a number of contradictory consequences for civil society. In some contexts it weakened predatory state structures and limited the scope for "rent-seeking behaviour" by political and bureaucratic elites. It is clear that some groups are better placed than others to exploit the opportunities created by liberalization for advancing their own economic agendas, and organizations representing their interests can wield considerable influence over decision making.

The removal of price controls and other restrictions on economic activity are often accompanied by the growth of the informal economy, and the emergence of a dense network of groups and associations geared toward the advancement of collective economic interests. The removal of safety nets and the reduction of government welfare spending give rise to a proliferation of self-help groups and development associations whose mandate is to provide relief and services to people marginalized or impoverished by market reforms.

Deregulation

State-led development is predicated on government regulation of private economic activity and markets in the public interest. However, from the perspective of firms concerned with maximizing their profit-making opportunities this policy is viewed as an intolerable attack on freedom that inevitably results in "inefficiency" and a distortion of market forces which, if unhindered, produce an optimal distribution of society's productive resources and incomes. In the 1980s, the perceived "failure" of the state in the form of a widespread fiscal crisis (an inability to finance from government revenues costly social and development programs) created political conditions for a reversal of this regulatory approach and the implementation of a deregulation policy.

The Economic and Political Dynamics of Civil Society-Led Development

As noted in chapter 1, by the end of the 1980s, most countries had been brought into line with the "new world order" of neoliberal globalization and free-market capitalism. In the 1970s, in the first phase of neoliberal experiments the implementing agency was a series of military regimes in the southern cone of South America in Chile, Argentina, and Uruguay (Veltmeyer and Petras, 1997). When these experiments with neoliberal policies crashed and burned in the early 1980s, a new crop of liberal democratic regimes, forced into line by the realities of a regionwide debt crisis of historic proportions, initiated a second round of neoliberal policy reforms. They did so with the assistance of an emerging civil society in the so-called third sector of nonprofit, voluntary associations and NGOs. These organizations, formed in response to a generalized retreat of many governments from their erstwhile primary responsibility for economic development and social welfare, were enlisted by International Financial Institutions (IFIs) such as the World Bank and the international community of development associations and aid donors to mediate with the poor, to assist them in their self-development efforts in return for an acceptance of their policy advice (Carroll, 1992).

The scholarly literature on these issues is divided. Some see the development of NGOs as "saviours" rescuing the capitalism system from itself (Carothers, 1999; Hayden, 2002; Kamat, 2003). These authors emphasize the role of NGOs not so much in delivering economic assistance (microdevelopment projects or poverty alleviation funds) but in democracy promotion, which, Ottaway (2003: vi) notes, is a "new activity in which the aid agencies and NGOs [originally] embarked [upon] with some trepidation and misgivings" but that in the early 1990s (came) of age. Others, however, like the authors, see them as stalking horses for global capitalism and neoliberalism— Trojan horses to facilitate the entry of foreign investment and the domestic operations of multinational corporations and, in the process, to help bring to realization the dream of some for world domination (Petras and Veltmeyer, 2001, 2005, 2007).

NGOs: Catalysts of Development, Saviors, or Agents of Imperialism?

The major expression of civil society in the 1980s was the "voluntary private association" or "nongovernmental organization," formed in what at the time was defined as the "third sector" (versus the "private sector," composed of profit-making economic enterprises, and the "public sector," referring to state institutions).

At the beginning of the decade there were relatively few such organizations, most of them voluntary associations to provide poverty relief or to assist communities in their adaptation to the forces of change. By the end of the decade, however, these NGOs had mushroomed, responding as they did to the vacuum left by a retreating state and assuming responsibilities hitherto given to the state.

Although there were barely several hundred NGOs in the early 1980s at the outset of the new imperial world order, it is estimated that by the mid-1990s, a decade into the neoliberal era, there were tens of thousands of development NGOs, organized to assist poor communities in their quest for self-development. And, of course, there were all those NGOs formed in the struggle against the violation of human rights, for environmental protection and to address other such issues of concern to the urban middle class. As mentioned earlier, some political sociologists holding postmodern political ideas saw this development as the emergence of "new social movements," concerned with an array of non-class issues (Escobar and Alvarez, 1992) rather than state power and transformative social change.

NGOs were enlisted by the international cooperants in the development project as a strategic partner in the war against poverty, to act as intermediaries between the providers of financial and technical assistance and the poor communities ravaged by the forces of modernization and change, and abandoned by their governments (at the behest of these "development associations"). "Development" in this context was seen within the optics of a new paradigm that conceived of and valorized "popular participation" and grassroots self-development that is initiated "from below" and "from within" civil society.

To create an appropriate institutional framework for such an "alternative" form of development, the IFIs and the development associations engaged in "international cooperation" promoted a policy of administrative decentralization, which in short order was incorporated into the new economic model together with the structural reforms mandated by this model as the cost of admission into the new world order: privatization of public enterprises, financial and trade liberalization, deregulation of markets and private economic activity, and democratization of both the state-civil society relation and the political regime, replacing authoritarian rule with liberal democracy and the rule of law.

NGOs in this context were recruited not only to mediate between the aid donors and the poor communities but also to carry into the localities and communities of the poor the gospel of capitalism and democracy, the virtues of private enterprise and reform. By the end of the decade and into the 1990s, the marriage between economic and political liberalization had been consummated in many countries with the NGOs acting as midwife. In the process the NGOs helped dampen the fires of revolutionary ferment among the rural poor, who were encouraged to turn away from the confrontational politics of class-based organizations and antisystemic social movements. The dynamics of this process can be traced out in Latin America in the wake of the Cuban revolution and within the institutional and policy framework of the Alliance for Progress, and the agency of USAID

(Veltmeyer and Petras, 2005). However, the 1990s provided conditions for a renewed and more extended development of this strategy. It can be traced out throughout the region, but the cases of Bolivia, Ecuador, and Brazil (in relation to the land struggle of the MST) stand out.

Neoliberalism, NGOs, and the State

There is a direct relation between the growth of social movements organized to challenge the neoliberal model and the growth of NGOs, used by the "overseas development associations" to subvert these movements by providing the rural poor alternative forms of social action. As opposition to neoliberalism grew, governments in the global north (basically the United States, Canada, and Europe) and the World Bank increased their funding of the NGOs.

The convergence between the NGOs and the World Bank was their common opposition to "statism." On the surface the NGOs criticized the state from a "leftist" civil society perspective, while the Right did so in the name of the market. But in reality, the World Bank, the neoliberal regimes, and the Washington-based foundations and financial institutions coopted and encouraged the NGOs to undermine the welfare-development state by providing social services to compensate the victims of the multinationals. In other words, as the neoliberal regime devastated communities by inundating the country with cheap imports, extracting external debt payments, abolishing labor legislation, and creating a growing mass of low-paid and unemployed workers, the NGOs were contracted to provide the poor "self-help" projects, "popular education," and job training—to temporarily absorb small groups of the poor, co-opt local leaders and undermine emerging antisystemic social movements.

In this connection, it is possible to view the NGOs not as they view themselves, as agents of social change and democratic development, but rather as Wallace does, as a Trojan horse for global capital. It is also possible to see them as we do—as agents of imperialism, and as a sort of prophylactic, allowing the agents of imperialist exploitation a good screw without an unwanted outcome.

The NGOs also became the "community face" of neoliberalism, intimately related to those at the top and complementing their destructive work with local microprojects. In effect the neoliberals organized a "pincer" operation or dual strategy, using the State or local governments to pave the road for capital, and the NGOs to pacify the resistance. Unfortunately many on the left focused only on "neoliberalism" from above (the State) and the outside (IMF, World Bank) and not on neoliberalism from below (NGOs, microenterprises). A major reason for this blind spot was the conversion of many former Marxists to the NGO formula and practice. *Anti-Statism was the ideological transit ticket* from class politics to community-based local development—from Marxism to the NGOs.

Typically, the partisans of "civil society" and the NGO ideologues counterpose "state power" to the "empowerment of the poor." State power, they argue, is distant from its citizens, autonomous, and arbitrary, and it tends to develop interests different from and opposed to those of its citizens, while local development empowers the poor, capacitating them to act in their own interests, to become subjects of their own history. But apart from historical cases where the reverse has also been true, this leaves out the essential relation between state and local power—the simple truth that state power, wielded by a dominant and exploiting class, will undermine progressive local initiatives, while that same power in the hands of progressive forces can reinforce such initiatives.

Counterposing state and local power has been used to justify the role of NGOs as brokers between local organizations, neoliberal foreign donors (the World Bank, Europe, or the United States), and the local free market regimes. But the effect is to strengthen neoliberal regimes by severing the link between local struggles and organizations and national/international political movements. The emphasis on the "local" (from global capital to local development) serves the neoliberal regimes well, since it allows its foreign and domestic backers to dominate macro-socioeconomic policy while channeling the bulk of the state's resources toward subsidies for export capitalists and financial institutions.

So, while the neoliberals were transferring lucrative state properties to the private rich, the NGOs were *not* part of the trade union resistance. On the contrary they were active in *local private* projects, promoting the private sector (self-help) discourse in the local communities via a focus on microenterprise. The NGOs, in this context, built an ideological bridge between the small-scale capitalists and the monopolies benefiting from privatization—in the name of "anti-statism" and strengthening civil society. Although the rich accumulated vast financial empires from the privatization policy, the NGO-based middle-class professionals mediated the delivery of poverty alleviation funds, small amounts of money to finance offices, transportation, local projects, and small-scale economic activity.

The political point here is that the NGOs effectively if unwittingly *depoliticized* sectors of the population, undermined their commitment to public employees, co-opted potential leaders in small projects, and demobilized the social movements. Thus, NGOs have generally abstained from public school teacher struggles as neoliberal regimes attack public education and public educators. Rarely, if ever, have the NGOs supported strikes and protests against low wages and budget cuts. Since their educational funding comes from the neoliberal governments in the north and the south, they avoid solidarity with public educators in struggle.

In reality, NGOs are *not* nongovernmental. They receive funds from overseas governments, as well as (increasingly) from the state,[4] in effect serving as private subcontractors of government service. Indeed, they frequently openly collaborate with governmental agencies at home or overseas. This "subcontracting" undermines professionals with fixed contracts, replacing them with contingent professionals. But the NGOs cannot provide the long-term comprehensive programs that the welfare state used to and can furnish. Instead they provide limited services to narrow groups of communities. More importantly, their programs are not accountable to the local people but rather to overseas donors. In that sense, NGOs undermine democracy by *taking social programs out of the hands of the local people* and their elected officials to create dependence on nonelected, overseas governors and their locally anointed officials.

Neoliberalism, the NGOs, and the Social Movements

The NGOs and their post-Marxist professional staff directly compete with the sociopolitical movements for influence among the poor, women, and other socially excluded groups. Their ideology and practice diverts attention from the source and possible solutions of poverty (looking downward and inward instead of upward and outward). To speak of microenterprises, instead of the elimination of exploitation by the overseas banks, as the solution is based on the notion that the problem is one of individual initiative rather than the transfer of income overseas. The "aid" or poverty-alleviation funds mediated by the NGOs affect or benefit small sectors of the population, setting up competition between communities for scarce resources, generating insidious distinctions and inter- and intracommunity rivalries, thus undermining class solidarity. The same is true among the professionals: each sets up their NGO to solicit overseas funds. They compete by presenting proposals more congenial to overseas donors, while claiming to speak for their followers.

The net effect is a proliferation of NGOs that fragments poor communities into sectoral and subsectoral groupings, unable to see the larger social picture that afflicts them and even less able to unite in struggle against the system. Recent experience also demonstrates that foreign donors finance projects during "crises"—political and social challenges to the status quo. Once the movements have ebbed, they shift funding to NGO-style "collaboration," fitting the NGO projects into the neoliberal agenda. Economic development compatible with the "free market" rather than social organization for social change becomes the dominant item on the funding agenda.

But while the majority of NGOs increasingly serve as instruments of neoliberalism, as a Trojan Horse or condom, there is a small minority which attempt to develop an alternative strategy that is supportive of anti-imperialist and class politics. None of them receive funds from the World Bank, or from European or US governmental agencies. They support efforts to link local power to struggles for state power. They link local projects to national sociopolitical movements: occupying large landed estates, defending public property and national ownership against multinationals. They provide political solidarity to social movements involved in struggles to expropriate land. They support women's struggles linked to class perspectives. They recognize the importance of politics in defining local and immediate struggles. They believe that local organizations should fight at the national level and that national leaders must be accountable to local activists. Unfortunately, these NGOs are in the minority.

Let us take a few examples of the all-too-standard "best practice" of many NGOs in the development field.

Bolivia

In 1985 the Bolivian government launched its New Economic Policy (NEP) by decree: freezing wages for four months while inflation raged at a 15,000 percent annual rate. The NEP annulled all price controls and reduced or ended food and fuel subsidies. It also laid the basis for the privatization of most state enterprises and the firing of public-sector employees. Massive cutbacks in health and education programs eliminated most public services. These neoliberal policies were designed and dictated by the World Bank and the IMF, and approved by the US and European governments and banks. The number of poverty-stricken Bolivians grew geometrically under the influence of these policies. Prolonged general strikes and violent confrontations followed. In response the World Bank, European and US governments provided massive aid to fund a "poverty alleviation program." Most of the money was directed to a Bolivian government agency (the Emergency Social Fund—ESF), which channeled funds to the NGOs to implement its program. The funds were not insignificant: in 1990 foreign aid totaled $738 million.

The number of NGOs in Bolivia grew rapidly in response to international funding: before 1980 there were 100 NGOs; by 1992 there were 530 and growing. Almost all the NGOs are directed toward addressing social problems created by the World Bank and the Bolivian government's free market policies, which the dismantled state institutions could no longer deal with. But of the tens of millions allocated to the NGOs, only 15 to 20 percent reached the poor, not an unusual circumstance in the delivery of "foreign aid." The rest was siphoned off to pay administrative costs and professional salaries. The Bolivian NGOs functioned as appendages of the state and served to consolidate its power. The absolute levels of poverty stayed the same and the long-term structural causes—the neoliberal policies—were cushioned by the NGOs. Although not solving the poverty problem, the NGO-administered poverty programs strengthened the regime and weakened opposition to the SAP. The NGOs, with their big budgets, exploited vulnerable groups and were able to convince some leaders of the opposition that they could benefit from working with the government. According to one observer, commenting on the NGO role in the "poverty program": "If this (NGO program) did not create direct support, it at least reduced potential opposition to the government and its program."

When the public school teachers of La Paz went on strike to protest $50-a-month wages and crowded classrooms, the NGOs ignored it; when cholera and yellow fever epidemics raged in the countryside, the NGO self-help programs were helpless where a comprehensive public health program would have been successful in combating them. The NGOs absorbed many of Bolivia's former leftist intellectuals and turned them into apologists for the neoliberal system. Their seminars on "civil society" and "globalization" obscured the fact that the worst exploiters (the private mine owners, newly rich agroexport-ers, and high-paid consultants) were members of "civil society" and that the neoliberal policies were cut to an imperial design to open the country's mineral resources to unregulated pillage.

Chile

In Chile, under the Pinochet dictatorship from 1973 to 1989, the NGOs played an important role in denouncing human rights viola-tions, preparing studies critical of the neoliberal model, and sustaining soup kitchens and other poverty programs. Their numbers multiplied with the advent of the massive popular struggles between 1982 and 1986 that threatened to overthrow the dictatorship. To the extent that they expressed an ideology, it was oriented toward "democracy" and "development with equity." But of the close to 200 NGOs in the country, fewer than 5 provided a clear critical analysis and exposition of the links between US imperialism and the dictatorship or the ties between World Bank-funded free market policies and the 47 percent level of poverty.

In July 1986 there was a successful general strike, a guerrilla group almost succeeded in killing Pinochet, and the United States sent a representative (Gelbard) to broker an electoral transition between the more conservative sectors of the opposition and Pinochet. An elec-toral calendar was established, a plebiscite was organized, and elec-toral parties reemerged. An alliance between Christian Democrats and Socialists was forged and eventually won the plebiscite, ending Pinochet's rule (but not his command of the armed forces and secret police); this alliance subsequently won the presidency and remained in state power until 2010.

As for the social movements that played a vital role in ending the dictatorship, they were marginalized. The NGOs turned from sup-porting the movements to collaborating with the government. The Socialist and Christian Democratic NGO professionals became gov-ernment ministers. From being critics of Pinochet's free-market poli-cies, they became its celebrants. Alejandro Foxley, a former President of CIEPLAN (a major research institute), publicly promised to con-tinue managing the macroeconomic indicators in the same fashion as Pinochet's Minister of Economic Affairs. The NGOs were instructed by their foreign donors to end their support for independent grass-roots movements and to collaborate with the new civilian neoliberal regime. *Sur Profesionales*, one of the best-known research NGOs, carried out research on the "propensity for violence" in the shantytowns—information that was useful to the police and the new regime in repressing independent social movements. Two of its chief researchers (specialty: social movements) became government ministers administering economic policies that created the most lopsided income disparities in recent Chilean history.

The NGOs' external links, and the professional ambitions of its leaders, played a major role in undermining the burgeoning popular movement. Most of its leaders became government functionaries who co-opted local leaders while undermining rank-and-file-style community assemblies. Interviews by the authors with women active in the shantytown Lo Hermida revealed the shift in the postelectoral period. "The NGOs told us that because democracy has arrived there is no need to continue the (soup-kitchen) programs. You don't need us." Increasingly the NGOs conditioned their activities on supporting the "democratic" free-market regime. The NGO functionaries continued to use their participatory rhetoric to hustle votes for their parties in the government and to secure government contracts.

One striking and not atypical effect of the NGOs in Chile was their relationship to the "women's movement." What started as a promising activist group in the mid-1980s was gradually taken over by NGOs that published expensive newsletters from well-furnished offices. The "leaders" of these NGOs, who lived in fashionable neighborhoods, represented a shrinking number of women. During the Latin American Feminist Conference in Chile in 1997, a militant group of rank-and-file Chilean feminists ("the autonomists") provided a radical critique of the NGO feminists as sellouts to government subsidies.

Brazil

As we have observed, the most dynamic social movement in Brazil is the MST, a movement of proletarianized rural workers in Brazil. With more than five thousand organizers and several hundred thousand sympathizers and activists, it has been directly involved in hundreds of land occupations over recent years. At a conference organized in May 1996 by the MST, at which author Petras was invited to speak, the role of NGOs was one of the subjects of debate. A representative from a Dutch NGO appeared on the scene and insisted on participating. When he was told the meeting was closed, he told them that he had a "proposal" for funding (with US$300,000) various community development projects, and insisted on entering. In no uncertain terms the MST leaders told him that they were not for sale and that the MST designs their own "projects" according to their own needs and did not need NGO tutors.

Later the women's caucus of the MST discussed a meeting they had had with a rural-based feminist NGO. The MST women, it turned out, pushed for a class struggle perspective in combining direct action (land occupations) and the struggle for agrarian reform with gender equality. But the NGO professionals insisted that the MST women break with their organizations and support a minimalist program of strictly feminist reforms. The end result was a tactical agreement opposing domestic violence, registering women as heads of families, and encouraging gender equality. The MST women, mostly daughters of landless peasants, perceived the NGO professionals as divisive careerists, unwilling to challenge the political and economic elite that oppressed all peasants. Despite their criticisms of their male comrades, they clearly felt greater affinity with the movement than with the class-collaborationist "feminist" NGOs.

In our discussion, the MST members distinguished between NGOs that contributed (money, resources, etc.) to the movement to finance class struggle, and those that were essentially missionary outfits working (often unconsciously or unwittingly) to fragment and isolate peasants, as in the case of many Pentecostal, USAID, and World Bank sponsored NGO projects.

Peasants Take Action and the State Responds: The New Development Paradigm

Michel Camdessus, the IMF's Managing Director from 1987 to 2000, on a visit to Mexico, a client of the US imperial state, announced publicly that the IMF no longer espouses neoliberalism as a national policy; IMF policy now rested on three pillars, namely (1) "the invisible hand of the market," (2) "the visible hand of the state," and (3) "social solidarity of the poor and the rich."

What Camdessus failed to note is the difficulty of securing the third objective even by means of a strategic engagement of "civil society" in a policy of "popular participation." It was the UNDP that assumed responsibility for designing an economic model that could serve as a guide to state action in this area. The linchpin of this model ("Sustainable Human Development," in UNDP lingo) is a policy of administrative decentralization pioneered by Augusto Pinochet in the

1970s as a means of "increas[ing] government responsiveness to local needs."[5] As conceived by economists at the World Bank (Rondinelli, McCullough, and Johnson, 1989) and designed by the UNDP, the policy of administrative decentralization was designed as a means of ensuring both a participatory form of development vis-à-vis stakeholders in civil society and a "good governance" regime (Goss, 2001; UNDP, 1997). Within the framework of this regime in the 1990s a decentralized "no-power" approach toward social change was widely implemented with variable but little overall success in alleviating rural poverty and bringing about change. As noted earlier, the "success" in the strategy lay in its capacity to divide the popular social movement and demobilize the forces of resistance.

The strategic objectives of this "no-power" local development microproject approach are to turn the rural poor away from the social movement, away from a confrontational approach and a "revolutionary" path to state power; to encourage the poor to use the market in their economics and elections in their politics; to seek change and improvements in their lives within the local spaces of the power structure rather than challenging it; and to change themselves (to empower or capacitate themselves to "act") rather than the system.

Focused on the promotion of local development via the accumulation of social capital, this "no power" approach to social change has been advanced via the agency of NGOs enlisted as cooperants in the development process. The NGOs are drawn into the service of the state and its diverse agencies and partners as frontline soldiers in the war against poverty waged in the localities and within the communities of the rural poor.

The mandate of these frontline soldiers (it could be argued, in the war on the poor) is to mediate between the demands and microproject funds of the donor organizations and the needs and desires of the rural poor in their marginalized communities—to help them adjust to the new world order. In effect, as Wallace (2003) argues, the development NGOs function, albeit in many cases unwittingly, as a stalking horse for global capital and assist in the delivery of the good word about the virtues of capitalism and democracy, and in the process helps dampen the fire of revolutionary fervor.

As the objects of this strategy, the peasants and the rural poor are encouraged, and where possible led, to substitute social action for political action—to build on their cooperative culture by "scaling up" their social capital from the local level "small community" to leadership at the regional (and even national) level (Durston, 1999).

The problem is—and this is where the NGOs come in—the "constructability" of social capital is based on a commonality of interest and a culture of solidarity. And it appears that more often than not the requisite "culture of solidarity" (and sense of "community") does not exist, creating the problem not only of how to "scale up" the self-development efforts of the rural poor but also of how to build social capital where it does not exist.

Under these conditions the accumulation of social capital is necessarily impeded. Nevertheless, Durston, an ECLAC economist committed to the "new paradigm," argues (albeit without any supporting evidence) that even under these conditions it is possible for the rural poor to build on their social capital in their localities and communities and subsequently to scale-up the resulting "development." The key, he argues, is for rural landless workers and other categories of the rural poor to "form alliances with reformist sectors in government" and to take advantage of the "opportunities" provided by "changes in national elites." These unspecified "changes," he says, produce "windows of opportunity for the *emergence* of local social capital" while "reformist alliances" open the way to "capital *building.*"

From the Global to the Local: NGOs versus the Social Movements

The combination of market-assisted land reform and local development was a strategic and political response to the social movements mounted by the indigenous communities and popular-sector organizations of peasants and rural landless workers. The strategic aim of this response was to demobilize the forces of peasant resistance and to provide the "rural poor" with an alternative road to social change, one that was paved not with state power or a confrontational politics of direct action but rather a market-assisted search for social change within the localities and communities of the poor. In the space allowed for by this response of the neoliberal state and the "international development community," the rural poor, in their diverse social and political forms, essentially have three options on the road to social change. One is to adjust to the forces of agrarian transformation unleashed by the neoliberal globalization process by resorting politically to electoral mechanisms and economically to market mechanisms. The second is to redouble their efforts to mobilize the forces of resistance against neoliberalism—to advance the popular movement. And the third option, one designed by and opened up for them by the World Bank and its strategic partners in "the war on poverty," is to take a "no power" approach: in the words of John Holloway (2002), "to change the world without taking power."

Throughout the 1990s and into the new millennium the dominant popular approach to social change was to mobilize the forces of resistance and take direct action as a social movement. Considerable gains were made by means of this approach—both in improving the situation of members (regarding access to land) and in setting back the neoliberal state. However, the neoliberal state and its strategic allies (particularly the World Bank and other intergovernmental and nongovernmental "cooperants" in the development project) also succeeded in diverse contexts in dividing the popular movement, demobilizing the forces of resistance, and paving alternative roads to social change (participation in the electoral process, market-assisted land reform, local development). Subsequent political developments in Bolivia and Ecuador are eloquent testimony concerning the relative success of the establishment in defusing pent-up pressures for radical change and dividing the popular movement by channeling these pressures in three directions. In the mid-1990s the popular (indigenous and peasant) movements in Bolivia and Ecuador set up a political apparatus to contest local and national elections, and the World Bank successfully intervened to turn important if not leading elements toward the no-power approach to social change, a road paved with microprojects, the "assistance" of "civil society," and the mediation of the urban middle class in the form of NGOs.[6]

The MST in Brazil and the Zapatistas in Mexico made a similar strategic decision as did the Cocaleros in Bolivia and CONAIE in Ecuador—to turn toward "civil society" for political support. In the case of the MST, and other organizations in the popular movement (CONAIE in regard to the *Coordinadora de Movimientos Sociales*), this move was a matter of fundamental strategy involving a politics of broad intersectoral alliances with non-agrarian, urban-based social organizations, seeking to coordinate the forces of resistance to government policy while advancing the struggle for land and land reform, bringing this struggle to the cities—to the streets, government offices, and the media. In the process of this struggle, the MST for example, concerted actions with a myriad of civil society organizations and movements, including CUT and a spectrum of neighborhood and civic associations, women's groups, developmental and human rights NGOs, a global advocacy network, as well as the media—organizations that make up "civil society" broadly defined (but not so broad as the UNDP has it, to include the business associations and other organizational forms and political expressions of the "private sector").

Changing Political Dynamics of the Class Struggle

At the time several strategic political questions arose along the following lines, many of which led to decisions with negative consequences for the movement's dynamics. Is the political evolution of the MST in this new politics atypical or is it shared with that of other organizations in the popular struggle? If typical, what are the social and political dynamics of struggle and action involved? Are these dynamics rooted in conditions that are conjunctural and episodic, or are they becoming more widespread and generalized, likely to provoke similar or other forms of organization and further action along the same lines? If so, what forces are generated in the process? And in what direction, if any, are the forces of resistance and opposition being mobilized?

Given the present state of rural development/agrarian transformation studies, the answers to these questions have to be tentative at best. At the moment, answers have to be given in terms of the specific contexts that have given rise to them. In these contexts, the most dynamic sociopolitical movements, those that have the capacity to address the central concerns of their members and advance the popular struggle, appear to be peasant-based (and led) sociopolitical movements, such as the MST, *Ejército Zapatista de Liberación Nacional* (EZLN), the Cocaleros, and CONAIE. However, the dynamics of these sociopolitical movements pose more problems and raise more questions than solutions or answers.

As for CONAIE,[7] in the context of conditions found in Ecuador—and similar conditions found in Bolivia, Peru, and Mexico, to name but a few countries—the critical and at times dominant issue in the orchestration—and, at times, coordination—of collective actions within the popular movement was that of national or ethnic identity and its associated rights.[8] In terms of this issue, which also related to social movements in Mexico as well as several countries in Central America (Honduras, Guatemala, El Salvador, and Nicaragua) and the Andes (Bolivia, Colombia, Ecuador, and Peru), the central struggle revolves around issues not of land or land reform but of ethnic identity, democracy, and autonomy, liberation from relations of oppression, respect for indigenous cultures and forms of organization—and, in some contexts, the struggle for a multiethnic or plurinational state, and in others, for social transformation—a fundamental change in the structure of the national economy and the nation-state.

In terms of this struggle, leaders of the indigenous organizations and movements frequently register complaints against other organizations on the social or political Left, their potential allies in the popular struggle for systemic change—that they persist in viewing indigenous peoples only as peasants.

By some accounts, this has been a primary obstacle in the endurance or even formation of any strategic alliances among indigenous organizations and civil and political organizations on the Left. It is also likely a critical factor in the recent trend within the indigenous movement to ally with a broad network and coalitions of international advocacy or activist organizations and other forms of a "global civil society." These organizations have sometimes assisted the popular movement in creating conditions of broad public support and thus political pressures on the government relative to campaigns launched in the struggle.

On the other hand, the action of the guerrilla movements—the Fuerzas Armados Revolucionarios de Colombia (FARC) and the Ejército de Liberacion Nacional (ELN)—exemplify conditions of struggle that were widespread in the 1970s, in a very different regional context, primarily as a result of political reaction and repression by the state, but have disappeared or radically changed elsewhere in Latin America. In the 1970s, in Uruguay, Argentina, Brazil, and Chile, and other countries in the throes of a counter-revolution and dirty war prosecuted by the armed forces of the state, the popular struggle was largely located in the urban centers. It was in the more rural societies of Central America and the Andes, particularly those with a significant indigenous population, that the popular struggle was centered in the countryside and took the form of a revolutionary armed struggle and a guerrilla organization, much like that which erupted in Chiapas on the first of January 1994. In the 1970s various rural fronts of such organization and revolutionary movements were formed but with very few exceptions (e.g., Colombia) were either destroyed or did not survive the changing conditions.

In the 1980s, in a very different context, peasant and indigenous movements reorganized. In Central America they engaged in both a class war and a war of national liberation—a confrontation of belligerent social and political forces that was not settled until well into the 1990s at enormous human and social cost. But in Brazil, Ecuador, Mexico, Paraguay, Bolivia, and elsewhere, these movements took another direction, generating sporadic outbreaks and another wave of "rural activism" across the region—coinciding with a wave of protests against the neoliberal agenda of the governments that hit the major urban centers. These movements were generally concerned with action on the critical issues of land and democracy, and in some contexts the cause of indigenous rights, a cause that contributed to the growth, even proliferation, of NGOs with a human rights agenda. By 1990 in Mexico there were at least thirteen NGOs with a human rights agenda active just in Chiapas.

In previous studies (2005, 2009) the authors have argued the obvious point that market-driven globalization, that is, neoliberal capitalist development, was the primary factor responsible for the renewed activism of social and political movements in the early 1990s. The Zapatista movement in the form of the EZLN is a case in point. Its irruption in 1994, after a decade of organizational development, on the very day that the North American Free Trade Agreement (NAFTA) took effect, was strategically timed to coincide with a development that was regarded as "the death knell" of the economy on which indigenous communities depend on for livelihood.[9]

Since 1994, an important watershed in the resurgence of the popular movement in the current context (the indigenous uprising in Ecuador in 1990 is another), agrarian social movements rooted in the indigenous community and the peasantry have washed across the Latin American political landscape. Although the success of these movements in bringing about change has been variable, they undoubtedly contain the most dynamic force of resistance against the neoliberal agenda, managing to put the neoliberal state very much on the defensive, or, as in Brazil, Bolivia, Ecuador and, for a time, Chiapas, forcing the government to negotiate if not come to terms with the demands of the movement. As mentioned, in Ecuador several heads of state were forcibly removed from office, the neoliberal agenda regarding privatization was thwarted, and the indigenous movement even managed to encircle and capture the state apparatus, albeit for a matter of hours only (Petras and Veltmeyer, 2005). In Bolivia active mobilizations against the neoliberal agenda of the state resulted in the defenestration of several heads of state, effectively stalled the government's plan to privatize not only the country's reserves of natural gas and oil but even access to water, and produced a quasi-revolutionary situation that created conditions allowing Movimiento al Socialism

(MAS) to come to power by electoral means (Petras and Veltmeyer, 2005).

In Brazil, the *Movimento dos Trabalhadores Rurais Sem Terra* (MST), the region's largest and most powerful "peasant" social movement has managed to effectively confront the state without being able to change its neoliberal policy orientation (even under a purportedly "leftist" Worker Party regime). But the movement has continued to make gains for its members in the land struggle on the basis of a tactic of direct action ("occupations"). More generally in Latin America the momentum of active resistance and mobilization has created conditions for the emergence of the center-left in politics. Although the political significance of this tilt to the left is ambiguous at best and debatable (see chapter 6), there is no question about the contribution of the peasant-based and -led movement to the demise of neoliberalism as an economic model.

Conclusion

The dominant expression of "civil society"—the NGOs—for the most part tend to serve (whether unwittingly or consciously) as agents of imperialism, as in the form of local development. The managers of the NGOs in this service are skilled in designing projects, and they transmit the new rhetoric of "identity" and "globalism" (from the global to the local) into the popular movements. Their activities and texts promote self-help and adjustment to, rather than resistance against, the forces of change (capitalist development, neoliberal globalization).

After two decades of NGO activity, these professionals have "depoliticized" some of the social movements and deradicalized entire areas of social life, such as women, neighborhoods, and youth organizations. In Peru and Chile, where the NGOs have become firmly established, radical social movements have declined. In Ecuador, where they gained a major foothold in the 1980s in response to a strategy of ethnodevelopment designed by the IDB and World Bank economists, the NGOs have created a serious division within what was one of the powerful social movements in Latin America—CONAIE.

Local struggles over immediate issues include basic food, subsistence, and jobs that nurture emerging movements. NGOs emphasize the "local." But the crucial question is what direction local actions should take: whether they will raise the larger issues of the social system and link up with other local forces to confront the state and its imperial backers, or whether they will turn inward, while looking to foreign donors and fragmenting into a series of competing supplicants for external subsidies. The ideology of NGOs encourages the latter.

The discourse of NGO intellectuals is about "cooperation"—but without dwelling on the price and conditions for securing the cooperation of neoliberal regimes and overseas funding agencies. In their role as mediators and brokers, hustling funds overseas and matching these funds to projects acceptable to donors and local recipients, the "foundation entrepreneurs" are engaged in a new type of politics that harkens back to the "labor contractors" (*enganchadores*) of the not too distant past: herding together women to be "trained," and setting up microenterprises subcontracted to larger producers or exporters employing cheap labor.

The politics of many NGOs is essentially not to promote national economic development but to link foreign funders with local labor (self-help microenterprises) to promote economic development and seek improvement in people's lives within the local spaces of the existing power structure, rather than challenging that structure. The managers of NGOs are fundamentally *political* actors whose projects and training workshops do not make any significant *economic* effect in raising workers' and peasants' incomes. But their activities *do* make an effect by diverting people from the class struggle and into forms of collaboration with their exploiters and oppressors.

To justify this "no-power" approach to social change, NGO ideologies often invoke "pragmatism" or "realism," citing the decline of the revolutionary Left, the triumph of capitalism in the East, the "crisis of Marxism," the absence of any alternatives, the power of the United States, and the importance of not provoking state repression. This "possibilism" is used to convince the left to work within the niches of the free market imposed by the World Bank and structural adjustment and to confine politics to the electoral parameters imposed by the military.

The pessimistic "possibilism" and pragmatism of the NGOs are matched by the extremism of the neoliberals. The 1990s witnessed a radicalization of neoliberal policies, a third cycle of "structural reforms" designed to forestall crisis by handing over even more lucrative investment and speculative opportunities to overseas banks and the multinationals: petroleum in Brazil, Argentina, Mexico, and Venezuela; lower wages and lower social security payments; more tax exemptions; and the implementation of "labor reform," including the elimination of protective labor legislation. The result, ironically enough—from a civil society perspective—was a more rigid class structure, and a state that was more directly tied to the ruling classes than ever. The irony is that the neoliberals in state power, and the NGOs in their promotion of local development, have created a polarized class structure that is much closer to the Marxist paradigm than to the NGOs' visions.

6

A Turn of the Tide:
The Center-Left Comes to Power

Today, so-called leftist or "progressive" political forces have formed governments in eleven Latin American nations, and social movements continue to challenge neoliberalism in several other countries. This situation contradicts the prognosis of Jorge Castañeda (1993: 3) made in the opening of his well-known but misbegotten and now largely forgotten book on the Latin American Left:

> The Cold War is over and Communism and the socialist bloc have collapsed. The United States and capitalism have won, and in few areas of the globe is that victory so clear-cut, sweet, and spectacular as in Latin America. Democracy, free-market economics, and pro-American outpourings of sentiment and policy dot the landscape of a region where until recently left–right confrontation and the potential for social revolution and progressive reform were widespread. Today conservative, pro-business, often democratically elected and pro-US technocrats hold office around the hemisphere. The US spent nearly 30 years combating nationalist Marxist revolutionaries where the Left was active, influential, and sometimes in control, and where it is now on the run or on the ropes (quoted in Barrett, Chávez, and Rodríguez-Garavito, 2008: 1).

Rodríguez-Garavito and his colleagues have used this quote to launch a different assessment of the fortunes of the Latin American Left over the course of the 1990s and into the new millennium, which they view as the rebirth of the Left—"utopia reborn" (with reference to Castañeda's "correct diagnosis" that the Left's utopian dream had come to an end). This view of the rebirth of the Latin American Left is widespread, based as it is on the dynamism of the social movements in the 1990s and the emergence of a red or pink tide of left-leaning regimes in the new millennium—regimes that rode the widespread disenchantment with neoliberalism to state power. Even the 2003 electoral victory in Ecuador of the now disgraced Gutiérrez, who upon his election immediately scampered off to Washington for advice and tutelage, was greeted by many on the Left at the time with the same sense of optimism and wild expectation of a new direction and alternative politics that had greeted the election to the presidency of Lula in Brazil and surrounded Hugo Chávez's declaration of the Bolivarian Revolution. Each of these and other such events was seen as a setback to the efforts of the US administration to dominate economic and political developments in the region—to reassert its hegemony and what even some of its advisors see as a project of imperial domination.

To all appearances there would seem to be little question as to the correctness of this view of political developments in the region over the past decade, a view reflected in the widespread concern in neoliberal policymaking and political circles, and in the evident glee on the Left that their fortunes are on the mend in this turning of the political tide. This turn in the tide can be traced back to the election of Hugo Chávez to state power in 1999. This now perhaps transcendental event was followed by the election to power of the following self-styled progressives: in Brazil, Da Silva ("Lula") in 2002, backed by the PT, CUT, and the Movimento dos Trabalhadores Rurais Sem Terra (MST); in Argentina, Kirchner Fernandez in 2003, backed by the Confederación General del Trabajo de la República Argentina (CGT); in Uruguay, Tabare in 2004, and Mujica in 2010, backed by PIT-CNT; in Chile, Bachelet in 2005, a socialist member of the *concertación* regime in power since Pinochet's loss of the si/no campaign in 1989; in Bolivia, Morales, in 2006 and 2010, backed by MAS, the COB, and the indigenous social movements; in Nicaragua, Ortega in 2006, backed by the trade unions and the social movements; in Ecuador, Correa in 2006 and 2008, backed by the citizens alliance, trade unions, and CONAIE; in Honduras, Manuel Zelaya in 2006, a liberal backed by the social movements; in Paraguay, Lugo in 2008, backed by the peasantry and other progressive forces; and in El Salvador, Funes in 2009, backed by the FLMN, the peasants and the trade unions. In addition, progressive forces almost came to power in Mexico in the form of López Obrador and the PRD (and would have, if not for electoral fraud) and also captured important cities in Latin America, from Bogotá and Mexico City to Montevideo, Caracas, Rosario, San Salvador, and Belo Horizonte.

Notwithstanding the loss of state power to the political Right in Chile, and the solid line-up of neoliberal regimes close to Washington on the Pacific rim of Latin America (Mexico, Colombia, Peru, and now Chile), we have the appearance in the region of a leftward tilt in national politics—"economic rebels" in the words of Mark Weisbrot (2009), "anti-imperialists" in the conception of Hugo Chávez, critics of the neoliberal world order of capitalist development. This appearance raises a number of questions that we propose to address in this chapter. First, what conditions brought about or facilitated this political development, this turn in the tide? Second, what does the label "Left" or "progressive" or "pragmatic left" mean in the context of regime politics? Is it a question of a center-left concerned to open up or tread the narrow path between neoliberalism on the Right and socialism on the Left, or a more radical Left concerned to not merely reform or humanize capitalism with greater expenditures on poverty alleviation programs harnessed to neoliberalism but to establish "the socialism of the 21st Century"? Can the political Left in state power best be viewed, as Weisbrot does, as "economic rebels" and social democrats? Or is *Newsweek*'s Mac Margolis (2009) closer to the mark in describing the center-Left regimes and politicians in power in Latin America as "sheep in wolf's clothing," tilting to the right rather than to the left?[1]

We will return to this issue at various points below, but the answer to these questions turn on the way that virtually all of the politicos on the left capitalized on the wave of social mobilizations, uprisings, and class struggle to attain state power but then used electoral politics to demobilize and diminish the social movements. As for the movements, they managed to bring down the neoliberal stooges of US imperialism, but they lacked the leadership and a political strategy for taking power, and for the most part ended up supporting the emerging center-left regimes. In the process we can identify a shift in the balance of power between the movements to the left and the right. We will observe that the locus of struggle shifted from an anti-capitalist and anti-imperialist leftist politics toward a vague, ideologically undefined concern with "another world" (beyond neoliberalism).

Political Regime and Ideology: The Center-Left and the State

Despite the worsening of the world and regional economy, "the Left," Weisbrot (2009) noted, "keeps winning in Latin America." The "latest Left victory" he was referring to was that of President Rafael Correa of Ecuador, an economist who was first elected at the end of 2006 and was reelected in 2009 under a new constitution designed, as in Bolivia, to establish a plurinational or multiethnic state, giving representation and power to the country's indigenous nationalities. The election gave the charismatic forty-six-year-old four more years of state power, and, Weisbrot noted, he may be reelected once more for another term.

There are a number of reasons, Weisbrot continues—ignoring or ignorant of the explicit repudiation of Correa's policies by CONAIE in its Asamblea Extraordinaria in Ambato on February 25–26, 2010—that most Ecuadorians might want to "stick with their president." As in Bolivia under Morales, some 1.3 million of Ecuador's poor or poverty-stricken households (some 6 million in a country of 14 million) now get a stipend or *bono* of $30 a month, a "significant improvement" in their situation, according to Weisbrot. In addition, social spending as a share of the economy, as well as public investment, increased by more than 50 percent in Correa's two years in office. In 2008, in the maelstrom of the global financial crisis, the government invested heavily in public works, with capital spending more than doubling.

Correa, Weisbrot adds, has delivered on other promises that were important to his constituents, not least of which was a referendum allowing for a constituent assembly to draft a new constitution, which voters approved by a nearly two-thirds majority. It is seen by many as one of the most progressive constitutions in the world, with advances in the rights of indigenous people, civil unions for gay couples, and a novel provision of rights to nature. The latter would apparently allow for lawsuits on the basis of damage to an ecosystem.

Many thought Correa was joking when he said during his presidential campaign that he would willingly keep the US military base at Manta if Washington would allow Ecuadorian troops to be stationed in Florida. But he was not, and the base was scheduled to close later in the year. Correa also resisted pressure from the US Congress regarding a multi-billion-dollar lawsuit in which Chevron is accused of dumping billions of gallons of toxic oil waste that polluted rivers and streams. And in an unprecedented move last November, Correa stopped payment on $4 billion of foreign debt when an independent Public Debt Audit Commission, long demanded by civil society organizations in Ecuador, determined that this debt was illegal, having been illegitimately contracted.

In the United States these policies have been dismissed as "populism" or worse. A *New York Times* editorial in November 2007, entitled "Authoritarians in the Andes," summed up the US foreign policy establishment's view that Correa, Bolivia's President Evo Morales, and Hugo Chávez of Venezuela were "increasingly interested in grabbing power for themselves." For Morales and Correa, wrote the editorial board, "their confrontational approach is also threatening to rend Bolivia and Ecuador's fragile social and political stability."

The *Times* (and Washington's foreign policy establishment), however, were proven wrong, as Ecuador and Bolivia are now more politically stable than they have been for decades. (Ecuador has had nine presidents over the last fifteen years.) They are also, as Weisbrot (2009) notes, more democratic than they had ever been. And, as for the economy, growth has been steady, joint ventures have been signed with multinationals, trade has been diversified, and pillage of the financial sector, all too common under previous US-backed regimes, has ended.

Indeed, Weisbrot opines, Latin America is experiencing a democratic transition that "is likely to prove every bit as important as the one that brought an end to the dictatorships that plagued many countries through the first four decades of the post-second world war era." "Ironically," he adds, "the region's economic performance was vastly better in the era of the dictatorships, because the governments of that era generally had more effective economic policies than the formally democratic but neoliberal governments that replaced them." What governments Weisbrot might be referring to here is unclear—those of General Rodriguez in Ecuador or General Velasco in Peru, both of them national populists more than developmentalists? Surely not the governments of Augusto Pinochet in Chile or Martinez De Hoz in Argentina, pioneers of liberalism at the level of national policy who halted and reversed the gains in living standards made under previous regimes? Possibly Weisbrot had in mind the welfare-development capitalist states of earlier years in Mexico and elsewhere, which, as in East Asia, had to some degree assumed the responsibility for social welfare and economic development.

"A few years ago," Weisbrot continues, "there were fears, backed by polling data, that people would become nostalgic for the days of real (not imagined) authoritarian governments because of the much greater improvements in living standards during that era. Instead, they chose to vote for left governments who extended democracy from politics to economic and social policy."

Political Regimes and Economic Policies

The Left-leaning governments in the region, Weisbrot (2009) observes, in regard to the economy, "have mostly succeeded where their neoliberal predecessors failed." This is in part, he acknowledges, because they have benefited from the acceleration in world economic growth over the last five years. But, he argues, "they have also changed their economic policies in ways that increased economic growth."

To elaborate on and critically examine this point, Argentina's economy grew more than 60 percent from 2003 to 2007, recovering from the deepest and most severe crisis in its history. As for Venezuela its economy expanded by 95 percent. Table 6.1 provides some more data on this process of economic growth for these and other countries in the region. These growth rates, Weisbrot notes, are impressive even when the prior recession and the crisis of 2001–2002 are considered. Statistics provided by ECLAC on Latin America's "social panorama" in recent years suggest that these growth rates—and presumably the economic policies responsible for, or accompanying, this growth—allowed for or created conditions that led to large reductions in poverty. On this issue, table 6.2 shows a significant reduction in the Latin American poverty rate, especially regarding extreme poverty over the course of the past decade, most of which with the center-left in power.

Note that the measures of poverty in these statistics are based on an extremely low World Bank standard of $2 a day ($12 for extreme poverty), which is not only entirely misleading in not considering or

Table 6.1 Growth rates of GDP (percent), selected countries, Latin America, 1995–2009

	1995	2000	2003	2004	2005	2006	2007	2009	
Argentina	−2.1	4.8	8.8	9.0	9.2	8.5	8.6	0.9	
Bolivia	4.9	2.5	2.7	4.2	4.0	4.6	3.8	3.5	
Brazil	4.2	4.3	1.1	5.7	2.9	3.7	5.3	−0.2	
Chile	10.6	4.5	3.9	6.0	5.7	4.0	5.3	−1.5	
Colombia	5.2	2.9	4.6	4.7	5.7	6.8	7.0	0.4	
Cuba	–	3.8	5.4	11.8	12.5	7.0	4.5	1.4	
Ecuador	–	1.8	2.8	3.6	8.0	6.0	3.9	2.7	0.4
Mexico	–	−6.2	6.6	1.4	4.2	2.8	4.8	3.3	−6.5
Peru	8.6	3.0	4.0	5.1	6.7	7.6	8.2	0.9	
Venezuela	4.0	3.7	−7.8	18.3	10.3	10.3	8.5	−3.3	
LA	0.6	3.9	2.1	6.2	4.7	5.5	5.6	−1.9	

Source: CEPAL, 2007: 85; ECLAC, 2010: 20.

Table 6.2 Rates of poverty(P) / indigence(I) in Latin America, 2002, 2004, 2006 (percent)

	2000–2002		2003–2004		2007	
	P	I	P	I	P	I
Argentina	45.4	20.9	26.0	9.1	21.0	7.2
Bolivia	62.4	37.1	63.9	34.1	54.0	31.2
Brazil	37.5	13.2	36.3	10.6	30.0	8.5
Chile	20.2	5.6	18.7	4.7	13.7	3.2
Colombia	51.1	24.6	46.8	20.2	–	–
Ecuador	49.0	19.4	45.2	17.1	38.8	12.4
Mexico	39.4	12.6	37.0	11.7	31.7	8.7
Peru	54.8	24.4	48.7	17.4	39.3	13.7
Venezuela	48.6	22.2	37.1	15.9	28.5	8.5

Source: ECLAC, *Social Panorama of Latin America*, 2007b; *Social Panorama of Latin America*, 2008.

controlling for different income thresholds in different countries, but also grossly unrealistic. A more realistic measure based on real basic needs would indicate poverty at twice the rate as that measured by CEPAL. Moreover, by providing a statistical average of national incomes per capita income figures define a fictional, nonexisting individual. If we were to take per capita income as a percentage of growing national income, or in terms of the actual social distribution of this income, then poverty rates are in fact rising.

However, even if we were to acknowledge that progress has been made at the level of extreme poverty—and the evidence for this is stronger, at least in the case of Chile and Brazil—the question is: To what can this change in the "social panorama" (to use ECLAC's phrase) be attributed? Is it the result of changed conditions in the global economy, the growing demand for natural resources—agromineral commodities—and the resulting increase in the world price for these commodities? Without a doubt, the economies in the region oriented toward commodity exports have benefited hugely from the primary commodities boom. Agromineral exporters took advantage of this boom, with resulting windfall profits for themselves, as well as a significant increase in fiscal revenues derived from these exports by the governments. As for Bolivia, Ecuador, and Venezuela, the three countries that dominate an emerging anti-neoliberal, anti-imperialist axis, being regimes that have been and might well be labeled "national populist," it would seem that to varying degrees they delivered on their promises to take greater control over their natural resources on behalf of the people and to share the income from these resources with the poor. But yet the revolutionary spirit was stilled. The movements demobilized and retreated. The wave of hopes and expectations died. Dreams ended.

Political Regimes and Fiscal Expenditures

A closer look at the pattern of fiscal expenditures and public investments over the course of the primary commodities boom that coincided with the advent to state power of the political Left suggests that the issue of social change is not as simple or straightforward as Weisbrot and others on the intellectual left imagine or think.

First, there is little difference in the actual policies pursued by the ostensibly anti-neoliberal regimes on the center-left and those, such as found in Mexico, Colombia, and Peru that are overtly neoliberal in their policies and aligned with the United States. The dominant feature of these policies is their origin in what has been described as a post-Washington Consensus on the need to "bring the state back in" and for a more pragmatic, more socially inclusive form of neoliberalism and development (Ocampo, 2006, 2007; Sunkel and Infante, 2009). Under this consensus, virtually all governments, regardless of ideological orientation or regime type, introduced a new poverty-targeted social policy and pursued a "pro-poor" approach in the implementation of neoliberalism.

Second, an examination of actual fiscal expenditures of governments across Latin America for their "social programs" (health, education, housing, security, welfare) shows that even in ostensibly leftist regimes such as Morales's Bolivia, and certainly pragmatic neoliberal (center-left) regimes (such as in Chile, Argentina, and Brazil), there has been no significant change in the distribution of income. Indeed, table 6.3 shows that, perversely, the highest income quintile of households benefited more from fiscal expenditures on social programs than the bottom quintile.

Expenditures in some areas (e.g., welfare) are indeed poverty-targeted, benefiting disproportionately (by redistributing income) more to the poorer households, but populist programs in this area are by no means given greater priority in left-of-center popular nationalist regimes such as Bolivia and Ecuador than in centrist (pragmatic neoliberal) regimes such as Argentina, Brazil, and Chile.[2] Although in the case of Bolivia the data reflect barely a year of Morales in power, it is revealing that the incidence of poverty over that year actually

Table 6.3 Latin America: Distribution of benefits from social spending percent, top and bottom quintiles (percent share)—2006

	Poorest 20 percent	*Richest 20 percent*
Education	20.2	20.4
Primary	29.0	7.9
Secondary	13.2	18.3
Tertiary	1.9	52.1
Health	20.6	17.6
Social security	5.6	51.2
Total social spending	15.0	30.4
Share of quintiles in primary income	3.6	56.4

Source: Alier and Clements (2007: 4–5), based on ECLAC (2006) data.

increased—from 59.6 percent in 2005 to 60.1 percent in 2007. As for extreme poverty, while considerable improvements were being made in a number of countries such as Chile and Brazil, in Bolivia the situation actually worsened—from a rate of 36.7 percent in 2005 to 37.7 percent in 2007. This worsening situation, when other countries were making improvements in ameliorating poverty, undoubtedly reflects the absence of any state-led social reforms at the time. However, it also reflects a decline in the government's expenditures on social programs as a percentage of GDP—down from 13.3 percent in 2003 to 11.2 percent in 2008. And the context for this relative decrease in social expenditures[3] was a growing trade surplus and an increase in international currency reserves from $1.8 billion in 2005 to $8.5 billion in 2009.

Third, none of the governments, with the notable exception of Venezuela, implemented any fundamental change in the social and institutional structure of the dominant capitalist system. As a result, notwithstanding the alleviation of conditions of extreme poverty in a number of countries, no regime—again with the exception of Venezuela under Chávez—implemented changes that would result in a significant redistribution of society's productive resources, wealth, and income. In the 1960–1975 period of state-led development many governments used instruments of state power, such as progressive taxation, to create a "secondary distribution" of national income. However, under much more favorable economic conditions no such "structural" change was either contemplated or induced in any of the countries. In Bolivia, for example, the Morales government legislated that the natural resources of the country belonged to the "Bolivian people," but beyond the extraction of a higher royalty share on the extraction of these resources by the multinationals that continue to operate in the country, and an increased taxation regime, to date there is no visible change either in access to the country's productive resources or in the distribution of income by sector and class. In the agricultural sector, for example, despite the announcement two years ago of "agrarian revolution," to date there has been no change effected in the land tenure system in which large tracts of land are owned by a small elite of major landowning families.

The Left as a Political Class: From Theory to Practice

The "left" is generally understood as an ideological orientation toward socializing the means of production, preventing the exploitation of labor for the sake of private profit, ensuring a more equitable distribution of the social product, agrarian reform, and indigenous autonomy. In political practice this orientation is reflected in a policy of increased state spending, which reinforces the power of the state and augments its role in the economy; the rejection of free trade in favor of fair trade; improving working conditions and ensuring a decent wage for the working class; public investment in economic and social infrastructure and social services to ensure that basic needs are met and fundamental human rights (access to means of production or meaningful employment, decent housing and shelter, meaningful employment, health, education and housing, etc.) are protected; reversal of the neoliberal policy of privatization with a policy of nationalization, increasing public ownership of economic enterprise in strategic sectors of the economy; regulating in the public interest private economic activity and the labor, product, and capital markets; and an "authoritative re-allocation of wealth and income," placing a cap on wealth and ensuring that the basic needs of the population are met.

If we were to apply these criteria in assessing "what is left of the Left today," how might we understand the contemporary Latin American political left and assess and evaluate the ideological and political character of the leftist or center-left regimes that have emerged in the past decade? What regimes might we consider to be truly on the "left"?

Let us first consider Lula in Brazil. In practice he supports and has even extended the neoliberal policy of privatization. He has rejected the demand of the social movements for substantive land reform, supporting instead the demand of the agromineral elite and capitalist exporters and industrialists for improved access to the US market and other forays into the world market. In terms of this policy Lula's PT government prefers to finance the productive transformation of the large soy plantations of the agro-exporters rather than the productive transformation of the land settlements formed by the MST. In terms of wage and income policies, the government headed by Lula, who was once a trade unionist but spent twenty-five years as a party official before assuming state power as president, is closer to the IMF than organized labor. He has doubled the minimum wage over the past eight years and provides a $40 poverty subsidy, even as he sharply reduced public sector pensions, tripled the mass of profits of the financial and agromineral export sectors and oversaw the criminalization of the social movements, including the arrest and prosecution of MST activists.

In what sense might we then consider Lula a Leftist? Certainly not by reference to his origins and background as a metallurgical worker and a trade unionist. People change, and so do organizations such as the PT, which has transformed over the years from a labor party into a thoroughly bourgeois party. The PT has a left wing, but Lula represents the right wing, which has become increasingly distanced from the workers at the base of the party and the movement of organized labor, such as it is in Brazil today

Bachelet's Socialist Party in Chile has nothing to do with the party of the former Socialist President Salvador Allende. The regimes under the presidencies of Lagos and Bachelet, closer to a socialites than a socialist party, have espoused a policy of free trade and a special relationship with the United States, rather than joining Venezuela, Bolivia, Ecuador—and Cuba—in an alternative regional trading arrangement based on socialist principles. Chile's macroeconomic and social policies can best be described as pragmatic neoliberalism or a new form of social liberalism—leaving the strategic heights of the economy in the hands (and financial institutions) of the capitalist investors, bankers, and industrialists, but supplementing the neoliberal agenda at the level of macroeconomic policy with a social policy designed to reduce the incidence and alleviate the conditions of extreme poverty. At the level of international relations Bachelet collaborated with the United States and Canada in an imperialist offensive against Aristide, and they joined Brazil in sending troops to Haiti to keep the peace (i.e., to massacre Aristide's supporters). In what sense is this leftist, to collaborate with US imperialism and the occupation forces that overthrew Aristide?

As for Correa's policies in Ecuador, the position of CONAIE, the most consequential albeit diminished social movement in the country, was unambiguous regarding his so-called citizen's revolution, as noted, at its assembly in Ambato on February 25–26, 2010. Correa in his years in office has not modified in any substantive way the colonial nature of the so-called plurinational state and continues to "consolidate the neoliberal model, betraying [in the process] the Ecuadorian people, the communes, the communities, peoples, indigenous nationalities, Afro-Ecuadorians and Montubios." In response to this betrayal, the Assembly of indigenous nationalities convoked a "plurinational uprising" (*levantamiento*), articulated with other social sectors, in protest against the neoliberal policies applied by the government. At the same time, CONAIE, as the effective government of Ecuador's indigenous nationalities and peoples, categorically rejected the state system of indigenous institutions and demanded autonomy for these institutions. It also demanded the expulsion of the mining corporations, both national and multinational, operating in indigenous lands and territories, and demanded that the Correa government's concessions to these corporations and the oil companies and others be declared null and void. So much for Correa's leftist credentials, his socialism and his "citizen's revolution."

And the Revolutionary Left?

The genuine Left movement maintains a presence in several countries, not only in Ecuador in the form of CONAIE, but also in Colombia with the FARC, sectors of the MST in Brazil, in some union sectors and among farmers in Bolivia who are demanding both the nationalization of the mining and agro-business multinationals that dominate the economy and the expropriation of the big landed estates; and in Mexico in the movement of electrical workers—the Sindicato Mexicano de Electricistas (SME). In the SME the neoliberal government of Felipe Calderón faces the broadest, deepest, and most unified resistance movement in decades. The government was able to severely weaken the SME by closing a public power facility and firing 44,000 workers. While the fightback was massive, the SME did not have the strength to force a quick reversal of the government's actions. The government's actions and policies advanced the neoliberal project by securing the backing of its big business base. The SME defeat resulted in the loss of jobs, benefits, and rights held by its members and retirees. In Mexico as in the rest of Latin America the radical social movements are on the defensive if not in retreat, an unequal stalemate, without any clear avenue for political alliances that do not compromise their basic programmatic demands.

The Political Left and the Social Movements

In the 1990s and at the beginning of the new millennium the peasant and indigenous movements were playing a major role in some countries in Latin America. In Bolivia, Ecuador, Colombia, Mexico, Peru, Brazil, Central America, and Paraguay, peasant and indigenous movements were involved in either overthrowing neoliberal regimes, building powerful regional movements with impacts on national policy, helping to elect center-left presidents and/or, in a few cases, providing mass support for guerrilla movements. Most of these social movements were effective "veto groups" in the making of national political agendas. As important political actors, these movements were allies much sought after by self-declared center-left electoral politicians and parties to counteract the patronage politics of right-wing agromineral elites. The moment of triumph of the movements, their recognition as central actors in national politics, as potential makers and breakers of the electoral fortunes of urban-led political parties and leaders, was also the beginning of the end of their role as representative agents of the mass base.

Peasant and indigenous leaders were divided. Some maintained their principled demands and remained loyal to their constituents, while others succumbed to the blandishments or political favors of government jobs, EU- and US-supplied NGO funds, or microproject loans administered by international banks. Social movement leaders, activists, and supporters witnessed their center-left political allies turn to the right, embracing an agromineral export strategy and abandoning promises of land reform, food security, and funding for cooperative agriculture. The result was a visible loss of political initiative, internal divisions, and mass defections and, in some cases, the transformation of the movements into transmission belts of official policies leading to partial demobilization and the loss of "street power."

The United States, in this context, as in Bolivia for instance, has favored rightist oligarchy-led separatist movements (in the *media luna* and the regional capital of Santa Cruz) and has funded those NGOs working to strengthen "civil society" on the Right. The Obama administration has also continued the policy of previous administrations by providing massive funding to opposition movements on the pretext of "strengthening democracy." It is pursuing this policy not only in Bolivia, where Morales has had to expel the US ambassador for political interference, but also in Ecuador (in Guayaquil, and Guayas province) and in Venezuela (in the oil-producing state of Zulia).

The emphasis on "autonomy" and the ethnodevelopment and ethnic politics strategy promoted by the NGOs and their funders also caused the indigenous movements to move away from class politics in favor (in some cases) of a separatist regional politics. In Bolivia, for example, this shift toward identity politics isolated the movements from the trade unions, the miners, and urban working class and provided the powerful regional agromineral elites with a pretext to seize control of the most productive and rich regions of the country that contain the most fertile soil and concentrations of minerals and major gas and oil fields.

Despite the relative decline of some of the peasant and especially the indigenous movements, and their increasingly marginal role in national politics in most countries, Bolivia's indigenous movements are still relatively strong. CONAIE, once the most powerful popular movement in the region, is making a slow recovery and mounting action against Correa in alliance with urban movements, while an army of leftist and progressive journalists, NGOs, academics, and writers continue to prattle on about "Latin America's powerful social movements," a "pink tide," the "advance of the Left," and so on.

As the agromineral bourgeoisie and the Far Right in Bolivia passed separatist referenda in provinces that they dominated or controlled, and peasants and indigenous supporters of the central government were savagely beaten by neofascist thugs backed by the provincial separatist regimes, the Morales-Linares regime in Bolivia abandoned any pretext of defending the physical security of its followers while making every effort to placate the agromineral elite. In Ecuador, subsequent to the CONAIE's disastrous (2003) electoral alliance with the pseudopopulist, turned-rightist Lucio Gutiérrez, the popular movement declined, divided, and demoralized in its mass base, reaching its nadir in the 2007 vote for the constituent assembly where it secured barely 2 percent of the vote for its candidates. But since then it has regrouped, and in coalition with urban movements in the CMS, it has begun to organize mass regional protests.

As for the Zapatista movement, it marginalized itself in refusing to support the multitudinous protest movement against the presidential fraud of 2006, giving only minimal token help to the mass urban-rural uprising in Oaxaca, which lasted for six months despite severe state repression. The Zapatistas also offered no sign of solidarity with the ongoing struggles of indigenous and peasant communities all over the country (movements such as El Campo No Aguante Más) against the economic and environmental ravages of capitalism and neoliberalism. As discussed in the next two chapters, the resistance has not been cowed by the counteroffensives of the neoliberal state and US imperialism, and these struggles are mounting across the region in response to new and changing conditions of capitalist development that are reaching crisis proportions.

Conclusion

There are powerful left-wing forces in Latin America, and sooner or later they will rekindle the revolutionary spirit, contest and challenge the power of the neoliberal converts and their allies in Washington and in the multinational corporations. Perhaps sooner in the case of Bolivia, where the scale and scope of Morales's broken promises and embrace of the business elite has already provoked the mobilization of the class-conscious trade unions, the mass urban organizations, and the landless peasants. The insurrectionary movements on whose back Morales rode to office are intact if demobilized, their coopted leaders replaced by new militants. The populist "gestures" and "folkloric" theater have only a limited time span for diversion in the face of the grinding poverty of class-conscious miners and the indigenous militants in El Alto. The insurrectionary forces that brought Morales to power can also bring him down.

In Brazil, Lula's regime, and its control and co-optation of the class-collaborationist labor confederation CUT, has led to the formation of a new militant confederation called ConLuta (founded in May 2006), which is based mainly on public sector workers and has failed to make inroads in the factories. The MST's critical collaboration with the Lula regime has led to a political impasse, internal debates, and a decline in support outside of the organization, hopefully leading to a political rectification and reorientation toward autonomous class politics. The Brazilian Left faces a "long march" toward regaining its formidable presence. The case is similar in Uruguay and Argentina: the new "center-left" neoliberals, unlike the old right, have co-opted many of the leaders of the major trade unions and some of the unemployed workers groups through government posts, inclusion in Congressional electoral slates and generous stipends.

Hugo Chávez stands as the major political figure representing a real challenge to US imperialism. He has led the fight against "Free Trade Agreement of the Americas" or ALCA and the US invasion of Haiti; he defeated a US-sponsored coup attempt and has demonstrated that social welfare, nationalism, and political independence is viable in the Hemisphere. But like Cuba, Chávez has to contend with not only US aggression from the outside but also contradictions from within. Many officials in his party (The Fifth Republic), the state apparatus, and sectors of the military are not in favor of his proposed twenty-first-century Socialism. Between Chávez and the 10 million voters who support him is a political apparatus of dubious political credentials. Likewise, Fidel Castro has spoken of a profound internal threat from a "new class" of rich emerging from the scarcities of the Special Period (1992–2000) and the opening to tourism. He has called for a "revolution within the revolution." If there are "new Left winds blowing in Latin America" they are coming from a new generation of militants engaging in direct action politics, from Chávez's insistence that socialism is the only alternative to capitalism, from the new mass leaders in Bolivia, Brazil, and elsewhere, as well as from insurgent movements in Colombia.

The center-left regimes and their intellectual supporters on the Left represent a sad epitaph on the fate of the radical generations of the 1970s and 1980s. But they are a spent force, lacking critical ideas or audacious proposals for challenging imperialism and capitalist rule. They will not fade away—they have too much of a stake and are well ensconced in the current system. A new generation of popular leaders, self-taught, and young intellectual militants are emerging within the urban councils of Bolivia's El Alto, the community councils and self-managed factories of Venezuela, the new class-oriented trade unions of Brazil, the popular movements fighting the US-backed golpista regime in Honduras, the peasant fighters in the jungles of Colombia, and elsewhere. These are the winds of social change on the Left.

By the commonly understood criteria of the Left, the Latin American regimes that have been hailed by many intellectuals as "new winds from the Left" fail to meet the test: none pursue redistributive policies; most have implemented regressive budgeting policies, subsidizing big business and reducing expenditures for social policy; class selective austerity programs have been applied prejudicial to minimum-wage earners and low-paid public employees in health and education; privatizations—legal and illegal—have been extended and deepened, even in lucrative publicly owned mineral and energy sectors; and foreign investors have been given privileged access to local markets, cheap labor, and privatized enterprises and banks.

But while none of the so-called center-left regimes can be considered "leftist" there are variations in the degree of conformity to the neoliberal model. The Kirchners have channeled some of the economic surplus toward funding national capitalist development and supported some price controls on basic foodstuffs and electricity rates. Lula has been at the other extreme prejudicing national manufacturing with an overvalued Brazilian Real and exorbitant interest rates favoring financial capital. As for Morales, he combines Lula's pro-foreign investment policies, especially in minerals and petrol, with a policy of increasing tax rates on foreign-owned mining, gas and oil producers. Although most have provided troops for the US-sponsored occupation of Haiti, they are unanimous in their opposition to the US military bases in Colombia and of US direct intervention in Venezuela. While most promote minimalist subsistence antipoverty programs, none pursue structural changes in land tenure and public investments toward creating employment to get at the root of poverty.

US foreign and imperial policy, until recently designed and executed by one of the most extreme rightist regimes in recent Western history, has led to frictions, particularly in its attempt to impose non-reciprocal free-trade agreements and a legal basis to punish electoral regimes for not conforming to US dictates. Within the framework of neoliberal politics, these regimes face strong pressures from popular organizations and threats of renewed mass direct action. This in itself has served to pressure these regimes into making symbolic gestures of independence and opposition to extreme demands from the militarist-imperialist Bush and Obama regimes. It would be a mistake, however, to consider these regime gestures as a sign of a major revival of the Left when in fact the credit is due to the mass movements outside the regime who demand more than symbolic gratification and a sharp turn toward substantial socioeconomic transformations.

7

Social Movements in a Time of Crisis

A striking aspect of the present world global crisis has been the passivity of the working and middle classes (with a few exceptions) in the face of massive job losses, big cuts in wages, health care and pension payments, and mounting housing foreclosures. Never over the past two centuries of capitalist development has an economic crisis caused so much pain and loss to so many workers, employees, small business operators, and farmers with so little large-scale public protest. The crisis is multifaceted, reaching well beyond the financial system, the machinations and conditions of which have riveted the attention of so many analysts of the global crisis. Although most academics, policymakers, and politicians fret about the financial aspects of the crisis and its ramifications, ordinary citizens, the small direct producers, and the mass of workers that dominate the economy all over the world struggle to make ends meet, feed their families, and survive the onslaught of a major capitalist production crisis.

An irony—or rather, and more to the point, a fundamental contradiction of capitalism—is that the very system that produced so much private wealth over the past decade, sprouting super-billionaires all over the world and fueling the growth of a substantial middle class of high consumers (reflected in the rapid expansion of the economies that catered to these classes), has generated so much insecurity and misery. The surge in recent years in the price of fuel and food is a clear case in point. Surging prices have ignited inflation throughout Latin America, driving up the cost of food, thanks in part to the Chinese demand for Latin American farm products. In some countries, a gallon of gas now costs more than a typical day's wages. Food prices, according to ECLAC, have escalated at a yearly average of 15 percent since 2006 (years before the putative "global financial crisis"), and the prices of many staples have increased much more than that.

The International Monetary Fund (IMF) estimated that the regional average inflation rate in April 2008 was 7.5 percent, compared to 5.2 percent a year earlier, and the World Bank (*La Jornada*, July 29, 2008) estimated that in Mexico the 2008 inflation rate would reach a level not seen since 2002, erasing any wage gains made by workers and likely to produce strike actions to recover the value of wages and pensions. And by some accounts these were gross underestimates. In Argentina, for example, the official inflation figure of 9.1 percent at the time was less than half the actual rate. In 2010, inflationary pressures intensified, eroding the nominal increases in the minimum wage in Brazil, Argentina, Bolivia, and elsewhere (*Financial Times*, March 7, 2010). Also, for some reason (probably political), economists do not include the cost of food and fuel in their measure of the "core inflation rate." According to DIEESE, a Brazilian research outfit linked to the labor movement, in some areas of the country the effective cost of the "*canasta básica*" (basic needs basket) rose by 50 percent from 2008 to 2009.

These cost increases and inflation are leeching workers' paychecks and eroding the limited progress made in reducing the incidence and alleviating the conditions of extreme poverty such as hunger and indigence. Already in 2007, according to the UN's World Food Program, at least 500,000 people in El Salvador and Guatemala had toppled into poverty. Across Latin America, if prices keep rising, an additional 15 million people could fall back into poverty, adding to a total count of 190 million poor.

They are not alone. If gasoline, food, and grocery prices continue their relentless climb, and farmland is increasingly converted for biofuel production, an additional 100 million people worldwide, according to a leaked secret World Bank report (Engdahl, 2007), could well be sucked into the same downward spiral. In Africa, food riots have erupted in Egypt, Cameroon, and Burkina Faso. Consumers have staged demonstrations in India and Indonesia to protest fuel subsidy cuts. And in the Caribbean as well as Central and South America, food riots have led to the overthrow of regimes, mass protests, and road blockages.

"There is," notes Carlo Scaramella, who heads the World Food Program in El Salvador, "a whole combination of factors that are putting a tremendous amount of pressure on the poor." He adds, "We haven't had an economic shock of this magnitude in years." But it is one thing to compile the statistics; it is quite another to live the reality behind them.

In this connection, consider the following. Maria and Jose Lopez, who live with their three children in a two-room cinderblock house on a hillside in San Salvador, are among many millions to feel the strain. Early in 2008, before the perfect storm of the global crisis, they scraped together $148 for a downpayment on their own place in a hard-luck area aptly named "Thin City." But with the onset of the crisis the dream of home ownership vanished. The new priority was simply to eat. They need to spend a large and growing chunk of their wages on food. When the price of rice and beans, both staples, and cooking fuel jumped by more than 30 percent in just a few months of 2008, it cut deeply into the family's $500 monthly income. José, a laborer, pawned his wedding ring to buy groceries following a short bout of unemployment. Maria, who works in the central market downtown, cadged a loan from her employer and took a weekend job as a domestic. They pulled Laura, 14, and Kimberly, 10, out of Catholic school. Only Bryan, 7, still attends classes. But the family can no longer afford $17 per month tuition for each girl on top of their debts, childcare, and ballooning food bills. "I'm frightened," Maria said. "I'm working seven days a week, and it's still not enough."

She has good reason to be frightened. The power of capital and its social consequences is truly frightening. However, this power is not immutable. In this connection, we have already made reference to, and reviewed some of the dynamics of, the class struggles that derive from diverse strategic and political responses to the systemic crisis that brought an end to the so-called golden age of capitalism. Given the scope of this book, we have not fully examined the actual dynamics of this struggle, but we are able to conclude and assert that in general terms the working class bore the brunt of the offensive, and that as a result its organizational and political capacity was seriously compromised.

Nevertheless, a subsequent offensive in the form of neoliberal global-ization and international development generated new forces of resistance, forces that were mobilized by social movements in the 1990s. Chapters 4 and 5 reviewed some of the major dynamics, and political outcomes, of these forces of resistance under conditions of a major incursion of capital and US imperialism into Latin America. Chapter 6 took up this story of capitalist development as in the form of neoliberal globalization under radically changed economic and political conditions—in the con-text of economic crisis. In this chapter, we take up several issues of class struggle as it has unfolded under conditions of another systemic crisis, global in scope, multidimensional in form, and expressive of the capac-ity and disposition of people to organize, resist, and fight back.

One issue relates to transformative changes to, and within, the neoliberal world order wrought by the crisis. Any crisis is disruptive of the existing "structure"—the institutionalized practices that make up the "social and the institutional structure" of the system. A crisis also generates forces of change in this structure that can be mobilized in one section or another, depending on the class nature of these forces. Thus, the second issue taken up in this chapter is to determine and briefly examine the diverse strategic responses made to the crisis and to the system behind it. Of course the guardians of the neoliberal world order will seek to consolidate the system, making the adjustments to it necessary for the system to survive the challenge presented by the crisis. Another strategic response relates to the concern of some to find a solution to the crisis within the system—to place some limits on greed, to reestablish regulatory control over speculative capital, and to construct a system of good global governance. This is perhaps the dominant strategic response of most governments, both in the North and in the South of the global divide in wealth and development. However, the focus of the authors, and this chapter, is on the strategic response of organizations and classes in the popular sector.

In this connection there are three major issues. The first is to explain the continuing decline and weakness of labor vis-à-vis the forces of resistance—working-class passivity and impotence. The second is to establish the nature of the diverse strategic responses to the crisis by social and political sector, particularly the strategic response of the social movements. The third issue is to assess, where and when possible, the precise correlation of forces in the strategic responses to the crisis of the system.

This chapter seeks to advance our argument regarding these issues in three parts. First, we will review the dynamics of the social movements under conditions of the 2000–2002 crisis. Then we will review the social movement dynamics at the time, and under the conditions of a primary commodity boom from 2003 to 2008. Finally, we will briefly review the movement dynamics at the current conjuncture, under the conditions of, and in response to, the current financial and economic crisis.

The Social Movements and the 2000–2002 Crisis

Major social movements that challenged neoliberalism, class rule, and imperialism emerged in response to the economic crisis of the 1990s and the early 2000s. The most successful of these movements were formed in Brazil, Ecuador, Venezuela, Bolivia, and Argentina.

Brazil: The Rural Landless Workers Movement (MST), with over 300,000 active members and over 350,000 peasant families settled in cooperatives throughout the country, represented the biggest and best organized social movement in Latin America. The MST built a broad network of supporters and allies in other social movements, such as the urban Homeless Movement, the Catholic Pastoral Rural (Rural Pastoral Agency), and sectors of the trade union movement (CUT), as well as the left wing of the Workers Party (PT), progressive academic faculty, and students. The MST succeeded through "direct action" tactics, such as organizing mass "land occupations," which settled hundreds of thousands of landless rural workers and their families on the fallow and surplus land of the giant latifundistas. They successfully put agrarian reform on the national agenda and contributed to the electoral victory of the putatively leftist PT presidential candidate Ignacio "Lula" da Silva in the 2002 elections.

At the turn of the new millennium, during Cardoso's second administration, and under conditions of a mild recession (relative to Argentina at the time), the rhythm of class struggle and land occupations in Brazil had slackened, in response in part to a disposition of the government to negotiate a "market-assisted" approach to land reform via loans provided by a newly instituted system of Land Banks, and also in response to pressures from the NGO sector for the MST to moderate its class actions. The Cardoso government initiated its own land settlement program, distributing land to some 48,000 landless peasants a year, which compared favorably to the land distribution program instituted by the subsequent PT government headed by Lula. Lula's promise to his "ally," the MST, to distribute land to 100,000 families a year was totally disregarded once he became president and the PT formed the government. Under his government, more than 200,000 families camped by highways under plastic tents, and millions of landless families lived with little hope.

Ecuador: CONAIE played a central role in the overthrow of two neoliberal Presidents—Abdala Bucaram in 1997 and, in January 2000, Jamil Mahuad, who had been implicated in massive fraud and was held responsible for Ecuador's economic crisis. In fact, during the January 2000 uprising, the leaders of CONAIE briefly occupied the presidential palace. In the mid-1990s, CONAIE formed the electoral party Pachakutik to serve as the "political arm" of the movement.

However, the formation of a party to contest elections had a very different outcome than in Bolivia, where a combined strategy of mobilization by the social movements, and the contestation of national and local elections via Movement to Socialism (MAS), created conditions that allowed the indigenous communities and nationalities to achieve state power. In Ecuador, the formation of Pachakutik brought about a major internal division and a close to fatal weakening of the indigenous movement. What was responsible was the decision to form an alliance with the rightist-populist former military officer Lucio Gutiérrez in the 2002 elections, on the basis of which CONAIE briefly held several cabinet posts, including those of Foreign Relations and Agriculture. CONAIE's shortlived experience in government was a political disaster. By the end of the first year, the Gutiérrez regime allied with the multinational oil companies, the US State Department, and the big agribusiness firms to promote a virulent form of neoliberalism that forced the resignation of most CONAIE-backed officials. Widespread discontent and internal divisions within the popular movement were exacerbated by the army of US- and EU-funded NGOs that had infiltrated the indigenous communities as the foot soldiers of US imperialism in the form of "international cooperation" for development.

Venezuela: Major popular revolts in 1989, and again in 1992, culminated in the election of Hugo Chávez in 1999. Chávez proceeded to encourage mass popular mobilizations in support of a referendum for constitutional reform. A US-backed alliance between the oligarchy and sectors of the military mounted a palace coup in April 2002 that lasted only forty-eight hours before being reversed by a spontaneous outpouring of over a million Venezuelans supported by constitutionalist soldiers in the armed forces. Subsequently, between December 2002 and February 2003, a bosses' lockout of the petroleum industry, designed to cripple the national economy, supported by the Venezuelan elite and led by senior officials in the PDVSA (the state oil company), was defeated by the combined efforts of the rank-and-file oil workers and the support from the urban popular classes. The failed US-backed assaults on Venezuelan democracy and President-elect Chávez radicalized the process of structural change: mass community-based organizations, new class-based trade union confederations, and national peasant movements sprang up, and the million-member Venezuelan Socialist Party was formed. Social movement activity and membership flourished as the government extended its social welfare programs to include free universal public health programs via thousands of clinics, state-sponsored food markets selling essential food at subsidized prices in poor neighborhoods, and the development of universal free public education, including higher education. At the same time numerous enterprises in strategic economic sectors such as steel, telecommunications, petroleum, and food processing, and landed estates, were nationalized.

Although the ruling class continues to control certain key economic sectors and highly paid officials in the state sector retain powerful levers over the economy, the Chávez government and the mass popular movements have maintained the initiative in advancing the struggle throughout the decade from the late 1990s into the first decade of the new millennium.

The Venezuelan social movements have retained their vigor—unlike the situation in most countries where the emergence of the political class in state power coincided with or led to the decline of the social movements, a loss of dynamism. This was in part because of Chávez's leadership and support—his need for a social base for the policies that he proposed to institute. But the movements are also held back by powerful reformist currents in the regime that seek to convert the movements into transmission belts of state policy. The movement-state relationship is fluid and reflects the ebb and flow of the conflicts and threats emanating from the US-backed rightist organizations.

The regime-movement relationship deepened in the aftermath of the popular defeat of the bourgeois-military coup of 2002 and the bosses' lockout of 2002–2003. Those ties were further strengthened by the rise in oil prices during the world commodity boom of 2003–2008, which led to massive government social expenditures favoring the poor. With the unfolding of the world economic crisis in late 2008–2009, the relationship between the state and the movements was increasingly strained.

Bolivia: Bolivia has the highest density of militant social movements of any country in Latin America, including high levels of mine and factory worker participation, community and informal market-vender organizations, indigenous and peasant movements, and public employee unions. However, the long years of military repression from the early 1970s to the mid-1980s weakened the trade unions and were followed by an intense application of neoliberal policies that weakened them further.

By the end of the 1990s, new large-scale social movements had emerged, but the locus of activity shifted from the historically militant mining districts and factories to the sub-proletarian or popular classes engaged in informal, "marginal" occupations, especially in periurban areas such as El Alto where an estimated 70 percent of a population of a million move back and forth each week from the countryside and rural communities to the streets and urban slums. Located on the outskirts of La Paz, El Alto is densely populated by rural migrants, displaced miners, and impoverished indigenous people and peasants with access to few public services. The new nexus for direct action challenging the neoliberal regimes emerged from the coca farmers and Indian communities in response to the brutal implementation of US-mandated programs suppressing coca cultivation and the displacement of small farmers in favor of large-scale, agribusiness plantations. In the cities, public sector employees, led by teachers, students, and factory health worker unions fought neoliberal measures privatizing services such as water and cutting public budgets for education and healthcare.

The economic crises of the late 1990s and early 2000s led to major public confrontation in January 2003, followed by a popular revolt in October, an insurrection that spread from "El Alto" to all over the country. Before being driven from power, the Sánchez de Lozada regime murdered nearly seventy community activists and leaders. Hundreds of thousands of impoverished Bolivians stormed the capital of La Paz, threatening to seize state power. Only the intervention of the coca farmer leader and presidential hopeful Evo Morales prevented the mass seizure of the presidential palace. Morales brokered a "compromise" in which the neoliberal Vice President Carlos Mesa was allowed to succeed to the presidency in exchange for a vaguely agreed-upon promise to discontinue the hated neoliberal policies of his predecessor, Sánchez de Lozada. The tenuous agreement between the social movements and the "new" neoliberal president survived for two years due to the moderating influence of Evo Morales.

In May and June 2005, a new wave of mass demonstrations filled the streets of La Paz with workers, peasants, *indios*, and miners, forcing Carlos Mesa to resign. Once again, Evo Morales intervened and signed a pact with the Congress calling for national elections in December 2005 in exchange for calling off the protests and appointing a senior Supreme Court judge (Rodriguez) to act as interim president. Morales diverted the mass social movements into his party's campaign machinery, undercutting the autonomous direct action strategies that had been so effective in overthrowing the two previous neoliberal regimes. The result was his election as president in December 2005.

Although the economic crisis abated with the boom in commodity prices, President Evo Morales' social-liberal policies did little to reduce the gross social inequalities in the distribution of wealth and income, the lack of access by most of the indigenous population to the country's vast reservoir of natural and productive resources, the concentration of fertile land among the small number of plantation elite, and the dispossession of the majority of Indian communities from their lands. The regime's policy of forming joint ventures with foreign multinational gas, oil, and mining companies has done little to end the massive transfer of profits from Bolivia's natural resources back to the home offices of the multinationals. Even so, the tepid nationalist gestures of the regime led to major confrontations with the US-backed coup led by the Santa Cruz oligarchy and the agribusiness bourgeoisie of adjoining provinces who were flush with the profits derived from their agroexports during the "commodity boom."

Argentina: The strongest link between a severe economic crisis and a mass popular rebellion could be found in Argentina on December 19–20, 2001, and throughout 2002. The conditions for the economic collapse were building up in the 1990s during the two terms of President Carlos Menem. His neoliberal regime was marked by the corrupt "bargain basement" sale of the most lucrative and strategic public enterprises in all sectors of the economy. The entire financial sector of Argentina was deregulated, denationalized, dollarized, and opened up to the worst speculative abuses. The national economic edifice, weakened by the massive privatization policies, was further undermined by rampant corruption and gross pillage of the public treasury. Menem's policies continued under his successor, De la Rua, who presided over the banking crisis and the subsequent collapse of the entire national economy, the loss of billions of dollars of private savings and pension funds, a 30 percent unemployment rate, and the most rapid descent into profound poverty among the working and middle classes in Argentine history.

In December 2001 the people of Buenos Aires staged a massive popular uprising in front of the presidential palace, and the demonstrators took over the Congress building. They ousted President De la Rua and subsequently three of his would-be presidential successors in a matter of weeks. Hundreds of thousands of organized, unemployed workers blocked the highways and formed community-based councils. Impoverished, downwardly mobile middle-class employees and bankrupt shopkeepers, professionals and pensioners formed a vast array of neighborhood assemblies and communal councils to debate proposals and tactics. Banks throughout the country were stormed by millions of irate depositors demanding the restitution of their savings. More than 200 factories, which had been shut down by their owners, were taken over by their workers and returned to production. The entire political class was discredited and the popular slogan throughout the country was: *"!Que se vayan todos!"* ("Out with all politicians!"). While the popular classes controlled the street in semispontaneous movements, the fragmented radical-left organizations were unable to coalesce to formulate a coherent organization and strategy for state power. After two years of mass mobilizations and confrontation, the movements, facing an impasse in resolving the crisis, turned toward electoral politics, and elected center-left Peronist Nestor Kirchner in the 2003 presidential campaign.

The Formation and Dynamics of Low-Intensity Social Movements

The entire Latin American continent and the neighboring regions have witnessed the significant growth of social movement activity of greater or lesser scope. What differentiated these movements from their counterparts in Brazil, Argentina, Ecuador, Bolivia, and Venezuela was the absence of political challenges and regime change, and the limited scope of their social action. Nevertheless, mass popular movements continued to challenge the reigning neoliberal hegemony. In Haiti, a mass popular rebellion to reinstate the democratically elected President Jean Bertrand Aristide, who had been taken hostage and flown into exile by a joint US-EU-Canadian military operation, was brutally repressed by a multinational mercenary force led by a Brazilian general. Subsequent massacres in crowded slums by the occupying troops aborted the resurgence of the popular *"Lavelas"* movement protesting the foreign imposition of neoliberal "privatization" and austerity measures.

Mexico witnessed a series of localized rebellions and mass uprisings against the neoliberal regimes that dominated the country. In 1994, the Zapatistas, based in the indigenous communities of rural Chiapas, rose and temporarily succeeded in gaining control of several towns and cities. With the entry of many thousands of Mexican Federal troops, and in the absence of a wider network of support, the Zapatistas withdrew to their jungle and mountain bases. An unstable truce was declared, frequently violated by the government, in which an isolated EZLN continued to exist, confined to a remote area in the state of Chiapas. In Oaxaca, an urban rebellion backed by trade unions, teachers, and popular classes in the capital city and surrounding countryside organized a popular assembly *(comuna)* and briefly created a situation of "dual power" before being suppressed by the reactionary neoliberal governor of the state using "death squads" and Mexican troops. Faced with the repressive power of the state, the insurgent popular movements shifted toward the electoral process and succeeded in electing center-left Andres Manual Lopez Obrador in 2006 in the midst of the neoliberal economic debacle. Their victory was short-lived, with the election results overturned through massive fraud in the final tally of the votes. Subsequent peaceful protests involving millions of Mexicans eventually lost steam and the movement dissipated.

In Colombia, mass peasant, trade union, and Indian protests challenged the neoliberal Pastrana regime (1998–2002) while the major guerrilla movements (FARC/ELN) advanced toward the capital city. Fruitless peace negotiations, broken off under US pressure and a $5 billion dollar US counterinsurgency program, dubbed "Plan Colombia," heightened political polarization and intensified paramilitary death-squad activity. With the election of Alvaro Uribe, the Colombian regime decimated peasant, trade union, and human rights movements as it advanced its neoliberal policies.

The political effects of the economic crisis at the end of the 1990s, which had precipitated social movement activity throughout the hemisphere, led to brutal repression in Haiti, Mexico, and Colombia for the neoliberal regimes to continue their policies.

In several other Latin American countries, namely Peru and Paraguay, as well as in Central America, powerful rural-based peasant and Indian movements engaged in rural road blockages and land occupations against their governments;' neoliberal "free trade" agreements with the United States. Since these rural movements lacked nation-wide support, especially from the urban centers, their struggles failed to make a significant effect even as their national economies crumbled under neoliberal policies.

The Social Movements and the Commodity Boom of 2002–2008

The sharp rise of agricultural and mineral commodity prices between 2003 and 2008, along with the election of center-left politicians, had a major influence on the most active and dynamic social movements. We here illustrate this point regarding some of the most important of these movements and the relation between these movements and the left-of-center political regimes that were formed under these conditions.

Brazil: In Brazil the election of "Lula" Da Silva (2002–2006) was backed by all the major social movements, including the MST, under the mistaken assumption that he would accelerate progressive structural changes such as land redistribution. Instead, Lula embraced virtually the entire neoliberal agenda of his predecessor, Cardoso, including widespread privatization and tight fiscal policies, which, with the rise of agro-mineral prices, led to a narrowly focused agro-mineral export strategy centered exclusively on the interests of the large agribusiness and mineral extractive elites to the detriment of small businesses and rural producers. Even before his election, Lula signed a letter of understanding with the IMF (June 2002) to pay on the foreign debt, to maintain a budget surplus of 4 percent (up to 4.5 percent subsequently), to maintain macroeconomic stability, and to continue neoliberal "reforms." Upon election he slashed public employee pensions by 30 percent and bragged that he had the "courage" to carry out IMF "reforms" in which previous right-wing presidents had failed. As for the government's agrarian policy, it has been directed toward financing and subsidizing agri-business exports rather than land reform.[1]

The MST's efforts to influence Lula over the past decade have been futile, as state, local, and federal governments criminalized the movement's direct action tactics of land occupation. Also, several tactics cost the MST hard-won public support. Lula's policy of granting subsistence federal food allowances to the extremely poor and his success at co-opting movement leaders, especially from the huge trade union federations, neutralized the landless peasants and organized workers' capacity to protest and strike. Lula's policies also isolated the MST from its "natural" urban allies in the labor movement.

Lula's right turn and the vast increase in export revenues from high commodity prices led to increased social expenditures and reduced the level of activity and support for the MST in its struggle for agrarian reform. Although retaining its mass base and continuing its land occupations, the MST no longer had a strategic political ally in its quest for social transformation. Subsequently it pursued more moderate reforms to avoid confrontation with the Lula regime, to which it still offered "critical support."

Lula introduced labor legislation increasing the power of employers to fire workers and lowering the cost of severance pay. Social programs in health and education were sharply reduced by more than 5 percent during the first three years, while foreign debt creditors received punctual (and even early) payments of $150 billion dollars, making Brazil a "model" debtor. Past privatizations of dubious legality of lucrative petrol (Petrobras), mining (Vale del Doce), and banks were extended to public infrastructure, services, and telecommunications—reversing seventy years of history—and making Brazil more vulnerable to foreign-owned relocations of production. Brazil's exports increasingly took on the profile of a primary producer; exporters of iron, soya, sugar, citrus juice, and timber expanded while its industrial sector stagnated due to the world's highest interest rates of 18.5 percent and the lowering of tariff barriers. Over 25,000 shoe workers lost their jobs due to cheap Chinese imports.

The government's key economic ministers and central bankers were dominated by right-wing bankers, corporate executives, and neoliberal ideologues linked to the IMF and multinational corporations occupied the Finance, Economy, Trade and Agriculture ministries and the Central Bank.

In foreign policy, as mentioned, Lula sent troops and officials to occupy Haiti and defend the puppet regime resulting from the US orchestrated invasion and deposition of elected President Aristide. Lula's differences with the United States over ALCA were clearly over US compliance with "free trade" and not over any defense of national interests. As Lula stated, "Free trade is the best system, providing everyone practices it"—meaning his opposition revolved around US subsidies and protection of agriculture. Although Lula opposed the US-sponsored coup against Venezuela in April 2002, as well as other extremist measures, and spoke for greater Latin American integration via MERCOSUR, in practice, his major trade policies focused on extending and deepening economic ties outside the region.

The empirical data on key indicators show that Lula's political profile is closer to a pragmatic neoliberal than a "center-leftist." Those who classify Lula as a leftist focus on, and attach undue significance to, his background as a worker some twenty to thirty years back, his social origins as a trade union organizer, and his rather theatrical populist rhetoric and symbolic gestures.

Argentina: In Argentina the massive wave of direct action social movements in 2001–2002 subsided with the election of Nestor

Kirchner in 2003 and a recovery from the dramatic economic melt-down with a 7–8 percent economic growth rate stimulated by the commodity boom. With the recovery of employment and the return of their savings, the middle class demobilized and their "assemblies" rapidly disappeared. Kirchner offered subsidies to the unemployed and co-opted their leaders, which led to a sharp reduction of road blockages and membership in the militant unemployed workers organizations.

Kirchner won over part of the human rights movement with his policies, which included a public purge of some of the more notorious military and police officials and the granting of subsidies to certain sectors of the human rights movement, including the Madres de la Plaza de Mayo. With the decline of the radicalized movements of 1999–2002, the economic recovery of 2003–2008 led to a partial recovery of trade union activism, whose demands were mostly economic, focusing on the recovery of workers' wages and benefits lost during the systemic crisis.

Compared to Lula's ultra-liberal policies, Kirchner, and his wife Cristina Fernández, who succeeded him, gave the appearance of progressive leaders on the left of the political spectrum. From a Leftist perspective, however, the Kirchner regime has fallen far short. The Kirchners have not reversed any of the fraudulent privatizations of Argentina's strategic industries in the energy, petroleum, and electrical sectors. Under Nestor Kirchner's regime in particular, profits of the major agroindustrial and petroleum sectors skyrocketed, with no commensurate increases in wages and salaries. While the Kirchners financed and subsidized the revival of industry and promotion of agroexports, salaries and wages have barely returned to the level achieved in 1998, the year before the economic crisis. Moreover, while poverty levels have declined from their peak of over 50 percent in 2001, they are still close to 30 percent (according to unofficial yet reliable sources)—in a country that produces enough grain and meat to supply a population six times its size.

The regime's central banker and economic and finance ministers have long-term ties to international capital and banks, as reflected in President Cristina Fernández's parliamentary battle with the conservative (and neoliberal) opposition.[2] Although economic growth and some social amelioration have taken place, they can be attributed to the favorable world commodity prices for beef, grains, petroleum, and other prime materials. At no point have the Kirchners shifted any of the budget surplus now used to pay the foreign debt to fund the deteriorating health and educational facilities or to provide better salaries for personnel in those vital public sectors.

In foreign policy the Kirchners, just as Lula, have opposed ALCA because the United States has refused to reciprocate by lowering its tariff barriers. But the regime's foreign policy is hardly anti-imperialist. Argentine troops continue to occupy Haiti at the behest of the United States and to engage in joint maneuvers with the United States. Criticism of Washington only extends to the most extreme interventionist measures that prejudice Argentine big business interests in regional trade. Hence Argentina's opposition to the State Department's attempt to form an anti-Chávez bloc. The regime's rejection is based almost exclusively on the facts that Argentina receives oil and gas from Bolivia and Venezuela at subsidized prices and has secured a major shipbuilding contract with Venezuela and signed lucrative trade agreements with that country to market Argentina's agricultural and manufactured products. Regarding Cuba, the Kirchners have opened diplomatic relations but have maintained their distance. While on excellent diplomatic terms with Chávez, neither of them share his socialist principles or redistributive policies.

In conclusion, the Kirchners meet none of our criteria for defining a leftist. They could be more accurately described as pragmatic conservatives or neoliberals who, like Lula, are willing to dissent from US hegemony when it is in the economic interest of the agrobusiness elite and the industrial capitalist class behind the government's agenda.[3]

Uruguay: Tabare Vazquez was elected by an electoral coalition (the Broad Front and Progressive Encounter), which included Tupamaros, Communists, Socialists, and an assortment of Christian Democrats and liberal democrats. However, his key appointments to the Central Bank and the Economic Ministry (Danilo Astori) are hardline neoliberals and defenders of continuing previous budgeting constraints toward social spending while generously financing the agroexport elites.

During the Economic Summit in Mar de Plata, Argentina, in November 2005, while tens of thousands protested against Bush, and Chavez declared ALCA dead, Tabare Vazquez and Astori signed a wide-reaching "investment protection" agreement with the United States, which embraced the major free-market principles embodied in ALCA. Astori, with Tabare Vazquez's backing, has not only rejected renationalization of enterprises, but also proposed to proceed to privatize major state enterprises, including a water company, despite a popular referendum vote that exceeded 65 percent in favor of maintaining state ownership. The Tabare Vazquez regime has taken no measures to lessen inequalities and has put in place a paltry "job creation" and emergency food relief program that covers only a small fraction of the poor, indigent, and unemployed Uruguayans.

Meanwhile the government has laid down the royal carpet for a Finnish-owned, highly contaminating cellulose factory that will prejudice fishing communities and perhaps even the important tourist facilities downstream. Tabare Vazquez and Astori's unilateral signing off on the controversial factory has resulted in a major conflict with Argentina, which borders on the Uruguay River, where the plant will be located.

The Tabare Vazquez regime has repudiated every major programmatic position embraced by the Frente Amplio in its thirty years of existence: from sending troops in support of the occupation of Haiti, to privatizing public properties, embracing free trade, welcoming foreign investment, and imposing wage and salary austerity controls on the working class. Tabare Vazquez, like Kirchner, reestablished diplomatic relations with Cuba, but he avoids getting too close to Chávez and Venezuela. Probably the most bizarre aspect of the Broad Front government is the behavior of the Tupamaros, the former urban guerrilla group converted into senators and government ministers. Minister of Agriculture Mujica supports agribusiness and foreign investment in agriculture while upholding the law on evicting landless squatters in the interior. Senator Eleuterio Huidobro attacks human rights groups demanding judicial investigations of military officials implicated in assassinations and disappearances of political prisoners. According to Huidobro, the "past is best forgotten." He embraces the military and turns his back on scores of former comrades who were tortured, murdered, and buried in unmarked graves.

Bolivia: One of the most striking examples of how the "center-left" regimes formed in the context of the primary commodities boom (and widespread disenchantment with neoliberalism) has embraced the neoliberal agenda is the Morales regime in Bolivia. Between October 2003 and July 2005, scores of factory workers, unemployed urban workers, and indigenous peasants were killed in the struggle for the nationalization of petroleum and gas, Bolivia's most lucrative economic sector. Two presidents were overthrown by mass uprisings in two and a half years for defending foreign ownership of the energy resources. As mentioned earlier, Evo Morales did not participate in either uprising and, in fact, supported the hastily installed neoliberal President Carlos Mesa until he too was driven from power.

As president, Evo Morales has categorically rejected the expropriation of gas and petroleum, providing explicit long-term and large-scale guarantees that all the facilities of the major energy multinational corporations will be recognized, respected, and protected by the state. Consequently, the multinationals not only support Morales but also have lined up to extend and deepen their control and exploitation of these nonrenewable resources. The government, through a not-too-clever semantic manipulation, claims that "nationalization" is not expropriation and transfer of property to the state. In the government's lexicon, minority state ownership of shares, tax increases, and promises to "industrialize" raw materials are equivalent to nationalization. Although the exact terms of the new contracts have yet to be published, all the major multinationals are in full agreement with Morales's policies. The proof is that Petrobras, the primarily privately owned Brazilian oil and gas giant, was prepared to invest $5 billion over the next six years in the exploitation of gas and petroleum and the construction of a petrochemical complex. Repsol (a Spanish multinational corporation [MNC]), has promised to invest $150 million; Total (a French MNC), BP (a British MNC), and every other major energy and mining multinational have expanded investments and reaped billions in profits under the protective umbrella of the MAS regime. No previous regime had opened the country to mineral exploitation by so many multinationals in such lucrative fields in such a short period. In addition to oil and gas sell-offs, the government has declared that it will proceed to privatize the Mutun iron fields (60 square kilometers with an estimated 40 billion tons of iron with an estimated worth of over $30 billion dollars), following the lead of earlier neoliberal predecessors. The only change introduced in the bidding was to raise the share of taxes that Bolivia would receive from US$0.50 a ton to an undisclosed but "reasonable" amount.

Contrary to earlier promises, Morales has refused to triple the minimum wage. Indeed the Ministry of the Economy has promised to retain the previous regime's policies of fiscal austerity and "macro-economic stability" even though the legislated increase in the minimum wage was less than 10 percent. The Morales government did raise the teachers" base salary but only by a meager 7 percent—in real terms less than 2 percent. The teachers' base salary is US$75 a month, so their net gain under the new social movements' "revolutionary" regime is less than US$2 a month—and this at a time of record prices for Bolivian raw material exports and a budget surplus.

In Morales' first administration formed in January 2006, appointments to the economic, defense, and other ministries were linked to the IMF, World Bank, and to previous neoliberal regimes. Morales and his agricultural minister are opposed to any expropriations of the property of large landowners, "whether they are owners of...5,000, 10,000, or 25,000 or more acres, as long as they are productive." This effectively puts an end to the hopes of millions of landless indigenous peasants for a "profound agrarian reform" as promised in the "agrarian revolution" announced in mid-2007. Instead, the government has promoted agroexport agriculture with generous subsidies and tax incentives.

To date, notwithstanding several progressive developments in the agrarian sector—particularly the formation of community-based enterprises (*empresas comunitarias*)—there has been next to no advance on the "agrarian revolution" declared by the government over two years ago. A key measure in this "revolution" was a policy of *sanamiento*—expropriating any land that does not have a productive or social function. This is an excellent measure, not unlike the Brazilian law used by the MST to force the government to negotiate land settlements after the MST has taken "direct action" in "land occupation." However, to date, no effective government action has been taken (although it seems that finally some "action" is being taken to expropriate some of the land held by Branko Marinkovic, the biggest agribusiness landlord in Santa Cruz—and a leader of the *media luna* opposition).

Particularly indicative of Morales' pro-big business policies was the February 2006 signing of a pact with the Confederation of Private Businessmen of Bolivia, in which he promised to maintain "macroeconomic stability" and the "international credibility" of the government. This meant, in effect, curtailing social spending, promoting foreign investment, prioritizing exports, maintaining monetary stability and, above all, promoting private investment—policies reflected in the actual fiscal expenditures over the course of the first administration from 2006 to 2009.

The servility of the government vis-à-vis the Bolivian capitalist elite was evident in the decision to reactivate the National Business Council, which would analyze—and even take decisions—on economic and political issues. Morales declared, "I am asking the businessmen to support me with their experience" (forgetting to mention their experience in exploiting the labor force). He went on to ask the businessmen to advise him on "ALCA, MERCOSUR...on agreements with China, the US...as to their benefits for the country." Guillermo Morales, President of the Business Confederation, immediately emphasized the importance of signing up on the free trade agreement (ALCA).

While Morales was signing a business pact he refused to meet with the leaders of FEJUVE (the Federation of Neighbourhood Councils of El Alto), the biggest and most engaged democratic urban organization in Bolivia, which was active in leading the struggle to overthrow the previous neoliberal presidents and demand the nationalization of gas and petroleum.

In his first election to the presidency (as in his second in December 2009), Morales received over 80 percent of the vote in El Alto, a predominantly Aymarian city on the upper reaches of La Paz, which had suffered scores of deaths and numerous injuries in the at times violent struggle in the run-up to the vote. He named two ministers from FEJUVE, Mamani (Water Minister) and Patzi (Education Minister), without consulting the organization, which takes all decisions via popular assemblies. Both ministers were forced to resign from FEJUVE, in part because Patzi rejected the long-standing demand to create a teachers college for the 800,000 residents of El Alto, claiming it was an "unacceptable cost for the system" (given Morales" selective austerity budget). Equally reprehensible, Mamani refused to expel the foreign multinational Aguas del Illimani, which overcharges consumers and fails to provide adequate services.

According to FEJUVE, the Morales regime has failed to deal with the most elementary problems such as the exorbitant electricity rates and the absence of any plan to connect households with heating gas and water lines. The major trade union confederations and federations (COB, miners, and others) protested the government's refusal to abrogate the reactionary (neoliberal) labor laws passed by previous regimes. These laws "flexibilized labour," empowered employers to hire and fire workers with impunity. In reward for these pro-business policies, Japan, Spain, and the World Bank have "forgiven" Bolivia's foreign debt.

Morales nevertheless excels in "public theatre," adopting a "populist" folkloric style that engages the popular classes. He delivered part of his Presidential Speech to Congress in Aymara; he danced with the crowds during carnival; declared a reduction of his presidential salary as part of an austerity program that lowered living standards for millions of poor Bolivians. He announced a "plot" against the government by unspecified oil companies to rally support among his followers, while preparing to sign away the country's energy resources to oil companies. Needless to say, neither the defense or interior ministries were aware of the "plot," nor was any evidence ever presented. But the nonexistent "plot" served to distract attention from the energy sellout.

Our analysis suggests that the Morales regime is following in the footsteps of its neoliberal predecessors in terms of a procapital big business outlook and acquiescence to the IMF's fiscal, monetary, and budgetary policies. The government's plans, appointments, institutional ties, and big business beneficiaries link him closer to the center-right than to any "left wing." Morales says, "we are a government of the social movements," but the relation between the social movements and the government is mediated by and through the development NGOs that dominate "civil society." The indigenous communities were well represented in the first cabinet, but for the most part indirectly by means of a connection to one NGO or the other rather than some indigenous organization.[4]

Ecuador: In Ecuador, the powerful indigenous movement CONAIE and its allies in the trade unions in their support of Lucio Gutierrez's neoliberal regime suffered a severe decline in power, support, and organizational cohesion. The recovery has been slow, hindered by interventions of numerous US- and EU-funded NGOs.

With the decline in militancy and autonomy of the established social movements, a new urban-based "citizens' movement" led by the self-styled "socialist" Rafael Correa overthrew the venal and corrupt neoliberal Gutiérrez regime and led the electorate to vote Correa into power in both 2006 and 2009. Correa adapted center-left political positions, financing incremental wage increases, and state-subsidized cheap credit to small and medium-size businesses. He also adopted a nationalist position on foreign debt payments and the termination of US military base rights in Manta. The boom in mining and petroleum prices, and ties with oil-rich Venezuela, facilitated Correa's capacity to fund programs to secure support from within the Andean bourgeoisie and the popular classes.

However, the capacity of the Correa regime to tread the fractured and rather narrow political line between the bourgeoisie and the popular classes has been severely tested by recent events and developments, including the onset of economic crisis in 2008, the struggle of indigenous communities against mining companies granted concessions to operate in their "territory" by the government, growing disenchantment with the "Citizens Revolution" that propelled Correa into office, and outright rebellion and opposition by CONAIE and a rejuvenated indigenous movement.

At the beginning of his fourth year as president (2010), and facing a downturn in the economy in the context of the global crisis, Correa confronted—and continues to do so—a major challenge from some of the very social actors that propelled him into office. In an address to the country in early January, Correa expressed his ire with a "coming series of conflicts...including indigenous mobilizations, workers, media communications, and even a level of the armed forces." A national assembly of CONAIE in March gave a sharp political voice to this concern in the form of a resolution condemning the government's neoliberalism and announcing a state of alert for the indigenous movement in its struggle for social change—against the government.[5]

Venezuela: The economic boom, namely the tripling of world oil prices, facilitated Venezuela's economic recovery after the crisis caused by the opposition coup and the bosses' lockout (2002–2003). As a result, from 2004 to 2008, Venezuela's economy expanded by nearly 9 percent a year. Thus, the Chávez government was able to generously fund a series of progressive socioeconomic changes that enhanced the strength and attraction of progovernment social movements. These social movements played an enormous role in defeating the opposition referenda that called for the impeachment of Chávez. Peasant organizations were prominent in pressuring recalcitrant bureaucrats in the regime to implement a new agrarian law with measures calling for land distribution. Trade union militants organized strikes and demonstrations and played a major role in the nationalization of the steel industry. Given the vast increase in state resources, the Chávez government was able to compensate the owners of the expropriated firms while meeting the workers' demands for social ownership.

The Social Movements and the Global Crisis

Similar to most economists in the area, the response of Latin American governments in general, regardless of ideology and regime type, was to view and diagnose the "crisis" at the end of the first decade of the twenty-first century as essentially financial in nature and to return to a policy of market regulation, credit expansion, and a Keynesian form of economic intervention—countercyclical spending on employment generation projects. The social movements, however, responded very differently. First, the crisis was diagnosed not as a financial issue but as a production issue, implicating not merely a new system for controlling and regulating "capital" that was inhibiting the freedom of capitalists to deploy their capital, but also the economic model used to guide policy, if not the system itself.

ALBA, the Bolivarian Revolution, and the Resistance

The struggle of the peoples of the Americas for their right to self-determination and control of their resources has produced many revolutionary processes in the early twenty-first century, their roots in the work of anti-capitalist organizations and activists, as well as peasants, landless workers, base communities, and oil workers. The coup against Zelaya in Honduras was a response ostensibly to his intention to change the constitution, but in reality the concern was Alianza Bolivariana para los Pueblos de América (ALBA), the Bolivarian project for the integration of the Americas launched in 2001, whose first signatories were Cuba and Venezuela. Unlike the US-backed Free Trade Area Agreement (FTAA), ALBA "is a strategic political alliance whose purpose is to harness the skills and strengths of its members with the aim of transforming our societies to produce the integrated development of free and just nations" (Abya Yala, 2009). The countries that have decided to introduce a new socialist constitution have been the victims of *coups d' etat*—Venezuela in 2002, Bolivia in 2008, and most recently Honduras.

Latin America's future will likely be intimately connected with the world prices of its agromineral and energy resources. It contains some of the world's largest reserves of oil, natural gas, and water, not to mention lithium, in the case of Bolivia, and nickel and cobalt in the case of Cuba. It is no coincidence that the US fleet is now in the Caribbean, while military bases in Colombia and Curacao, supposedly waging war against drugs and terrorism, threaten Venezuela and Ecuador, two of the region's largest oil producers. Bolivia has had to confront an extreme right-wing, intent on separating the *media luna* provinces, with their massive reserves of hydrocarbons, iron magnesium and fertile lands, from the rest of the country.

Some of the key factors in economic development in the next decade will be the proven reserves of oil (over 314bn barrels) in the Orinoco Basin in Venezuela, and Bolivia's enormous reserves of gas. Brazil's huge energy reserves, including Amazonia, the world's largest water source, are well documented; and Argentina and Uruguay could easily satisfy the food needs of the whole continent.

For the first time these countries are forming alliances and making agreements among themselves regarding trade—even an agreement to institute a new regional body exclusive of the United States and Canada (replacing the OAS)—a fundamental change in international relations that conflicts with the neoliberal agenda and the interests of the multinationals. In the twelfth annual *Encuentro Sobre Globalización* in Havana (March 1–5, 2010) the point was made that the formation of regional trade agreements exclusive of the United States and Canada was a significant, if not decisive, factor in the relative insulation of Latin America from the worst of the global crisis. It used to be said that when the United States sneezes Latin America catches a cold or, more often than not, contacts pneumonia. But the point was made by several economists at the Encuentro that the relatively mild outbreak of the global crisis in the region was directly related to the advances that have been made in new forms of regional integration— ALBA, la Comunidad Andina de Naciones, the Mercado Común Centroamericano, and MERCOSUR. ALBA was seen to have a particular significance in that it clearly breaks with capitalism and neoliberalism in the attempt to construct relations of *equal* exchange—an exchange of energy for food; creation of a *Banco del Sur* designed to promote genuine autonomous development based on socialist principles and a respect for nature and for indigenous and workers' rights; and considerations of external debt and development.

At a different level, developments in Venezuela based on Chávez's Bolivarian Revolution include the reversion of privatizations of not only strategic industries and the extension of nationalization, but also Venezuela's educational and health initiatives, communal councils, and "people's power initiatives (see the following below)—threaten imperialist interests by replacing neoliberalism with popular nationalism, and paternalism with class consciousness and revolutionary activism. With this new mode of national development, which harkens back to the initial and subsequent effect of the Cuban Revolution,[6] the next generation of Latin Americans will likely be much more independent and have a deeper sense of their own reality.

In 2010 oil production will reach its peak; after that there will be significant reductions, affecting the price of crude oil. The biggest oil consumers are the developed countries in the International Energy Agency; they are all experimenting with alternative energies, but there is none cheaper than oil and gas, especially as hydroelectricity is affected by shrinking water tables. Thus, there will be a permanent campaign to discredit OPEC as an organization that protects oil-producing countries; news reports always refer to it as a cartel, even though it only regulates oil production and not the price.

The United States will continue to intervene in Latin America by supporting the Latin American Right—coup makers, terrorists, and rightwing politicians such as Pinera in Chile, Cobas in Honduras, and Santos (a sub for Uribe) in Colombia.

But the social movements, and the revolutionary process of social change that they have incited, are producing new paradigms, new forms of production and social relations, and a different more respectful relationship between people and the planet. In this context people associated with the social movements speak of *Pachamama*—Mother Earth—and the need to protect and conserve it through relations of equitable development and respect for the right of national self-determination (alba@movimientos.org, 2010). A new form of social consciousness is in the offing and taking shape—shaped in a broad process of revolutionary change and class struggle.

In the decade to come there will be major contradictions to overcome, such as the capitalist legacy of class and imperialist exploitation, uneven development, oppression, social exclusion, and corruption. But at the same time, the crisis has loosened and weakened the institutional and social structure of the operative underlying capitalist system, generating in the process forces of change, new opportunities, and possibilities. Also, the effects of progressive developments instituted in Venezuela, Cuba, and elsewhere—including a decade of investments in health and education under the post-Washington consensus—will begin to be seen, to the benefit of those "hitherto excluded," bypassed or marginalized by the system. The organizations and social movements that make up the forces of resistance to neoliberalism, capitalism, and imperialism and which bid to overthrow those systems of exploitation and oppression are a fact and they cannot, or are not likely to, be decisively defeated, despite recent setbacks. As the slogan shouted by men and women all over Latin America has it: "Beware! Bolivar's sword is sweeping the continent."

A key element of the proposed new agenda and what amounts to a consensus in the movements is support of ALBA, a trade mechanism originally proposed by Chávez but now encompassing six countries, including Cuba and Bolivia, the initial partners of the project, and Nicaragua. The movement in its indigenous character understands and has constructed ALBA as a mechanism of "integration from below" based on a conception of "living well," the basic goal of "development" as understood by the Movement and embodied in Bolivia's new "National Development Plan." In this development paradigm, rooted in an indigenous worldview, "integration" is not just a matter of "trade" but is a means of "social, cultural, political and productive integration" of the people in the Andes, Amazonia, and the urban areas.

On the 29th of February 2009, a regional alliance of indigenous, peasant, and social movements convoked a "Minga of Resistance" in association with "other peoples and processes" in the region.[7] *Minga* is a Quechua word meaning "collective action" that has wide currency among the poor, both indigenous and mestizo, in the Andes. The call to join in a *Minga,* a name for collective action that is at once local and global, gains force from its cultural and historical references to shared experiences of subjugation. By calling their movement a *Minga,* the indigenous participants call attention to both the work that must go into politics and the need for collective action.

Thought and action in this direction—in search for an alternative to capitalist development and neoliberalism, the undoubted source of the current global crisis as it happens and is wisely understood—is underway in the popular sector of different countries in the region. See for example the Convocation (January 20, 2009) of the Social Movements of America at the World Social Forum in Belém. Departing from a diagnosis of the "profound crisis" of capitalism in the current conjuncture, a crisis that the agents and agencies of capitalism and imperialism are seeking to "unload" [*descargar*] on "our people," the representation of a broad regional coalition of American social movements announced the need, and its intention, to create a popular form of "regional integration" (ALBA) "from below"—"social solidarity in the face of imperialism."[8]

From this popular perspective the global crisis is not a matter of financial markets but rather a production and social issue—a matter of sustainable livelihoods, employment and the price of food, which is rapidly escalating under the conditions of the global and local crisis. In this connection, ECLAC Executive Secretary José Luis Machinea has noted that the steep and persistent rise in international food prices is hitting particularly hard on the poorest in Latin America and the Caribbean, worsening income distribution. Poverty and indigence will rise if urgent measures are not taken to reduce the effects of these hikes; nearly 10 million people would become indigent and a similar number would swell the ranks of the poor. This does not even take into consideration the aggravating social situation of those who were already poor or indigent before the price rises and the global crisis.

Another example of popular action against the production crisis is the peasant-worker alliance recently formed in Mexico to make available affordable food to workers in the cities.[9] Regarding the staple "tortilla," the prices of which have literally hit the roof over the past year, spokespersons for the alliance at a press conference announced that the producers in the alliance would deliver goods to workers and their families at cost or prices at least 20 percent below those at commercial enterprises—and there would be no taxes charged. Efraín García Bello, Director of the Confederación Nacional de Productores Agrícolas de Maíz de México (CNPAMM), a signatory to the production alliance, noted that actions of this sort would support the economy of both the workers in the urban areas and the inhabitants in the countryside.

Along the same line, and supportive of this popular action against the crisis, different organizations in Mexico's peasant movement, including those set up by or close to the government, proposed that the government's anti-crisis plan include a policy of local production in corn and rice, milk, vegetable oils, pork products, and so on, ending the policy of free agricultural imports under NAFTA, which, as the EZLN (the Zapatista Movement) had predicted, has been the cause of a major production crisis in the agriculture, if not its "death knell." In regard to the local production and import of vegetable oils, the president of the Senate's Rural Development Commission pointed out that in just this one case government policy (elimination of import duties) put at risk the livelihoods and direct employment of up to 10,000 jobs in the sector plus an additional 30,000 indirect jobs.

At issue in this and other such actions in the popular sector is whether the political and intellectual Left are up to the challenge leveled by Abya Yala (2009), an amalgam of popular movements in the Andes formed in the context of the global crisis—able and willing to actively support if not lead the forces of revolutionary change that are being formed in the popular sector.

As for the Mexican government it responded in the same way as other governments in the region by attempting to head off the possible political spread-effects of a growing crisis-generated social discontent via fiscal expenditures on a program of social and development assistance. In the case of Mexico, the basic mechanism of this anti-crisis response is *Oportunidades* (Opportunities), a program designed to assist those with scarce resources most directly affected by the global crisis. With a negotiated World Bank loan of US$500 million this program was expected in 2009 to pump US$4 billion into the countryside and the local economy, continuing the time-honored tradition (at least since the

1960s) of using rural development as a way of demobilizing the social movement and defusing revolutionary ferment in the countryside.

The Ecological Crisis of Capitalist Development and the Social Movements

The propensity of capitalism toward crisis is manifest not only at the level of finance and production but also in the ecological foundation of the system. The process of capitalist development unleashed by policies of neoliberal globalization over the past several decades, and the current global crisis, have not only exacerbated widespread conditions of poverty and hunger, pushing millions more into poverty, and jeopardized the livelihoods of millions of workers, peasants, and small-scale producers, but also led to a serious degradation of the environment and the ecosystem at the base of these livelihoods and economic activities. The same process, however, has also led to widespread and growing movements of resistance to the latest incursions of capital and neoliberal policies.

All over Latin America, particularly in countries with significant populations and communities of indigenous people—Bolivia, Ecuador, Peru, Guatemala, Mexico—there have emerged movements of local resistance. And, at the same time, there is a trend toward the organization of this resistance and forming connections among these organizations across the region. One of these connections, bringing together indigenous organizations in Bolivia, Ecuador, Peru, Colombia, Chile, and Argentina, is the Coordinadora Andina de Organizaciones Indígenas (CAOI), which in March 2010 announced a major congress of Andean indigenous organizations to consider and concert a collective response to the challenge of neoliberalism and corporate capitalism to their way of life and to mother earth.

What is emerging is a growing intraregional and international social movement of resistance to capitalist development under conditions of neoliberal globalization. This movement appears to be forming primarily along the lines of resistance against the environmental degradation caused by the operations of multinational corporations in hydrocarbon drilling, mining, and other sectors of mineral extraction and processing. Resistance against these operations, and opposition to the neoliberal policies of governments that facilitate them, have led to diverse local struggles as well as the formation of different social movements such as "the movement of those affected by the degradation of the environment" ("*el movimiento de los afecta-das...*") and a movement of organizations concerned with the negative effect of mining and extractive operations on their access to potable water, arguably the new central focus of the struggle against global capitalism, replacing land as the central issue of struggle.

A very important event in the formation of this intraregional movement was the organized political resistance of indigenous communities in Peru against the government's concessions to global capital.

In October 2007 Peruvian President Alan García, a former social democrat turned neoliberal, announced his strategy of placing foreign multinational mining companies at the center of the country's economic "development" program, justifying the brutal displacement of small producers from communal lands and indigenous villages in the name of "modernization." García pushed through congressional legislation in line with the US-promoted "Free Trade Agreement of the Americas" or ALCA. Thus, Peru was opened to the unprecedented plunder of its resources, labor, land, and markets by the multinationals. Later in the same year, García awarded huge tracts of traditional indigenous lands in the Amazon region for exploitation by foreign mining and energy multinationals.[10]

Under his "open door" policy, the mining sector of the economy expanded rapidly and huge profits were made from the record-high world commodity prices and the growing Asian (Chinese) demand for raw materials. The multinational corporations were attracted by Peru's low corporate taxes and royalty payments, virtually free access to water, and cheap government-subsidized electricity rates. The enforcement of environmental regulations was suspended in these ecologically fragile regions, leading to widespread contamination of the rivers, ground water, air, and soil in the surrounding indigenous communities. Poisons from mining operations led to massive fish kills and rendered the water unfit for drinking. The operations decimated the tropical forests, undermining the livelihood of tens of thousands of villagers engaged in traditional artisan work and subsistence forest gathering and agricultural activities.

Although the profit margins of the multinationals reached an incredible 50 percent on invested capital, and government revenues exceeded US$1 billion, the indigenous communities lacked paved roads, safe water, basic health services, and schools. Worse, apart from the horrendous damage to their habitat and environment, they experienced a rapid deterioration of their everyday lives as the influx of mining capital led to increased prices for basic foods and medicines. Even the World Bank in its Annual Report for 2008, and the editors of the *Financial Times*, urged the García regime to address the growing discontent and crisis among the indigenous communities. Delegations from the indigenous communities traveled to Lima to try to establish a dialogue with the president to address the issue of the degradation of their lands and communities. But the delegates were met with closed doors. García maintained that "progress and modernity come from the big investments by the multinationals...(rather than) the poor peasants who haven't a centavo to invest." He interpreted the appeals for peaceful dialogue as a sign of the weakness of the indigenous inhabitants of the Amazon and expanded the policy of concessions and grants to the foreign multinationals, allowing them to penetrate even deeper into the Amazon.

García having cut off all possibility for dialogue and compromise, the indigenous communities responded by forming the Inter-Ethnic Association for the Development of the Peruvian Rainforest (AIDESEP). They held public protests for over seven weeks, culminating in the blocking of two transnational highways, which enraged García, who referred to the protestors as "savages and barbarians" and sent police and military units to suppress the mass action.

What García failed to consider was the fact that a significant proportion of indigenous men in these villages had served as army conscripts in the 1995 war against Ecuador, while others had been trained in local self-defense community organizations. These combat veterans were not intimidated by state terror and their resistance to the initial police attacks resulted in both police and indigenous casualties. In June 2009, García, an ally of President Obama,[11] declared "war on the savages," sending a heavy military force with helicopters and armored troops with orders to "shoot to kill"—to assault and disperse a peaceful, legal protest organized by members of Peru's Amazonian indigenous communities protesting the entry of foreign multinational mining companies on their traditional homelands.[12] Martial law was declared and the entire Amazon region of Peru was militarized. Meetings were banned and family members were forbidden from searching for their missing relatives, the remains of many of whom are believed to have been dumped into ravines and rivers. AIDESEP activists reported over one hundred deaths among the indigenous protestors and their families, who were murdered in the streets, their homes, and their workplaces.

But this was one battle in the ongoing imperialist class war that the government did not win. Throughout Latin America, all the major indigenous organizations expressed their solidarity with the Peruvian indigenous movements and consolidated their organizational efforts to concert a collective action against the neoliberal regimes in the region. Within Peru, mass social movements, trade unions, and human rights groups organized a general strike. Fearing the spread of mass protests, *El Commercio*, the conservative Lima daily, cautioned García to adopt some conciliatory measures to avoid a generalized urban uprising. A one-day truce was declared on June 10, but the indigenous communities refused to end their blockade of the highways unless the García government rescinded its illegal land grant decrees, which in the end it was forced to do.

The events in Peru were an important moment in the contemporary reconstruction of the popular movement against the ravages of global corporate capital and the war launched against the rural poor by the forces of imperialism. Another was the action taken by the indigenous organizations against Texaco, the actions taken by the Correa government against Chevron in Ecuador, and the more recent (February 25–26, 2010) popular assembly of indigenous nationalities in Ambato, which announced the intention of CONAIE to launch a major offensive against the Correa government's neoliberal policies. Also, in Bolivia, Brazil, Mexico, and elsewhere in the region, a large number of indigenous organizations and communities have come together in the form of intraregional conferences and workshops, meetings and assemblies, to organize collective actions against the capitalist corporations and neoliberal governments responsible for the environmental degradation and the ecological crisis that is threatening the sustainability of their communities and livelihoods.

Conclusion

The economic boom and the ascendancy of a number of center-left (national populist and pragmatic neoliberal) governments have led to incremental increases in living standards, a decline of unemployment, and the cooptation of some movement leaders—and a resulting decline of radical movement activity and a revival of traditional "pragmatic" trade union moderates. During the economic boom and the rise of the center-left, the only major mass mobilization took the form of right-wing movements determined to destabilize the center-left governments in Bolivia and Venezuela.

A comparison of social movements in countries where they played a major role in the process of political and social change (Venezuela,

Ecuador, Brazil, and Bolivia), with movements in countries where they were marginalized, reveals several crucial differences. First, the differences are not found in terms of the number of public protests, militant direct actions, or participants. For example, if one adds up the number of social movement protests in Mexico, Peru, Colombia, and Central America, they might equal or even surpass the social actions in Brazil, Argentina, and Bolivia. What was different and most politically significant was the nature of the mass action. Wherever they were of marginal significance, the organizations were fragmented, dispersed, and without significant national leadership or structure and without any political leverage on the institutions of national power. In contrast, influential social movements operated as national organizations, which coordinated social and political action, and were centralized and capable of reaching the nerve centers of political power—the major cities (La Paz, Buenos Aires, Quito, and to a lesser degree Sao Paulo). To one degree or another, the high-impact social movements combined rural and urban movements, had political allies in the party system, and bridged cultural barriers (linking indigenous and mestizo popular classes).

8

Latin America in the Vortex of Social Change

The first decade of the new millennium opened, and threatened to close, with an involution in the system of global capitalist production—a multiple crisis of global proportions in the first instance and a region-wide crisis in Latin America in the second. Over the course of the decade, several years into the imperialist regime of George W. Bush, the region participated in a primary commodities boom on the world market, a development that changed and to some extent reversed a historic pattern in north-south trade, bringing windfall profits to the Latin American private sector in agroexport production and unanticipated gains in fiscal revenues for the center-left regimes that had formed in the wake of a spreading disenchantment and turning away from neoliberalism. Unfortunately for the Left and the popular sector organizations that had pinned their hopes on these regimes, the opportunity to change the course of national development in a popular or populist direction was missed.

It would take a global crisis to bring about a change in the pattern of deployment of fiscal expenditures, and then not in the interest of social justice (a more equitable distribution of the social product) but as part of a countercyclical strategy to pump prime demand and boost employment.[1] Throughout the decade, what has prevailed is an agenda engineered in Washington as part of a new policy consensus constructed as a means of saving capitalism from its own propensity toward crisis and from widespread forces of resistance.

US-Latin American relations in this new context—the imperialist system threatened from within and without, neoliberalism held at bay and in decline, the ascension of China, and the onset of a primary commodities boom—were shaped by conditions of what has been described as "neoimperialism," an imperialism based on "aggressive military unilateralism."

In the 1990s imperialism was ascendant in Latin America. In firm control of a string of neoliberal client regimes, US and EU-based capitalist enterprises pillaged Latin America under the cover of globalization and an imposed policy of privatization, financial deregulation, and denationalization of the economy. Under this cover and within the reach of imperial power, capitalists plundered the natural and financial resources of the region with the assistance and agency of state leaders—Menem in Argentina, Sanchez de Lozada in Bolivia, Cardoso in Brazil, Sagunetti in Uruguay, Perez and Caldera in Venezuela, and Zedillo in Mexico.

Given the Empire's loyal gatekeepers in the region there was no cause for military intervention in Latin America. The last skirmishes on this front were in 1983 and 1989, on the small Caribbean island of Grenada and in Panama. In the 1990s, and in the 2000s with the ascension to power of George W. Bush, the Empire was engaged elsewhere in the world, providing governments, parties, and movements in the region the freedom to conduct their affairs with relatively little interference.[2]

The depth and extent of imperialist exploitation, and the plunder of the region's resources, in the 1990s led to massive discontent as contradictions exploded, rocking the continent, and to the popular ousting of US clients and the total discrediting of neoliberalism and its development agenda. In addition, the projection and engagement of US power elsewhere resulted in the weakening of a number of the United States' strategic allies in Latin America and, as mentioned, the formation of a number of center-left regimes riding the wave of anti-neoliberalism to state power.

In this new and changing context of US-Latin American relations and US imperial power, political regimes in the region can be placed into three categories. First, there are regimes such as found in Peru, Colombia, and Mexico that are staying the course of neoliberal "structural reforms" and remain "on side" with US imperialism, recognizing and accepting its dominion and—with the collapse of the hemispheric free-trade project—disposed toward bilateral trade relations with the United States. Second, there are regimes such as Chile, Argentina, and Brazil pursuing a center-left path of pragmatic neoliberalism and, particularly in Brazil under Lula's PT regime, working to diversify trade relations and achieve a relative independence from the United States in national policy and international relations. A third bloc of countries, led by Venezuela and embracing Bolivia and Ecuador (as well as several countries in Central America and the Caribbean) have struck out against US imperialism in the direction of populist nationalism, countering the United States' proposed Hemispheric Free Trade Agreement with ALBA, an alternative mechanism of regional integration based on quasi-socialist principles. With the support of Cuba and a growing popular movement of resistance against neoliberal globalization, ALBA[3] has become a major focal point of resistance to US imperialism in the region.

Under these conditions the United States has lost a significant degree of influence in the region, certainly relative to the capacity it had in the 1980s and 1990s to dictate policy or even, in the case of Ecuador and Bolivia, to maintain its network of military bases.

A New Context for US Imperialism

In other parts of the Empire, since the 1960s (Vietnam, etc.) the United States has suffered a long series of major and minor setbacks and "blowbacks," as Chalmers Johnson terms the acts of resistance generated by the projection of imperial power. But in Latin America over the last decade, the US experience could better be described as a loosening of its hold on state power, a loss of influence that reflects in part its higher prioritized concern for developments in other parts of the Empire, and in part the strength of the resistance in the region against neoliberalism and imperialism. This loosening of the "ties that bind" is also evident in the increasing drive in the region for independence from Washington, Wall Street, and the International Monetary Fund (IMF), and in the growing divide in the policy stances and foreign relations of many governments in the region.

For example, on Cuba the United States is totally isolated, as it is on any attempt to interfere in the affairs of any government in the region. Notwithstanding the free trade agreements signed by the United States with its allies in the region (Colombia, Chile, Peru, Mexico) the dominant and growing trend is toward regional trade and international trade diversification, particularly in favor of China. Many governments are expanding ties and signing trade and investment pacts with governments, including Iran and North Korea that are hostile to the United States. ALBA is providing an important point of reference for a number of countries in the Caribbean and Central America in their pursuit of development paths and policies independent and different from those advocated by the United States.

All of the countries in the region in March 2010 went so far as to propose and set up an alternative (to the OAS) regional association exclusive of the United States and Canada, in reaction to the insistence of these countries on placing national interests above regional solidarity. And then there is a growing divide between the United States and the national bourgeosie in a growing number of Latin American countries, particularly in those governed by a party on the center-left. And as for the IMF, whose officials, together with those of the World Bank, have for many years managed to impose the Washington Consensus on governments in the region, many Latin American governments have either paid down their IMF loans or are refusing to borrow from it, drastically reducing Washington's leverage over policy and policymakers.

In this context of declining influence and power, widespread disenchantment with neoliberalism and opposition to its imperialism, the United States, under President Obama, has redoubled its efforts toward bilateral free trade agreements with its few allies in the region (Chile, Peru, Colombia, Mexico) and resorted to overt military pressure and intervention, via its remaining client states in the region. A central factor in this policy is the strengthening of relations with its major client state, Colombia, massively increasing funding and support to the Uribe regime as the nodal point of its regionwide hub of military operations.[4] A major example of the United States' use of military threat is not only the new development of seven military bases in Colombia, targeting Venezuela but also with a logistical reach across the entire continent. The Obama regime's policy and action on this issue was opposed by the major and most of the smaller countries in the region, another indication of the divergence between the center-left and US policymakers. The United States has stepped up the military phase of "Plan Colombia" (instituted a decade ago to tighten the noose around the neck of the one remaining "army of national liberation" in the region, FARC) and extended its potential military targets to Venezuela, Ecuador, and Bolivia.[5]

The agreement with the Colombian government to give the US access to those seven military bases is dramatic.[6] Despite the vehement opposition to this plan from most OAS member countries, the Colombian government signed the agreement, demonstrating both its subservience to the United States and the pivotal importance of Colombia in the US strategy, vis-à-vis Latin America, to protect its economic interests and contain the forces of resistance and subversion.

Battlefronts in the Imperialist Class War: Dispatches from Peru and Honduras

One of the ironies of the most recent pattern of regime change has been a weakening of the resistance against neoliberalism and a retreat of the social movements, sometimes, as in Argentina and Bolivia, in a context of revived dynamism on the Right. In part this development was the result of misplaced views of the Left that these regimes were progressive and "on their side"—anti-neoliberal in economic policy and anti-imperialist in their relations with the United States. But this is not necessarily the case. Except for Venezuela, and of course Cuba, and to some extent Bolivia and Ecuador, these regimes are not on the "left" and can best be characterized, as mentioned, as pragmatic neoliberal or *izquierda permitida*. In some cases, particularly those of Peru, Colombia, and Mexico, the current and recent regimes can even be described as dogmatically neoliberal. Unlike the governments formed in Chile, Argentina, and Brazil, incumbent regimes in Peru, Colombia, and Mexico are well disposed toward the United States and the post-Washington Consensus on the need for a more inclusive form of neoliberalism.

A clear example of this political and policy regime can be found in Peru, where the efforts of the government to protect the economic operations of the US empire in June 2009 resulted in a major confrontation with the indigenous communities adversely affected by these interests, leading the government to resort to its own repressive apparatus, and resulting in the deaths of twenty-four police and ten indigenous community members.[7] The day after President Garcia announced a new cabinet in response to the growing wave of social and class conflict, and a month into the wave of conflicts arising from the confrontation with the indigenous communities, the *Defensoría del Pueblo*, a movement-connected NGO that tracks the dynamics of social and political struggles in the region, identified up to 226 "active" social conflicts in the country. Transport and public sector workers struck, joining the march organized by the General Confederation of Workers (CGTP), the major workers' central in the country. Numerous streets blockades were reported on the periphery and outskirts of Lima, the country's capital city, harking back to the quasi-revolutionary situation that had emerged in Ecuador in 2000 and in Bolivia at various points between 2000 and 2005 (Webber, 2007).

As noted in chapter 7, at issue in this class struggle was the government's plan to grant free access for the multinational forms of capital operating in the country to the country's mineral resources and a guaranteed right to expatriate profits. The recent and ongoing resistance of the indigenous communities in Peru's Amazon is one manifestation of this struggle. Another is the antigovernment policy demonstrations of the country's cotton producers and textile workers. Peru, like several other countries in the region, has been subject to dumping by US cotton producers, whose product, grown with the aid of government subsidies, is able to enter the local market at superlow prices, undercutting and destroying local producers. This is similar to the situation confronted by corn producers in Mexico. In both cases, the governments, under threat of US trade sanctions, refused to provide a matching subsidy to protect local producers. In both cases workers and producers ("*no aguantamos más*") responded by taking their struggle onto the streets.

Similar situations are brewing elsewhere but none as meaningful for US imperialism as the situation in Honduras brought about by the military coup of the ruling class, in firm control of the Congress and the Supreme Court—and, it would seem, the Army—against a sitting and democratically elected president. For US imperialism, Honduras represented not so much a political crisis, or a crisis in US-Latin American relations, as a crossroads in imperial power and policy—a way in which the US administration might be able to recover its position and influence in the region.

In the 1990s the officials of the US administration under George W. Bush were too distracted by the greater game in Eurasia and the Gulf region, and too overextended in its operations in that part of the empire, to attend to its Latin American "affairs."[8] But various political developments in the new millennium (especially the emergence of a left-of-center axis of political power) forced the United States to concern itself with efforts to halt and reverse the decline of its influence and power, to renew and repair relations with its former allies (especially Chile, Peru, Colombia, and Mexico), and to counter the growing influence of Hugo Chávez and his Bolivarian Revolution. Under the new Obama administration these efforts were redoubled, thus far with limited and mixed results.

The significance of Honduras was that it represented an opportunity for the United States to reconstitute the contours of a new counter-reform offensive and to counter the growing influence of Chávez in the region. Particularly in the United States' Central American domain, Nicaragua and even El Salvador, not to mention Honduras, have fallen into the orbit of Chávez's Bolivarian Revolution and Cuba, the major irritant to US hegemony in the region for five decades.

When Chávez was deposed very briefly from power in 2002, the United States was forced to backtrack from its initial and swift recognition of the de facto regime. In the case of Honduras, however, the immediate and definitive demand of the OAS that Zelaya be restored to office presented the United States little room to maneuver, forcing the Obama administration to take its lukewarm public position that Zelaya should be allowed "to negotiate" his return to power, while working actively to prevent this from happening.[9]

The problem with Zelaya, from the standpoint of Honduras' ruling class as well as the United States, was that his proposal for a Constituent Assembly had all the markings of a Chávez-type move to extend his term in office as a means of pushing the country toward a socialist path like Venezuela's. Governing members of this class had no intention of allowing this, nor did the Obama administration. It was his alignment with Chávez on economic issues, and his criticism of US intervention, that turned Zelaya into a target for US coup planners, eager to make him an example and concerned about access to Honduras' military bases as a launching point for US intervention.

The shift in US policy toward Honduras occurred in 2007 when the liberal President Zelaya decided to improve relations with Venezuela and first joined "*Petro-Caribe*," a Venezuela-organized Caribbean and Central American association to provide long-term, low-cost oil and gas to meet the energy needs of member countries, and subsequently ALBA. This sealed Zelaya's fate as far both the Honduran ruling class and the US State Department were concerned. It is safe to assume that the State Department will stop at little or nothing short of outright support for a military coup in Honduras and elsewhere to prevent another Chávez. The lines of an emerging imperial war in the region have been drawn in the sands of class struggle in Honduras.

A number of observers of developments in Honduras have speculated on whether the political crisis in Honduras might create conditions for the use of military force by the ruling classes elsewhere in the region, working hand in glove with the US imperial state to help restore US dominion if not hegemony in the region. Quite apart from the anticipated albeit covert support from the United States for the "lesson in democracy" (democracy is good as long as the people do not mistakenly elect a potential despot) provided by the tilt to the Left in Latin American politics, it is conceivable that conditions for military solutions to political crises, namely class-divided countries, might materialize not only in Honduras but possibly in Ecuador, Bolivia, Nicaragua, perhaps El Salvador, and even Venezuela. This possibility is undoubtedly on the drawing-board used by the intelligence and security services of the imperial state to design covert responses and appropriate public policy stances.

Apart from Honduras, which provided the United States with both a challenge and an opportunity to recover lost political ground, other issues that the Obama administration will have to deal with in the near future include Cuba's increasing integration in the region; how to counter China's increasing economic role (displacing the United States in Brazil, Peru, Chile, and Argentina); and the widespread rejection of US military policies in the lucrative Middle Eastern markets. Since 2001 a growing number of countries in Latin America have been taking positions on policy and trade issues (the search to diversify trade relations, whether to join ALBA) that are not in the US national interest, most recently regarding Iran. Yet Obama is still stuck in the militarist mode that has isolated the United States from the biggest economies to its geographic south.

A complication for the United States is the apparent drive of Brazil to flex its muscles as a regional economic and political power, and as a potentially major player in the arena of world affairs. The government of Brazil has opposed several efforts by the United States to dictate developments and projects that undercut Brazilian capitalist expansion, as was illustrated most notably by Lula's victory at the WTO regarding cotton subsidies.

Of particular concern for the United States is the movement of more and more countries in its immediate backyard and former sphere of influence—the Caribbean and Central America—into the orbit of national capitalism and a relatively independent foreign economic policy. In this panorama, both Colombia and Honduras provide favorable conditions for a Washington-made solution—a US military base, intimate and day-to-day relations with Armed Forces personnel, a malleable and supportive Congress and Supreme Court, and a ruling class that shares its concerns about the actual and possible forces of subversion in the country and region.

In some ways the situation confronted by Obama in Central America is similar to that faced by Reagan in the early 1980s vis-à-vis Nicaragua. But Reagan had on his side a number of crony dictators— Alvarez in Uruguay, Videla in Argentina, Pinochet in Chile, and Stroessner in Paraguay. In this regard at least the political landscape in Latin America has changed. Today most countries in the region might be not only described as centrist and pragmatic in terms of macroeconomic policy, rather than leftist or rightist, but they are also concerned to keep the United States at bay on matters of foreign relations and policies. Thus, it is that a number of countries, and Argentina and Brazil in particular, are concerned to diversify their international trade relations, and even in some cases to align themselves with alternative mechanisms of regional integration such as ALBA and improved relations with Cuba. This is, in fact, the case for the countries in Central America and the Caribbean basin that have already joined ALBA.

What this means for the current Obama administration might be gauged by its initial reaction to the nomination for Secretary General of the OAS of José Miguel Inzulza, a conservative social democrat close to Michelle Bachelet, former president of Chile. It seems that the United States, as announced by Secretary of State Clinton, was implacably against this nomination, apparently (according to several Washington "insiders") because of Inzulza's support for Cuba's entry into the OAS (a consensus view today, except for the United States), his campaign against the "*golpistas*" in Honduras and his earlier denunciation of US intervention in Venezuela. If this is the attitude and position of the United States vis-à-vis a liberal social democrat, a representative of a centrist and pragmatic position in Latin American politics and the nominee of a country supportive of the United States and allied with it at the level of bilateral trade, what might be the position of the Obama administration regarding relations with regimes seeking to strike a more independent line and steer a leftward course? Needless to say, Obama's defense of old-fashioned imperialist intervention will produce one, two, or many more failed policies in the coming years.

The Obama administration has made several rhetorical overtures toward opening a new page in relations with Latin America. But his revival of hostility toward Cuba, Venezuela, and Bolivia and his refusal to break with the coup regime in Honduras provided a clear sign of the direction that US imperialism would take in the region. Apart from the handful of rightist regimes, no regional leader has any further illusions about Obama.

The Obama administration sees new sources of hope in the consolidation of right-wing governments in Mexico, Peru, Colombia, Panama, and, more recently, Honduras and Chile. New US military bases in Colombia and Panama illustrate the utility of such clients.

For another, Washington is also betting on its ability to turn a number of center-left regimes—Kirchner in Argentina, Funes in El Salvador, Colom in Guatemala, and Mujica in Uruguay, among others—against the relatively more independent regimes in Venezuela, Cuba, Bolivia, and Ecuador. Considering the lack of any new economic initiatives and despite the political opportunism exhibited by these regimes it is highly unlikely that the Obama regime will make much headway especially in light of a new regional alliance without the United States and Canada, the two imperial powers in the hemisphere.

US-Latin American Relations in a Time of Crisis and Realignment of Global Power

To elaborate further, one of the most striking aspects of contemporary US-Latin American relations is the divergence between the initial hopes, expectations, and positive image of the Obama regime and its actual policies, strategies, and political practices. In this connection many "progressive" North American commentators and not a few Latin American writers ignored the most elementary features of US foreign policy, focusing on the highly deceptive rhetoric of "change" and "new beginnings." The illusions of the Left here are of the same order as their illusion of progressive change engendered by the so-called red tide in Latin American national politics with the emergence of "center-left regimes" in recent years. However, recent "interventions" of the United States in the region provide a clearer window into the nature of the Obama regime and its imperialist policies.

First, to decipher the real content of the Obama regime's policy toward Latin America, one needs to look at foreign policy priorities, allocations of financial resources, and public policy commitments and to ignore inconsequential diplomatic rhetoric. The first major action, in line with US global military goals, was to militarize the US-Mexican frontier, allocating nearly one-half billion dollars in military and related aid to the right wing Calderon regime. The entire focus of White House policy toward the Mexican and Colombian regimes over the problems of narcotics and narco-violence is a military one, entirely ignoring their socioeconomic structural roots.

Millions of young Mexican peasants and small farmers have been driven into bankruptcy, unemployment, and poverty by the North American Free Trade Agreement (NAFTA), created a large pool of recruits for the narco-traffickers. The expulsion of hundreds of thousands of Mexican immigrant workers from the United States and the new militarized borders has closed off a major escape route for Mexican peasants fleeing destitution and crime. In contrast to the formation of the European Union, which provided tens of billions to the less competitive countries like Spain, Greece, Portugal, and Poland, who were entering, the United States has provided Mexico with no compensatory funds to upgrade its productive competitiveness and provide needed employment for its people. The highly militarized Colombian regime, notorious for its violations of human rights, is currently the biggest recipient of US military aid in Latin America. Under Plan Colombia, the US-financed counterinsurgency program, Bogota has received more than 5 billion dollars, the most advanced military technology and thousands of American military advisers and subcontracted mercenaries. Obama's support for the right-wing Colombian regime is his response to the emergence of democratically elected populist and radical governments in Ecuador and Venezuela.

Generally, Obama's policies toward Latin America are driven by his extension of the military defense priorities of the Bush administration, including its economic embargo of Cuba and its virulent hostility toward Venezuelan nationalism. There are no new economic initiatives. Beyond a rhetorical support for free trade, Obama upholds past quotas and tariffs on more competitive imports from Brazil, even adding new protectionist measures against Mexican trucks and truck drivers.

The Obama regime's relentless pursuit of military-driven empire building in the midst of an ongoing and deepening domestic economic depression forms the basis for understanding Washington's contemporary relations with Latin America today. The administration's military approach toward Latin America is reflected in Obama's inability or unwillingness to allocate new economic resources and underscores his concern to sustain two major US clients, Colombia and Mexico, through military aid programs. The limited interest and sparse commitment of non-military-directed monies to Latin America reflects the very low foreign policy priority the region has in the current White House. Latin America is a fifth-level priority after the US domestic economic depression, the Middle East and South Asian wars and nuclear issues, coordinating economic policies with the European Union, and formulating economic and military relations with Russia and China. With all these urgent priorities, the Obama regime has little time, interest, or programmatic offerings to help Latin America cope with the onset of the economic recession.

At the most basic level, the Obama regime is following a three-fold strategy of (1) retaining support from rightist regimes (Colombia, Mexico, and Peru), (2) increasing influence on "centrist regimes" (Brazil, Argentina, Chile, Uruguay, and Paraguay), and (3) isolating and weakening leftist and populist governments (Cuba, Venezuela, Ecuador, Bolivia, and Nicaragua). But what is most striking about the supposedly "progressive" Obama regime's policy for Latin America are its continuities with the previous, reactionary Bush administration in almost all strategic areas. These include:

- Latin America's very low priority in US global policy;
- an emphasis on "security," drug enforcement, and military collaboration over any long-term socioeconomic poverty alleviation and drug addiction treatment programs;
- close collaboration with the most rightwing regimes in the region (Mexico and Colombia);
- continuation of the US economic embargo of Cuba, despite the loss of its last two Latin American backers;
- a double discourse of talking free markets while practicing protectionism;
- financing and actions to strengthen the role of the IMF as an instrument of imperial expansion;
- a policy of driving a wedge between "centrist regimes" (Brazil, Argentina, Uruguay, and, until 2010, Chile) and left/center-left nationalist or populist regimes"; and
- support for the actions of separatist regional elites to destabilize center-left governments while operating from their traditional far right-wing bases in Santa Cruz (Bolivia), Guayaquil (Ecuador), and Maracaibo (Venezuela).

In short, the Obama regime has embraced the overall strategic agenda of the Bush administration while making several secondary changes having to do with adaptations based on the decline of US power. Obama has facilitated not only a few major negative changes, which go further than the Bush administration in harming Latin America's financial and trading position, but he has also made better use of the "soft power" of the United States. While reiterating the anachronistic demands for Cuba to convert to capitalism (dubbed a "democratic transition") as a condition for ending the US embargo, Obama has slightly eased travel restrictions for US-based Cuban families to visit relatives in Cuba and to send them money. The State Department relies less on confrontational diplomatic language and has made overt gestures to centrist regimes, including White House meetings with Lula (March 2009) and Vice President Biden's attendance at a meeting with centrist presidents in Chile (March 27–28, 2009). Obama's resort to "soft power," which is not backed by any new economic initiatives and which continues the basic policies of his predecessor, has gained him few new allies.

Because of the Obama regime's profound and costly commitment to military-driven empire building and the multitrillion dollar refinancing of its banking sector (while backing credit-financing protectionism), Latin America's ruling classes cannot expect and have not received any economic "stimulus" support from the United States.

The deep political divisions between the United States and Latin America (and between the classes within Latin America) and their divergent national and class strategies preclude any "regional strategy." Even among the left nationalist regimes, apart from some limited complementary initiatives among the ALBA countries, no regional plan exists. In this regard it is a serious mistake to write or speak about a "Latin American" problem or initiative. What we can observe today is a generalized breakdown of the export-driven model and divergent social responses, between the proto-socialist welfare policies of Venezuela and the export-subsidy policies of Brazil, Argentina, Chile, Peru, and Colombia. Throughout the economic downturn, as discussed in chapter 7, these regimes, no matter what their pronounced policy concerns or directions, have demonstrated a high degree of structural continuity, making no effort to deepen and expand the domestic market and public investment, let alone nationalize bankrupt enterprises. The crisis highlighted the process of *deglobalization* and the increasing importance of the nation-state.

The deepening economic crisis has adversely affected various incumbent regimes on both the center-left and the right, strengthening the opposition. In Argentina, for example, the right and far-right have dominated the streets in recent years, with a growing power base in the "interior" among the agrarian elite and the middle class in Buenos Aires. The progressive trade union, CTA, which has organized strikes and protests, is not connected with any new left alternative political organization.

Developments in Brazil have given rise to similar protests by social movements and trade unions against rising unemployment and the decline in export-oriented industries. But the principal political beneficiary of the declining popularity of Lula's self-styled "Worker's Party" (he himself has more or less retained popular support, primarily as the result of his foreign policy or his strutting on the international stage) has been the Right. However, wherever the political Right is in power, as in Mexico, Colombia, and Peru (and now Chile), the center-left has tended to benefit. But here as elsewhere, the mass movements lack an organized political response to take advantage of a system in crisis and the demise of neoliberalism. As a result, the pragmatic and social democratic regimes that have formed in current conditions of post-neoliberal capitalist development are reaping the harvest of the seeds sown by the forces of change.

In this conjuncture and under these conditions neither Cuba nor Venezuela offers a "model" for the rest of Latin America. The former is dependent on a highly vulnerable tourist-centered economy, while the latter is based on an abundant resource (oil) that no other country in the region can count on. For these countries to share in the possible benefits of a global realignment of state power and the "wealth of nations," they will need to move beyond piecemeal reform, such as the food subsidies and nationalizations instituted by Chávez, to move more decidedly in the direction of social transformation—toward a socialization of production and finance.

In the current context of Latin American politics and Latin America-US relations, mass protests, general strikes, and other forms of social unrest are beginning to manifest themselves throughout the continent. No doubt the United States in response will intensify its support for rightist movements in opposition and its existing rightist clients in power. US "hegemony" over the Latin American elite is still strong even as it is virtually nonexistent among the mass organizations in civil society. Given the overall militarist-protectionist posture of the Obama regime, we can expect intervention in the form of covert operations as class struggles escalate and move toward socialist transformation.

Holding to the Socialist Line in Cuba

The neoliberal imperialist world order installed in the 1980s was designed as a means of advancing capitalist development—reactivating the stalled accumulation process. At the time, the entire region was in the thrall of capital, with the exception of Cuba, which continued to press forward on a socialist path toward national development. Indeed, while virtually every other country in the region was pushed into the new world order under conditions of sluggish economic growth and an external debt crisis, Cuba was successfully advancing the socialist development of its forces of national production. While the other countries in the region were entering a decade "lost to development," Cuba had its best economic performance to date, posting rates of growth from three to 5 percent a year from 1980 to 1985 while the rest of the region was in the throes of a debt crisis under conditions of rampant inflation and a forced entry into the "new" imperial order of neoliberal globalization. This was not to last, however, and Cuba was slowly but surely drawn into the maelstrom of a growing global capitalist disorder and the political crisis that beset the socialist world. In the wake of the collapse of socialist system, the sluggish Cuban economy sailed into the stormy waters of a production crisis of such proportions as to seriously threaten the survival of the revolution. The subsequent "special period" (war in times of peace) was a critical moment in Cuba's revolutionary process, testing the resolve of the government and the resiliency of popular support for the revolution.

There is no space here to review the complex (and at times contradictory) dynamics of subsequent developments in Cuba. Suffice it to write that Cuba survived the challenge and by the end of the decade was on the road to gradual but persistent recovery, reflected in economic growth rates averaging 5 percent a year from 2001 to 2008.[10] In effect, Cuba participated in the benefits of the primary commodities boom in those years. Indications are that Cuba has also participated in the subsequent collapse of this boom.

To cope with and adjust to the dynamic forces released by and operating in the global economy, the government under the presidency of Raúl Castro had to institute a series of structural and economic policy reforms, ranging from reinstitution of private enterprise and the market in the agricultural and service sectors to an adjustment in government-set wage rates and measures designed to recover food security (Yepe, 2008).

Under the changing conditions of Cuba's structural adjustment to the global economy (see Bell Lara, 2002, on the dynamics of this adjustment), questions arise—as they have in the past—as to the political significance of recent developments in Cuba. In summary form—and with reference to ongoing debates on the Left, as well as the views articulated by social movement leaders in the region—the significance of these developments can be represented as follows.

Cuba has successfully held the line on socialism as a path of national development, providing an important point of reference for those wishing to define socialism and the forms that it might take.[11]

The Empire on the Offensive: Targeting the Bolivarian Revolution

Venezuela today is the major Latin American battleground in the imperialist war and the class struggle. Decisive battles between the forces of revolution and counter-revolution loom on the horizon in Venezuela. The campaign for the September 26, 2010, National Assembly elections will be a crucial battle between the supporters of socialist President Hugo Chávez and the US-backed right-wing opposition. But these battles, part of the class struggle between the poor majority and the capitalist elite, will be fought more in the streets than at the ballot box. As of the time of writing this book in 2010, there had been an escalation of fascist demonstrations by violent opposition student groups; continued selective assassination of union and peasant leaders by right-wing paramilitaries; and an intensified private media campaign presenting a picture of a debilitated government in crisis and on its way out.

Chávez warned on January 29, 2010: "If they initiate an extremely violent offensive that obliges us to take firm action—something I do not recommend they do—our response will wipe them out." The comment came the day after two students were killed and twenty-one police officers suffered bullet wounds in confrontations that rocked the city of Merida. Chávez challenged the opposition to follow the constitutional road and promote a recall referendum on his presidential mandate if they truly believe people no longer support him. Under the democratic constitution adopted in 1999, a recall referendum can be called on any elected official if 20 percent of the electorate signs a petition calling for one. He said if the capitalists continued down the road of confrontation, he would "accelerate the revolution," which has declared "21st century socialism" as its goal.

The stepped-up campaign of destabilization is part of the regional offensive launched by the opposition's masters in Washington. In 2009, as mentioned, the United States installed new military bases in Colombia and Panama, reactivated the US Navy Fourth Fleet to patrol Latin American waters, and helped to organize a military coup that toppled the left-wing Zelaya government in Honduras. In 2010 the United States occupied Haiti with 15,000 soldiers after the January 12 earthquake, and US warplanes have been caught violating Venezuela's airspace. A February 2 report from US National Director of Intelligence, Admiral Dennis Blair, labeled Venezuela the "leading anti-US regional force"—placing the Chávez regime in Washington's crosshairs.

A military invasion cannot be ruled out, but the main aim of the US military build-up and provocations is to apply pressure on those sections of Venezuela's Armed Forces, and others in the pro-Chávez camp, that would prefer to put the brakes on the revolutionary process to avoid a confrontation. This is occurring hand-in-hand with a campaign of media lies, combining claims that Chávez's popularity is rapidly declining with rumors of dissent in the military and government. The United States and Venezuela's retrograde elite still hope to isolate and ultimately remove Chávez. The ongoing campaign is similar to the one unleashed in 2007 to defeat Chávez's proposed constitutional reforms, a campaign that was narrowly defeated in a referendum called by Chávez himself.

The opposition hopes to fracture Chávez's base of support—the poor majority and the armed forces—to win a majority in the National Assembly (with which it is likely to move to impeach Chávez). At the very least, the opposition is seeking to stop pro-revolution forces from winning a two-thirds majority in the assembly, which would restrict the ease with which the Chavistas is able to pass legislation. The current assembly has a large pro-Chávez majority as a result of the opposition having boycotted the 2005 referendum.

The Revolution Advances

The global economic crisis is hitting Venezuela harder than the government initially hoped. Problems in the electricity sector, among others, are also causing strain. The government's campaign to raise awareness about the effects of climate change and wasteful usage has minimized the effect of the opposition and private media campaign to blame the government for the problems in the electricity and water sectors. But far from fulfilling right-wing predictions that falling oil prices would result in a fall of the government's fortunes, Chávez has continued his push to redistribute wealth to the poor—and increased moves against capital and corruption. This is occurring alongside important street mobilizations supporting the government (ignored by the international media, which gave prominent coverage to small opposition student riots).

Most important, however, have been the steps taken in the direction of grassroots participatory democracy or "people's power"— transferring power to the people via the construction of communal councils. Since the end of 200, when they were first instituted, these councils have developed and spread all around the country. Today, barely four years after the idea of Communal Councils was introduced, there are approximately 35,000 of them—grassroots organizations where the highest decision-making body is the General Assembly of the local community, with the ability to recall elected officials or elected spokespeople, a major democratic gain of the 1999 Constitution. A critical feature of these community councils is that they have emerged not by political fiat or from decisions made "from above." They emerged in the context of an explosion of community organizing in the 1990s, not only in the barrios of the poor in Caracas, but also in some of the other large cities. In the context of this political development there have emerged a lot of small, localized committees dealing with diverse local issues: health, education, housing, roads, water, and so on. The communal councils emerged out of the necessity to bring together all of these committees so that rather than being simply groups to campaign for or demand that the government do things, the communities could actually organize and empower themselves—assume decision-making power and take control over these issues.

Community-based organizing was not the only focal point of "public action"—combining actions at the levels of both the State and an actively mobilized population. In November, Chávez announced interventions into eight banks found to be involved in corrupt dealings. A majority were nationalized and merged with a state bank to form the Bicentenary Bank. Together with the Bank of Venezuela, nationalized in 2007, the state now controls 25 percent of the banking sector—the largest single bloc. Nearly thirty bankers were charged and face trial over corruption allegations. Significantly, a number of these had been closely aligned with the government. One of them, Ricardo Fernandez Barrueco, was a relatively unknown entrepreneur in the food sector who rose up through the ranks of the business elite to own four banks and twenty-nine Venezuelan companies.

State institutions, militants of the Chávez-led United Socialist Party of Venezuela (PSUV), and the National Guard have also moved to tackle price speculation following the decision to devalue the Bolívar. More than a thousand shops were temporarily shut down for price speculation in the first week after the announcement in 2007.

On February 13, 2010, Chávez announced that the government had come to an agreement with French company Casino to buy out 80 percent of its shares in the CADA supermarket chain, which has thirty-five outlets across the country. Together with the recently nationalized Exito supermarket chain and the mass importation of various essential goods, the government is moving to take up a much larger share of the retail and distribution sector.

The devaluation of the Bolívar meant that imported goods become more expensive, lowering workers' purchasing power. To compensate, the government decreed in January 2010 a 25 percent increase in the minimum wage (10 percent to be implemented in March and 15 percent in September 2010), made plans for a further wage increase and took steps toward establishing a state monopoly over foreign trade.

Grassroots Organizing

Despite the violent protests and slander campaign, a January 2010 poll by the Venezuelan Institute of Data Analysis (IVAD—generally accepted as one of Venezuela's least biased polling companies) found more than 58 percent of Venezuelans approved of Chávez's presidency. However, the same poll also found that 41.5 percent believed that the opposition should have a National Assembly majority, compared to 49.5 percent who did not. Some 32.6 percent said they would vote for pro-revolution candidates, 20.8 percent for the opposition, and 33.1 percent for "independents." The question is whether these "independents" or the undecided will abstain as they did in the 2007 constitutional referendum, or whether the revolutionary forces can organize to win them over and deal a decisive blow to the right.

It is likely that this battle will be fought more in the streets than through the ballot box. Three massive pro-revolution demonstrations had been already held by early 2010, dwarfing the small but violent opposition protests. A new grouping of revolutionary youth organizations, the Bicentenary National Youth Front, has also been created to organize the pro-revolution majority of youth and students. This injection of organized youth into the Revolution is vital for its future. This is needed, as Chávez noted in his February 12, 2010, speech to a mass demonstration of students in Caracas, to tackle the serious problems of reformism, bureaucratism, and corruption that continue to hamper the revolution.

Chávez has argued against those sectors of the revolutionary camp that insist that it is possible to advance by strengthening the private sector and wooing capitalists. Emphasizing that the "class struggle" is at the heart of the revolution, he has repeatedly argued that the "national bourgeoisie" has no interest in advancing the process of change. He has argued that it is vital to combat the inefficiency and bureaucracy of the state structures inherited from previous governments that hold back and sabotage the process. "We have to finish off demolishing the old structures of the bourgeois state and create the new structures of the proletarian state." To help achieve this, the government has encouraged the creation of 184 communes across Venezuela. Communes are made up of the communal councils mentioned earlier and other social organizations that are directly run and controlled by local communities. Chávez has referred to these communes as the "building blocks" of the new state, in which power would be progressively transferred to the people ("people's power").

The recent creation of peasant militias, organized for self-defense by poor farmers against large landowner violence, is also important. However, the biggest challenge is the continued construction of the PSUV, a mass party with millions of still largely passive members, as a revolutionary instrument of the masses. In its extraordinary congress, which began in November 2009 and continued to meet on weekends until April 2010, debates occurred among 772 elected delegates. Differences arose between those who support a more moderate reformist approach and those arguing for a revolutionary path.

An important emerging issue on the Left is whether to back Chávez's call for a new international organization to unite revolutionary forces globally to strengthen the fight for the "socialism of the 21st century." The debates also included whether party members will elect National Assembly candidates, or whether this important decision would be left in the hands of a select committee (as more conservative forces preferred). After the decision to hold primary elections for candidates was announced, Chávez said on February 11, 2010: "I have confidence in the people, I have confidence in the grassroots; they will not defraud us."

Winds of Rebellion within the Empire: The Rebirth of Class Struggle

A striking feature of political developments in Latin America in the current conjuncture has been the lack of an organized response and resistance from the working class to the actions and policies responsible for this crisis. In this book we have traced the lack of organized resistance to the multifaceted offensive leveled against the working class by the agency and workings of globalizing capital. Even so, it is difficult to explain the quiescence of organized labor in the face of this onslaught. On the other hand, we have pointed toward signs of a revival of the class struggle in other areas. Over the past decade several "observatories" of the class struggle—of relations of conflict under conditions of, and in response to, neoliberal globalization—have recorded a large and growing number of localized struggles all across the region.

Actually there is little or nothing new in this. Localized acts of rebellion or what Scott chose to conceptualize as "everyday resistance" against the oppression of the neoliberal model have been regular if sporadic occurrences throughout what Harvey views as "the short history of neoliberalism" in the region—a history that we ourselves in this book have conceptualized in terms of four distinct cycles. These acts of localized resistance surfaced in the wave of anti-neoliberal sentiment that brought the center-left of the political class to state power in the last decade. In some contexts (e.g., in Mexico over the past decade) we ourselves have recorded hundreds of outbreaks of rebellion a year. In the not atypical case of Guatemala more than 250 outbreaks of rebellion were recorded from 2004 to 2005. Many of these and other such struggles are undocumented and remain unstudied, "blushing"—as it were—"on the ocean floor unseen." But the pattern of Internet-facilitated communications among social movements across the region as of 1994,[12] and the construction of several observatories of the dynamics of the struggle and political conflict have led not only to greater awareness of how widespread the actual outbreaks of rebellion are and have been, but also to more coordination among these movements—and the formation of intraregional alliances. Further, the incidence of these rebellions, and the pattern of their growing frequency, is not new. What is new, however, and more specific to neoliberalism over the past decade (under changing conditions of crisis, recovery and crisis), is a growing trend toward linkages and alliances formed among these localized struggles.

It is possible to trace this development, which we briefly reviewed in chapter 3, back to 1994, to the irruption of the Zapatista movement and its initial efforts toward forging a national movement, the MST in its strategy of strategic alliances with civic society organizations, the formation of the Coordinadora de Movimientos Sociales (CMS), a social alliance of a broad spectrum of Ecuadorian social organizations and movements with CONAIE,[13] and the subsequent emergence of diverse intrasectoral or social alliances such as the Asamblea Nacional Indígena Plural por la Autonomía (ANIPA) and the Congreso Nacional Indígena (CNI) formed in Mexico soon thereafter (Bartra, 2005).

But the various "observatories" set up over the last decade of class conflict and the fight against neoliberalism suggest that there is a growing trend toward active resistance against the forces of capitalist development and the economic model used to advance these forces. The global crisis, if anything, has reactivated the resistance: for example, the Movimiento de los Afectadas (those affected by the environmental consequences of capitalist development and neoliberal policies). And then there is the Alianza Social Continental (the Hemispheric Social Alliance), a broad regional alliance of social organizations and movements formed to provide a collective response to the machinations of imperial power and the assault of capitalism.[14] Other examples of this trend are Red de Alternativas Sustentables Agropecuarias (RASA), a Mexican NGO whose membership and leadership include peasants and indigenous families, academics and social activists, and the Instituto Mexicano para el Desarrollo Comunitario (IMDEC)—an urban-based, middle-class NGO but even so helping to raise awareness of the issues of contamination and related health problems that affect a large and growing number of indigenous communities across the country and, more importantly, helping popular organizations engage in confrontational politics.[15] And then there is the peasant alliance El Campo No Aguanta Más (Mecnam) formed in 2002[16] and Via Campesina, formed as an international social movement of "peasant" organizations and social movements from across the world.

For El Campo No Aguante Más and Via Campesina, representing as it does the peasantry in the global class struggle, the key issues are land and rural livelihoods (food sovereignty, etc). However, for other emerging movements on the Left, the focus has moved from land to other issues affecting the livelihoods of the communities and classes affected by capitalism in its development of the forces of production.[17] But what defines, and in some contexts unites, these movements is not so much their concern for this or that specific issue (land, water, the habitat, food security or prices, conditions of work, human rights, or social welfare) but their united concern with the economic model used to advance capitalist "development" (neoliberalism), as well as the underlying system—and the machinations and conditions (exploitation, oppression) of state power and imperialism. In some situations (Mexico) the major protagonist in this struggle is the working class (the SME, in the current context); in others (e.g., Peru and Ecuador) it is the indigenous movement in instances such as the Coordinadora

Andina de Organizaciones Indígenas; and then there are the rural landless workers and "peasants" in the form of diverse national, regional, and international organizations and movements.

To Conclude: Ten Theses on the Social Movements

Just more than twenty years ago, at the threshold of a new period of neoliberal globalization and social movement resistance, Marta Fuentes composed "Ten Theses on Social Movements." Written with Andre Gunder Frank, her partner and well-known world system theorist, these theses reflected their understanding of capitalism as a world system (Fuentes and Frank, 1989).

The conclusion to our book reflects our contrary understanding of imperialism—not as a world system but as a policy pursued with the agency and under the changing conditions of capitalist development.

Thesis No. 1

Capitalism is a system of expanded commodity production based on imperialist and class exploitation—the pillage of resources and the extraction of surplus value from the direct producer, primarily but by no means exclusively in the form of wage labor. Radical egalitarian or national liberation social movements are the inevitable subjective, or political, response of the subaltern classes affected by the objective conditions of this exploitation.

Thesis No. 2

Neoliberalism emerged in a political reaction against advances made by organized labor in its class struggle with capital under conditions of state-led capitalist development of the forces of production.

Thesis No. 3

Globalization is a social-class project designed to facilitate and legitimate a program of structural reform in national policy, weakening thereby the capacity of the working and other subaltern classes to use the state as an instrument for advancing their collective interest in taming or overthrowing capitalism. The social movements that most effectively responded to this challenge were based on the agency of the proletarianized and semi-proleterianized rural landless workers—the dominant form of the "peasantry" in the current context of capitalist development and agrarian transformation.

Thesis No. 4

The strategic weakness of organized labor—the disarticulation of its forces of resistance—in the 1980s reflected both the *objective* conditions of capitalist development—the productive and social transformation of the system—and the *politics* of the capitalist class and its assault on labor. The absence of a dynamic response to these conditions of capitalist development—to the agency of imperialism used to advance this development—can be explained in terms of a particular correlation of class forces in the current conjuncture.

Thesis No. 5

The most dynamic forces of resistance in the 1990s—the popular movements—were formed by diverse organizations of landless or near-landless rural workers ("peasants") and, in some contexts, indigenous communities. These social movements directly challenged the power of capital and the agency of contemporary imperialism, and in some contexts were able to make substantial gains, slowing down and diverting the capitalist development process.

Thesis No. 6

The dynamic forces of resistance mobilized by the social movements under these conditions took three divergent political forms: (1) direct collective action against the neoliberal policies of the governments; (2) use of the electoral mechanism of democratic politics to contest national and local elections; and (3) local development—a nonconfrontational "no power" approach to social change, to bring about change without seeking or taking state power.

Thesis No. 7

Changing conditions in the new millennium have shifted the tide of national politics, bringing to power the political class on the Left, and a demobilization of the social movements and their retreat from the political arena. NGOs—not all of them by any means (some are aligned with and supportive of the popular movement in their struggle for substantive social change)—turned out to be a major instrument of this demobilization, the handmaiden of neoliberal globalization (from global capital to local development).

Thesis No. 8

The propensity of capitalism toward crisis, reflected in the contemporary outbreak of systemic crisis of global proportions, has generated movements to the Right as well as the Left, each seeking to mobilize the forces of change released by the crisis.

Thesis No. 9

The Obama administration of the US empire has taken action to reverse the decline of influence and power in Latin America. The linchpins of this strategy are a system of alliances with its neoliberal client regimes in the region and turning the center-left against the popular nationalist anti-imperialist axis led by Hugo Chávez in his project of Bolivarian Revolution.

Thesis No. 10

At the current conjuncture of neoliberalism in decline, multiple crises, and a renewed imperialist offensive in the region, winds of rebellion are once again stirring. The forces of resistance in this rebellion are being mobilized by a broad range of class- and community-based social movements, with the support of some progressive NGOs and the state of Venezuela. In this context the immediate prospects for substantive social change in the direction of radical egalitarianism and regional liberation—the socialism of the twenty-first century—are dim. The forces of resistance are resilient but the obstacles are formidable, demanding of the Left a response for which it has not yet demonstrated a capacity.

Conclusion

Our research has led us to several conclusions that challenge political and economic orthodoxy on the Right and Left. For one thing, the formation of neoliberal regimes and the implementation of neoliberal policies in Latin America resulted from sustained political and military intervention, at times directed but always backed by US imperial policymakers and their Latin American collaborators. The dynamic and dialectical relationship between the class struggle and the economic and political institutions of the imperial system set the stage for a neoliberal offensive. This offensive entailed a complicated multilevel restructuring of the system of global capitalist production, resulting in the privatization and deregulation of the economy, the concentration of income and property, and the polarization between the rich-and-powerful and the poor-and-powerless.

Contrary to the view of many mainstream and orthodox liberal economists, the neoliberal world order called for and put in place in the 1980s was not the product of market forces operating beyond anyone's ability to control. Rather, resulted from the machinations of a neoimperial strategy—the product of the economic, political, and military violence directed by the imperialist system and the capitalist class against the new global working class, labor, and direct production in its multitudinous forms. Not to mince words, class warfare, prosecuted by the state but aided and abetted by international financial institutions just as the IMF and the World Bank, weakened and destroyed the social movements, allowing the ruling classes to impose the new world order of neoliberal "globalization."

The implementation of IMF and World Bank policies of neoliberal reform, and structural adjustment to the requirements of the new (neoliberal) imperial order, were only and made possible by means of a multipronged assault on the working class and the new semiproletariat of rural landless workers, disarticulating the forces of resistance and demobilizing the social movements. On the other hand, the same forces and policies that destroyed the social movements of the 1960s and 1970s in conditions of capitalist exploitation and imperial rule gave rise to a new wave of social movements that in the 1990s would pose a serious challenge to the neoliberal world order.

The imposition of the imperial neoliberal model resulted in the productive and social transformation of agriculture and rural society, separating millions of peasants and small farmers from their means of direct production, not only proletarianizing and uprooting many of them but also fueling new forms of resistance in the form of popular sector social movements. To counter the rise of this popular resistance the World Bank and other agents of the neoliberal imperial order designed and implemented a new counterinsurgency strategy within the framework of a post-Washington consensus on the need for a more pragmatic form of neoliberalism, a more inclusive form of "development" and a new paradigm focused on the "empowerment of the poor," self-help, micro-projects and market-assisted land reforms.

In other words, the forces of capitalist development, seemingly undirected and arising from the depths of the underlying system rather than an imperial strategy, violently displaced the small producers that dominated the countryside, so that the state and other agencies of the imperial order could move in to help the victims of these "forces of change" by adjusting to them, via microprojects designed and funded by the international financial institutions in the lead of the "war against global poverty." The aim of this war (better understood as a war on the poor than poverty) was to demobilize the new social movements mounted by the rural landless workers, peasant farmers, and indigenous communities—providing the rural poor a less confrontational alternative ("change without state power," in one formulation). Contrary to progressive opinion and a widely held view on the Left, this "peaceful transition" was aided and abetted ("mediated") by an army of nongovernmental organizations that operated at the grassroots to undermine collective national resistance and facilitate an accommodation to the neoliberal imperial order.

Our research demonstrated that at each stage of the deepening and extension of the neoliberal order—1973–1982, 1983–1989, 1990–1999, and in modified form 2000–2010—new forms of class struggle and popular resistance emerged with overlapping and different sets of protagonists. In the earlier period, trade unions and urban industrial workers took the lead. Following the decapitation of the movements and massive urban unemployment, peasants, landless rural workers played a leading role in the run-up to the economic and political crises and partial collapse of the neoliberal model at the end of the 1990s.

The concentration of wealth and power at the top, especially within and among the sector of multinational corporations and the resulting social dynamics led to a highly polarized class structure and multiple forms of struggle—electoral, extra-parliamentary mobilization, and a self-help form of local development. The most effective forms of struggle, leading to the toppling of the neoliberal regimes in the period 1999–2003 were the extra-parliamentary struggles led by peasants, indigenous communities, rural landless workers, and the urban unemployed and impoverished public employees. Contrary to orthodox Marxist expectations, the industrial working class at best played a supplementary role, with the notable exception of the Bolivian factory and mining workers during the uprisings of 2003 and 2005.

What this suggests is that the principal axis of anti-neoliberal class struggle is contingent as much on subjective conditions of leadership and organization as it is on the "objective" position in the social structure and economic system. Contrary to the view of many leftist academics and journalists, the rising tide of popular movements, which overthrew the existing neoliberal rulers, did *not*, and could not overturn the existing economic system. At best, they set the stage for the emergence and election of new center-left regimes that proceeded to co-opt movement leaders and deradicalize the movements, aided immensely by the commodity boom of the period (2003–2008). In contrast to the conventional wisdom, which inflates the revolutionary potentialities of social movements, our study demonstrates that without a clear political agenda for state power, they are susceptible to political manipulation and marginalization.

In other words the outcome of each phase of the class struggle is somewhat indeterminate—contingent not only on socioeconomic conditions but also on intangible "subjective" factors, including the capacity to build social and political alliances across economic sectors. Our study demonstrates that for every imperial-led offensive designed to shape the economy and state to serve their interests, there is a counteroffensive by the exploited and dispossessed classes. Each imperial advance generates forces of popular resistance.

What has changed from the initial US-led neoliberal offensive of the 1970s to the first decade of the twenty-first century is the configuration of international and national power and economic relations.

US imperialism has lost its position as the predominant trading and investment power in South America as the new center-left and even rightist regimes turn to Asia, and within Latin America and elsewhere. The decline of US economic leverage has led Washington to emphasize its military and intelligence assets as weapons to regain influence, substituting military for declining market power, especially against the Chávez regime and administration in Venezuela. This military turn, while a physical threat to the social movements as evidenced by the US-backed military coup in Honduras and subsequent political assassinations, finds little support in the region.

Under conditions of the ascent of the new developmental and pragmatic center-left and even center-right regimes, in a time of high commodity prices, the dynamic of social movement has declined.

The popular movements have diminished in power but are resilient and retain the capacity to reactivate their constituencies when and if the current China-led growth slows and reduces the demand for commodities, which form the backbone of the Latin American exports and accounts in part for their relative stability of many economies in the region at the end of the decade. The social movements may have temporarily lost the class war, but they have repeatedly and successfully won numerous battles and struggles, imposing limits on the scope and depth of imperial pillage and at times toppling collaborator regimes in crisis. This study emphasizes the centrality of autonomous class-based movements, the successful exercise of extra-parliamentary class struggle politics, as well as the need for political leadership with a strategy for state power, one which anticipates the frontal political and military opposition of imperial collaborators.

Notes

Introduction

1. The strategy of local development based on the accumulation of social capital, constructed within the framework of a "new development paradigm" (Atria et al., 2004) is closely aligned with the earlier "community development" movement. The early history of the community development movement in the 1950s and the 1960s signified the emergence of a "pluralist democratic culture" in many developing countries as well as a concern for local development within the framework of liberal reforms of national policy. But the dominant trend was for economic and political development based on the agency of the central government and the state. However, in the new policy environment of the neoliberal world order ("structural" free market reform) this incipient democratic culture was cultivated by the return of civilian constitutional rule, and, at another level, by widespread policies of privatization and decentralization. With the retreat of the state from the economy and its social (and developmental) responsibilities, it was left to "civil society" to pick up the slack in the form of emergent self-help organizations of the urban poor and a myriad of community-based and nongovernmental organizations to deal with issues of social and economic development such as health, housing, food kitchens (*comedores* or communal dining halls), capacity building, and self-employment. The emergence of a "civil society" was a predominant feature of the 1980s.

2. The World Bank's economic logic flows from institutional economics and its concept of social capital as the source of a culture of cooperation and civism. As Portes (1998) points out the idea that social capital, embodied in norms of reciprocity and relations of solidarity, give rise to cooperation and civism so that if there is civism there will be social capital, is tautological to the extreme. Not only is the World Bank's reasoning hopelessly circular but it is also predicated on the unquestioned assumption that lies at the root of neoclassical economics, namely that allowing individuals in their economic exchanges and transactions to pursue their self-interest will somehow contribute to the common good. Thus the World Bank continues to persistently argue, against all sorts of empirical evidence, that a system of free market capitalism based on economic freedom and geared to private profit, like the policies that result in this system, is good for the poor.

3. According to Cockcroft (2008), 55 million indigenous persons, or 400 indigenous peoples, inhabit Indo-Afro-Latin America. Most are found in Mexico, Guatemala, Ecuador, Peru, and Bolivia. They generally reject the Europe-imposed term "Indians" (Indios). They call themselves "the native peoples" ("Ios pueblos originarios" in Spanish). They constitute an estimated 67 percent of Bolivia's population and 40 percent in Ecuador, mainly in the Andean highlands, or Sierra, and the Amazon, the tropical region regarded by the indigenous movement in the region as "the lungs of the planet," the common resource of all earth's peoples bestowed by "mother nature" (*Pachamama*).

I   US Imperialism and the Neoliberal Offensive

1. Quoted in *Guardian Weekly*, January 29, p. 19.
2. This system was governed by a set of rules and agreements overseen by three fundamental institutions: the World Bank—the Bank of International Construction and Development; the International Monetary Fund (IMF), and the World Trade Organization (WTO), which functioned as a free trade negotiating forum (GATT—the General Agreement on Tariffs and Trade) for 50 years before finally achieving institutional form. On the capitalist development dynamics of this institutional framework—the Bretton Woods sisters or, as some would have it, the "unholy trinity" (Bello (2010).
3. The US interventionist success in Guatemala (1954) led the United States to repeat its policy with Cuba in 1961—a policy that led to defeat. The successful US orchestrated military coups in Brazil (1964) and Indonesia (1965) and the invasion of the Dominican Republic (1965) encouraged the United States to deepen and extend its military invasion of Indo-China that led to a historic but temporary defeat of imperial policymakers and the profound weakening of domestic political support.
4. "Good governance" (see the multiple bibliographic references to various World Bank and UNDP reports) is generally understood to mean a broad array of practices, which maximize the common/public good. More specifically, the term denotes to a relation between social organizations and government that conforms to the following "democratic" principles: transparency, effectiveness, openness, responsiveness, and accountability; the rule of law, acceptance of diversity and pluralism, and social inclusiveness.
5. "Liberal" in academic discourse has both an ideological and theoretical center of reference. As "ideology" (belief in ideas used to promote action) liberalism is defined by the notion, and associated values, of the free individual, and the belief in the need for economic and social progress (slow incremental change or reform) in the direction of individual freedom. As "theory" it is associated with the notion of *homo economicus* that economic interactions among individuals in the marketplace are based on the rational calculus of self-interest by each individual. This notion is central to both classical and neoclassical economic theory and to the policies derived from this theory.

6. With the onset of the new world order of neoliberal globalization and financialization in the early 1980s, the level of capital formation and the growth rate in GDP per capita declined drastically from an annual average rate of close to 5 percent in the 1950s and 1960s, to an average rate of 3.2 in the 1970s, -0.6 in the 1980s, and 0.9 in the 1990s in the heyday of neoliberalism, and then 3.5 percent from 2002 to 2007 during the primary commodities boom, before collapsing in the mid-2008–2009 (CEPAL, 2009).

7. There is a strong evidence that the margin of difference for South America's commodities exports is a function of increased demand from China and India, and, to a much lesser degree, of other rapidly growing nations in Asia. For example, the average annual rate of growth of China's imports in the 1990s was 16 percent per year versus a 10 percent growth rate in exports. For some soft commodities, such as soybeans that were thought to have peaked in price around 2004, prices in 2007 once again soared, profiting directly the major soya producers (*sojeros*) of Argentina, Bolivia, Brazil, and Paraguay.

8. For the private sector the high growth rates have meant a massive increase of profits on sales for the agro-exporting oligarchic elites and conglomerates that dominate international trade. And for the governments it has meant windfall resource rents and additional fiscal resources, as well as a positive balance of payments on the current, trade and capital accounts.

9. *CEPAL News*, XXIV, no. 2, February 2009, p. 85.

10. *La Jornada*, March 17, 2009.

11. In fact, Brazil's brief recession was already over by the second quarter of 2009.

12. Inés Bastillo and Helvia Helloso, *The Global Financial Crisis: What Happened and What's Next*, Washington DC: ECLAC Washington Office, February 2009.

13. According to a recent ECLAC (2009b) study, the current global crisis will cause nine million people in the region to fall into poverty, an increase of 1 percent in the regional poverty rate. This effectively reverses the gains supposedly made over the past decade in which upward of 41 million, according to the same study, managed to overcome or move out of poverty—the combined result of actions taken by the poor themselves (to migrate) and by a number of governments (especially Brazil and Chile) under the post-Washington Consensus, via greater economic growth, expansion of social spending, improved income distribution, and what ECLAC defines as "the demographic bonus."

14. *Financial Times*, January 9, 2009, 7.

15. *Financial Times*, January 7, 2009, 5.

16. *CEPAL News*, XXIV, no.2, February 2009.

17. In the vortex of a economic crisis that has put at risk and threatens the livelihoods of hundreds of millions of the world's poor, the United Nations launched an online appeal for "individual [*sic*] donations" to fight hunger as for the first time in history more than one billion face starvation worldwide, a 100 million more than a year ago (CNN.com November 16, 2009).

2   Capitalist Development, Labor, and the Rural Poor: The Politics of Adjustment (Nonresistance)

1. On the recent debates and associated studies of the impact of neoliberalism on the peasant economy and society see Otero (1999).
2. W. A. Lewis, a West Indian development economist in his famous "Economic Development with Unlimited Supply of Labour" (1954) established what would become a model (dualism) for the analysis of the economic structure of developing societies.
3. See, for example, PREALC (1990), OECD (1994) and the World Bank (1993, 1995), the major object in this chapter. The term "labor market flexibility" has taken on a variety of meanings over time, prompting US Labor Secretary Robert Reich to remark at an ILO-sponsored meeting on June 10, 1994 that "rarely in international discourse has the [term] gone so directly from obscurity to meaninglessness without any intervening period of coherence" (quoted by Brodsky, 1994). What it means for the World Bank, however, as an overlooked precondition for successful structural reform is fairly clear: "A dynamic and flexible labour market is an important part of market-oriented policies. It helps reallocate resources and allows the economy to respond rapidly to new challenges from increased competition. Moreover, freeing the labour market of distortions improves the distribution of income because it encourages employment expansion and wage increases in the poorest segments of society" (World Bank, 1993: 92).
4. UNCTAD (1992), cited in Sagasti and Árevalo (1992: 1105).
5. On the model case of Chile see Agacino and Gonzalo Rivas (1995), Geller (1993), Herrera (1995), Leiva (1996), and Leiva and Agacino (1994).
6. The shift over the course of the 1980s in political conditions and climate relating to the labor question in Argentina is reflected well in a recent comment by the president of the Chamber of Deputies in the context of a heavy national debate and political struggle generated by the efforts of the government to legislate or decree a new labor code that extends the managers rights instituted in Law 20.744 (Labor Contracts and the National Law of Employment) and undermines further the advances made by labor over the years and that establishes the right of employers and managers to hire, fire, extend hours of work, and relocate workers in the production process without penalty. It was necessary, he argued, to support the government's proposed reform because "times have changed...The reality is [the need to make an effort] to obtain jobs; before it was to protect full employment" (*La Jornada*, October 7, 1996: 59).
7. Specifically, the Bank argues that minimum-wage legislation distorts factor allocation and punishes informal sector workers, high unemployment benefits reduce work incentives, job protection provisions and the high costs of dismissal make restructuring difficult and slow, and high non-wage costs and payroll taxes act as a disincentive for entrepreneurs to expand employment

and increase the international competitiveness of local firms. The Bank expands on these points in its annual (1995) *World Development Report* on *"Workers in an Integrating World."* However, its discourse is highly ideological, presented in the form of a manifesto, peppered with crude assertions and highly constructed and dubious data. On this see Veltmeyer (1997b).

8. In this connection, the economists of the World Bank depart from the neoclassical vision of the worker, seen not as the member of a class, acting in solidarity, and making gains on the basis of a long struggle with capital, but as an individual economic agent, capacitated as a social actor in the market, seeking and able to take advantage of the opportunities it provides. To this end, converting workers into self-seeking individual economic agents, the Bank has advocated reforms designed to strip the power of union over its members, its capacity to negotiate collective agreements on a sectoral or industry basis, mandatory dues checkoff, etc.

9. The literature on this redesigned model of the SAP and the associated agenda is voluminous. Inter alia see CEPAL (1992a, 1992b); IDB (1993); Lerner (1996); and Veltmeyer (1996).

10. This implementation of this agenda has also resulted in a huge and growing literature. Inter alia see Baros Horcasitas et al. (1991), Boisier et al. (1992), and Cook et al. (1996).

11. The importance and priority given to (1) the New Social Policy, designed to make the SAP more palatable and to defuse a mounting and destabilizing level of social discontent, and (2) the modernization of the state apparatus, is reflected in the distribution of funds by the IDB, the key financial institution charged with the responsibility of implementing the SAP within the region. In 1996, 40 percent of the Bank's portfolio was directed into social investment and program funds, 36 percent was directed toward the region-wide government decentralization process and the associated modernization of the state apparatus, another 16 percent went toward infrastructure support projects, and only 8 percent went toward agriculture and other productive sectors of the economy (IPS, Washington DC, March 14, 1997). This characteristic low priority given to production enhancement projects, also shared by public investments in the region, reflects the widely shared ideological orientation toward the neoliberal doctrine on the private sector as the motor of the development process.

12. The OECD, in its annual Economic Outlook (1996) defines "total productivity" as the weighted average productivity gains of capital and labor. However, more generally the modern (neoclassical) theory of economic growth holds that total factor productivity can be measured in terms of the difference between the productivity increase of direct production factors (capital and labor) and total productivity increase (FUSADES, 1996. In this context, total factor productivity relates to factors other than capital and labor such as the change in the organizations of production (increased flexibility) associated with what has been termed "postfordism" by French Regulationists.

13. This neoclassical theory (see ECA, 1995; 564: 940) basically holds that under free market competitive conditions each factor of production receive

in return for its contribution to production a commensurate return. In other words, the invisible hand of the market—according to Michel Camdessus, one of three pillars of IMF economic policy, the other two being (1) the visible hand of the state and (2) "solidarity between the poor and the rich"— has to be left alone...to assure an optimum, and equitable, distribution of the social product.

14. On this see Montesino and Góchez (1995: 940). The problem with the theory is that despite the centrality of this variable (the marginal productivity of labor) there does not seem to be any systematic or even casual effort to determine or measure it in a specific context. On this point see Montesino and Góchez (1995: 940) who point out that there exists neither an effective methodology nor any serious efforts to measure the marginal productivity of labor.

15. See Montesino and Góchez (1995: 945) who point out the similarities between the observations and recommendations arising from the Bogota Conference and the argument advanced by the ARENA government. More recently, the Menem government in Argentina has advanced the same argument in the context of its campaign to introduce a program of labor market flexibilisation. This argument was clearly made on the basis of the secret World Bank Report leaked to the media in the context of this campaign and the political struggle unleashed by it.

16. The idea of adjusting wages to productivity was, of course, a key element of the postwar labor-capital accord. But it was resurrected as a specific policy recommendation in the Latin-American context by the ILO (PREALC, 1990: 15) and CEPAL (1992a: 142).

17. The evolution of minimum wages has tracked the same pattern as average wages, although the tendency to fall has generally been even more pronounced. This fall in the purchasing power of wages reflects the effects of specific policies, as well as prevailing structural conditions, designed explicitly to compress wages as a mechanism of internal adjustment. The effects and social costs of this compression have been brutally severe, leading to a drastic reduction in consumption and standards of living, which is reflected in the fact that not even in 1996 had real per capita incomes in the region recovered their level achieved in 1980 and in some cases (Argentina, Peru, Venezuela) in 1970 (UN, 1996: 7).

18. *La Jornada* 5/11/96: 39; 15/3/77: 48.

19. In the not atypical case of Mexico, the number of workers in manufacturing within the formal production sector of the economy in the 1980s (from 1981 to 1989) declined dramatically, 4.5 percent a year on average, while production levels remained stagnant, with oscillations by industry, and productivity per worker increased by 5.1 percent, presumably to some extent related to the decrease in the number of workers (Morales, 1992: 64). According to a series of Industrial Surveys conducted over the period the same pattern held for the other branches of industry as well. In the industrial sector in 1989 the number of workers had declined 13 percent relative to 1981, while productivity rose 14.3 percent (Morales, 1992: 71).

20. Amsden and van der Hoeven (1994), based on data collected by UNIDO (1991, 1992), show that the growth rate of manufacturing output (taking manufacturing as a proxy for broader developments with respect to output and wage patterns) declined from an annually average rate of 6.6 percent from 1965 to 1980 to 1.2 percent in the 1980s, and that when value-added growth is considered—and the income associated with it, then the 1980s experienced a net decrease in output and income. Data assembled by FUSADES (1996) indicate that total productivity growth during the same period (the 1980s) was variable, reflecting in part the contribution of capital, but generally exceeded the growth of output. In the case of Mexico, an Industrial Survey showed that in 1988 the number of employed workers in the industrial sector was 87 percent of the number in 1981, but that productivity had risen 14.3 percent over the same period (Morales, 1992: 71).

21. In the case of El Salvador, for example, from 1980 to 1986 productivity on average increased by 8.4 percent while wages fell by 23.4 percent (ECA 564, 1995: 957). Subsequently, the rate of growth in average productivity slowed down while real wages recovered somewhat, but in either case there was clearly no systematic correlation between the two (see the detailed sectoral analysis of the dynamics of productivity and wages by Montesino and Gochez, 1995: 945–962). In the case of Mexico, a study by Guerrero de Lizardi and Valle (1995), showed that until around 1982 wage and productivity increases more or less were in tandem but that at that point they began to sharply diverge, wages falling drastically while average productivity tended to remain stable with a tendency for a gradual but persistent increase as of around 1987.

22. There is evidence that the Chicago Boys of Chile purposefully maintained unemployment at twice the historic rate as a means to pressure and discipline workers, undercutting and reducing their demands for decent or fair wage increases (Sanfuentes, 1987). As for inflation, there is similar evidence of it being used as a mechanism for compressing wages and transferring income from labor to capital. On this issue the economic policies of the current Zedillo regime are revealing. Since he came into office on December 1994, the Basic Basket (*canasta básica*) has increased by some 170 percent, while wages have been adjusted, allowed to increase, to a maximum of 71 percent, a difference of more than 200 percent (*La Jornada*, January 27, 1997: 42). The disarticulation and repression of working-class organizations have been well documented, albeit not analyzed in terms of a politically determined mechanism for compressing wages. For the case of El Salvador vis-à-vis the maquilladoras created in the mid-1980s see Arrida Palomares (1995 and the pioneering case of Chile see Leiva and Petras, with Veltmeyer (1994) and Leiva (1996).

23. Not only has the level of capital formation in Latin America over the course of neoliberal policies been generally and comparatively low but a significant part of the surge in FDI flows into the region was invested unproductively in the purchase of lucrative but privatized state enterprises (Petras and Veltmeyer, 2002).

24. This is particularly the case for Latin America, as we have argued elsewhere (Veltmeyer, 1996), but indications are the same applies elsewhere such as in the European Community where until the mid-1970s the share of capital in value added production in manufacturing, and the returns to capital invested in the sector had been declining, the 1980s turned these trends around.

25. In the case of Mexico, for example, the rate of investment and capital formation in 1988 was only 41 percent of that in 1981 (Morales, 1992: 69) and more recent studies (see, e.g., Petras and Veltmeyer, 1995) show that despite a resurgence of direct foreign investment as of 1992, with Mexico receiving close to half of all FDI flows into the region, the general level of productive investment in Mexico and the rest of the region (Chile excepted) remains low.

26. However, Leiva (1996), for one, discounts the effectiveness of this investment, emphasizing its many hidden and not so hidden costs such as the weakening and disarticulation of the labor movement, the disproportionate growth of precarious and poorly paid jobs, the dramatically increased rates of reliance on cheap female and child labor, the increase of job and economic insecurity, and an extension of inequality and poverty.

27. In 11 of Latin America's 20 economies the size of the external debt, measured in terms of the GDP or the rate of debt service, exceeds the World Bank's "crisis level" (over 50 percent of export earnings). It remains a substantial drag on the development process, explaining in part the low level of productive investment characteristic of economies in the region.

28. On the dynamics of this investment see inter alia Petras and Veltmeyer (1995). As for the high level of nonproductive consumption, a problem that was identified as early as the 1960s by CEPAL economists, it is reflected in the huge gap between the income disposed of by the richest households and individuals and the rate of investment. On this point, INEGI, Mexico's national statistics institute, has calculated that the 23 percent of the richest households in the country experienced an increase of 417 percent in their income from 1984 to 1994, while the share in national income of 10.4 million families earning the equivalent of from one to five minimum wages, and constituting 53.4 percent of all households, fell by 31 percent (*La Jornada*, September 23, 1996: an. supl. V).

29. The tendency for the technological restructuring of production to slough off and reduce the demand for labor is well-known, having been documented and analyzed from diverse perspectives as of the onset of the industrial revolution of the nineteenth century. Now as then it is possible to identify two major intellectual and political responses to this process: *techno-optimism*, to believe that the reduced demand for labor in the restructured sectors will be compensated for by an increased demand for labor in newly expanding sectors—that these expanding industries will absorb the labor released or expelled from the restructured industries; and *techno-pessimism*, the response of those who do not share this belief. In the current context, techno-pessimists do not believe in the existence of an automatic compensating mechanism between the loss and the generation of jobs, and they find it difficult to convince the mass of unemployed workers that their jobs will

be reconstructed some day, after a period of adjustment, benefiting their off-spring if not themselves. In this context, the techno-pessimist Jeremy Rifkin, in *The End of Work* (1996), goes so far as to expand on the argument that entire populations and nations are condemned to resign themselves to live and suffer the conditions of un- and underemployment. As he constructs this scenario, the technological process of job-destruction, and the incapacity of the system to regenerate jobs in the dynamic sectors of the economy, viz. the "jobless recovery," is leading to a definitive break with a historical cycle dating back to the industrial revolution. This is to say, there is no ground for optimism in the well-known history of technological restructuring of jobs destroyed in the process. Thus it is that Rifkin turns for hope toward what he calls the "third sector," the civil society which has demonstrated a greater capacity than either the state or the market to generate new forms of employment. In this connection, Rifkin has made an intellectual and political virtue out of the necessity experienced by millions of workers who, as a matter of survival more than the creative energy and ingenuity which he points to, are essentially self-generating jobs, an experience that is well-known in America where the so called "popular economy" in the informal sector has generated, it has been estimated, more than 90 percent of all net jobs in the 1980s.

30. The process of these developments has been well-documented and analyzed. It relates to what has been termed "The Golden Age of Capitalism" or what the French have dubbed "the thirty glorious years"—close to thirty years in the postwar context of continued and unparalleled annual growth worldwide of the social product (Glynn et al., 1990). One key element of the context for this growth was constituted by a labor-capital accord that provided conditions of social peace in exchange for a just share in any productivity gains and a guarantee of full employment, supported by labor-demanding spending policy of the state and the institution of a program of social welfare. In the late 1960s cracks began to appear in the foundation of this system with the onset of a "profitability crunch" reflected in conditions of stagnant production rates, a crisis of overproduction, and rising unemployment. As it happened, labor launched what turned out to be its last great offensive, from 1968 to 1973, in its push for higher wages and improved benefits precisely at the point of this crisis in capitalist production, provoking a counteroffensive, launched by capital in 1974 and continuing today. Key elements of this counteroffensive included a direct attack on wages and the power of unions, the welfare state, as well as the agreement to link wages to productivity gains. The rest, as they say, is history—a long history that is by no means at an end. For brief glimpses into this history see inter alia Aglietta (1982), Arrighi (1990), Davis (1984), and Veltmeyer (1996).

31. On this point, the extraction of absolute surplus value, a study by Arrida Palomares (1995 78–80) on the labor process of the maquilladores in El Salvador's San Bartolo Free Trade Zone found an extensive and abuse use of overtime, leading in many case of workdays of 9–10 hours per day or 55–60 hours a week. The extensive and abusive reliance on overtime and extended work-days does not even bring up the growing patterns of double- and triple-job holding, extensive self-exploitation in the context of households and

production units in the informal sector, and the dramatic growth of child and unreported female labor. For a statistical profile of these dimensions of absolute surplus value extraction see CEPAL (1995).

32. On this concept of "super-exploitation" see Marini (1981) and Veltmeyer (1983). It is based in part on what Meillasoux (1978) in a very different context conceptualized as "labour rents," extracted from migrant laborers on the basis of the assumption of the laborers' households outside the capitalist system of a part of the reproductive costs of the labor purchased by agro-capitalists on a seasonal base.

33. On this point see, inter alia, Veltmeyer (1983) and, with respect to Chile, which experienced a dramatic expansion of the *temporero* workforce in its privileged agro-export industries in the 1980s, Leiva, Petras, and Veltmeyer (1994).

34. With respect to the maquilladores, which in El Salvador and Mexico represent the most dynamic sectors of industrial growth, and in the case of Mexico accounting for 40 percent of total exports, see inter alia the study by Delgado Wise and Cypher (2005).

35. This problem is reflected in the general failure of economies in the region to recover let alone exceed the rates of growth (5.5–6.3 percent) that it had sustained for several decades under the previous now discarded state-interventionist, inward-oriented and populist strategy. As is well known the entire 1980s was "lost to development," averaging barely 1 percent growth per annum (-0.9 percent on a per capita basis), but each year into the 1990s, 10 to 15 years into the neoliberal era, and not withstanding the substantial recovery of foreign direct investment and inflow of capital since 1992, the expected or promised economic "recovery" and "activation" has failed to materialize. Once again, as in past years, an overall growth rate of around 3.0 percent (3.1, barely or less than 1 percent on a per capita basis) has been predicted for the following year, on the heels of an overall regional decline of 1 percent in 1995 (5.6 percent in the case of Mexico).

36. On this point, Leiva and Agacino (1994) contend that during the 1990–1994 period in Chile, employers in the manufacturing sector resorted to flexible labor practices such as temporary employment, subcontracting, homework, fixed-term employment, and the increased use of cheaper female labor, as means of increasing their control over the labor force by cutting production costs and weakening the negotiating power of workers. These variations in a labor flexibility strategy are also reflected in another characteristic feature of the production and labor process in the region: the wage discrimination against women, who make up the bulk of the labor force in the maquilladores, and who are on average paid at least 30 to 40 percent less than men in jobs of the same value and position. In the not atypical case of El Salvador, women are paid 53 percent less than men in industry and 47 percent less in commerce (*ECA*, 1994: 551: 911). On this point vis-à-vis Chile also see Henriquez and Reca (1994).

37. For example, in Mexico's manufacturing industry, the region's third largest, the total cost of labor in the production process has been reduced to 10 percent, with wages representing only 2.8 percent (*La Jornada*, April 18, 1996). Minimum wages per hour in the manufacturing sector are set

at $1.23 in Mexico (versus $12.60 in the United States, $20.80 in Japan, $11.93 in Canada, $8.85 in France, $6.10 in South Korea, and $2.75 in Chile). In the case of Mexico, this wage rate in real terms is lower than it was in 1965 and by no stretch of the imagination (or pocket-book) covers the cost of subsistence of the worker's family—and thus the reproduction of labor power. In this connection, it is estimated that a family of three to four, below the Mexican average in size, requires the equivalent to five minimum wages to pay for the *canasta básica*—the package of goods to meet its basic physical needs (*La Jornada*, 5/11/96: 40). According to the World Bank, 60 percent of Mexican families are unable to provide adequately for their basic needs, and half of this number are deprived to a level that seriously affects their health not to speak of any social capital.

38. The World Bank and neoclassical economists generally (Belassi, Bhagwati, Kreuger, Lal) have drawn a false and entirely misleading conclusions from the success of the rapidly growing economies of East Asia that have geared their economies to manufacturing exports. In no case was this export-oriented industrialization strategy pursued at the expense of the domestic market. In fact, this market was—and still remains—a protectorate of the state, as are the industries and enterprises that rely on it. In contrast, in Latin America the neoliberal reform process has prematurely exposed nascent and immature industries and enterprises to the forces of the world market, leading to the technological restructuring of a few but for the most part resulting in a policy of lowering the cost of labor in production and the weakening and destruction of domestic markets.

39. Under the conditions that we have identified it is possible to conclude that the phenomenon of low wages is functionally linked to a dynamic of export-oriented production, which is determined (limited) by the absorptive capacity of external rather than domestic demand: low wages provide a disincentive for the productive investment of surplus value and favors the unproductive consumption by capital.

3   Dynamics of Agrarian Transformation and Resistance

1. See the relevant sections in the collections edited by Stavenhagen (1970), Landsberger (1969, 1974) and Roseberry, Gudmundson, and Samper (1995).

2. The literature on the dynamics of these agrarian reforms is voluminous but see, inter alia, Stavenhagen (1970) and Veltmeyer (2005).

3. The 1986 rural Census estimated the rural population as 23.4 million people. By 1995, the rural population had declined to 18 million, *pointing toward* a massive exodus of more than five million people. Because of declining revenues, the compression of prices to below production 1972 costs, and massively increasing indebtedness among producers, an additional 800,000 families, that is, more than two million persons, are estimated by IBGE (the

Brazilian Institute of Geography and Statistics) to have abandoned the countryside in just five years (from 1995 to 1999) because of low prices and the lack of land and credit.

4. Carlos Menem, President at the time, declared that at least 200,000 small and medium-sized farms and rural "businesses" were productively marginal and surplus to the country's requirements, and could not be supported by government policy.

5. On the concept of "social exclusion" see Behrman, Gaviria, and Székely (2003), Lesboupin [2000], Paugam (1996), Pochman et al. (2006) and Wolfe (1994). Some of these scholars work for organizations such as the Inter-American Development Bank, the ILO, and ECLAC as project consultants or policy analysts while others are affiliated with a broad range of "independent" research institutions or universities. But they all seem to share this enthusiasm for "social exclusion" as the problem of poverty and the "social capital" of the poor as the solution.

6. UNICEF (Cornia, Jolly, and Stewart, 1987) conceptualized this process as "structural adjustment with a human face." CEPAL (1990), on the other hand, conceptualized the process as "productive transformation with equity" (to expand opportunities for the socially excluded to participate in the production process by improving their access to wealth- or income-generating assets). The UNDP (1996), for its part, conceptualized the process as "sustainable human development." On these efforts to move beyond the Washington Consensus without abandoning the fundamental pillar of neoliberalism in its prescribed "pro-growth" policies see Veltmeyer (2007).

7. After Cuba, state-led land reforms took place in Peru from 1958 to 1974, Brazil from 1962 to 1964, Chile from 1966 to 1973, Ecuador from 1964 to 1967, El Salvador from 1980 to 1985, Guatemala between 1952 and 1954 (and again after the civil war following the peace accords), Honduras in 1973, and Nicaragua from 1979 to 1986. These reforms were implemented by the state, regardless of its form (authoritarian, military, liberal reformist, proto-revolutionary). But they were undertaken in response to mass peasant mobilizations and the perceived threat of "social revolution" (Blanco 1972; De Janvry, Sadoulet, and Wolford 1998; Kay 1981, 1982).

8. In a number of systematic studies into the productivity of small versus large highly capitalized farms the general finding has been that in all cases relatively smaller, less capitalized farms are much more productive per unit area—200 to 1,000 percent greater—than the larger ones (Rosset 1999: 2).

9. Fujimori's poverty relief programs were similar to Salinas' PRONASOL (1992) in that it served primarily as an electoral mechanism for securing the rural vote.

10. This point is argued by Ulcuango (*Boletín ICCI*, 1, 5, Agosto 1999). In the view of this indigenous intellectual, organically linked to the indigenous movement and CONAIE, its representative body, NGOs wittingly or not have been called into arms and used as a "economic-political weapon" by the organizations of global capital (the World bank, the IMF, IDB, the

United States) for what in this antisystemic discourse appears as a struggle for "global domination."

11. On this argument see Marcos (1996) regarding Peru. The regional and global trend toward decentralization and the agency of local governments in the development process has been viewed in a similar light—as a means of disarticulating traditional forms of social and political organization of the indigenous communities, an opportunity for undermining their traditional authority and consolidating the economic and political power of the elite, regarding its capacity for manipulating the local politics process with its discourse on "modernity" (Editorial *Boletín ICCI "RIMAY,"* 2, 16, Julio; 2, 18, Setiembre). In all of the countries with a substantial indigenous population—Bolivia, Ecuador, Peru, and Guatemala—one of the more critical concerns with neoliberal policies relates to their negative impact on the relative autonomy of indigenous forms of community-based social, economic, and political organization.

12. Lest it be thought that this characterization of the NGOs formed in the 1980s and 1990s apply to all of them, a substantial albeit unidentified number (see the discussion in chapter 8) are indeed "progressive," concerned with genuine social change and working with rather than against the grassroots organizations or class-based social movements. A contemporary example of these more progressive NGOs, provided by a colleague Darcy Tetreault, would include the *Red de Alternativas Sustentables Agropecuarias* (RASA), whose membership and leadership include peasants and indigenous families, academics, and social activists. To qualify, if not nuance somewhat, our analysis of the political role played by many development NGOS as an unwitting (or witting) agent of imperialism, there are undoubtedly many other such genuinely "progressive" NGOs. However, there are precious few NGOs that are willing to go the distance—from a more humane form of capitalism to radical egalitarianism and socialism as a form of national development.

13. In the polarized political climate of the mid-1980s in Central America revolutionary movements and activists alike tended to view allies in the region and beyond as crucial for political success and even physical survival.

14. See, for example, the struggles of the indigenous movement in Ecuador against the government's various attempts, from 1994 to date, to implement a neoliberal program of structural adjustment. On the basis of its organizational and mobilizing capacity, and its capacity to concert an alliance of oppositional forces and popular resistance, this movement has been surprisingly successful in preventing the government from implementing its agenda. As noted by a number of scholars over the years the promulgation (in 1994) of the Modernization law failed to bring about the neoliberal transformation of Ecuadorian society. What was achieved was the structure of highly speculative economic activities that continues to generate the conditions of economic and betimes political crisis.

15. These linkages are horizontal and intersectoral and as such can be contrasted with the type of linkages advocated by the World Bank and the other IFIs (e.g., IDB) and ODAs, including the UNDP. These organizations, for the

most part, advocate the formation of a new form of tripartism—a "collab-orative triangle" between "the public sector, private business and civil soci-ety" (Atal and Yen, 1995; Bessis, 1995). However, as pointed out by some panelists at the Roskilde Colloquium of the UN's World Social Summit, the "necessary collaborative triangle" between public, private and "third sec-tor" organizations "may build up elements of resistance" within the social movements sector.

16. On this point note the view expressed by David Rockefeller of the Chase Manhattan Bank, the 174th richest person in the world and one of the archi-tects of the Trilateral Commission, to the effect that "in recent years there's been a trend toward democracy and market economies [which] has lessened the role of government...But...somebody has to take government's place, and business seems to me the logical entity to do it" (quoted by Herman Daly in his address, in 1999, to the International Society for Ecological Economics – http://www.feasta.org/article_daly.htm). This view is entirely consistent with what was termed (Williamson, 1990) the "Washington Consensus."

4   Neoliberalism and the Social Movements: Mobilizing the Resistance

1. A basic history of the MST can be found in João Pedro Stedile and Frei Sergio, *A Luta pela Terra No Brazil* (São Paulo 1993); and *Documento Basico do MST* (São Paulo, 1994).

2. Based on interviews with Pedro Stedile, leader of the MST, and Evo Morales, leader of the Cocaleros en Bolivia. Many of the names of the peasant unions were taken from mining centers of Oruro.

3. Interview with regional leaders of the MST of Brazil at the I Curso Latinoamericano de Formación, March19–29, 1995, Instituto Cajamar São Paulo.

4. Interviews with Brazilian rural women of the MST at a Conference on Peasant Women in Rural Struggles, June 22, 1996, Cajamar, São Paulo.

5. Based on interviews at the time with MST leaders João Pedro Stedile and Ademar Bobo Egidio Brunetto in March 19–29, 1995. See also *Documento Basico do MST*, pp. 24–30.

6. Interview with Ina Meireles, President of CUT, Rio de Janeiro, May 17, 1996, and Vito Giannotti, Educational Director, Aeronautical Workers, Rio de Janeiro, May 16, 1996.

7. In Bolivia, during a seminar presented by the authors in June 1996 at the training school for mostly coca-growing peasants in La Paz, the central topic of debate was the relation of class to nation. In Paraguay the issue was less clearly defined, although in everyday conversations with peasant leaders it was clear that the Guarani cultural-linguistic universe was central.

8. At a seminar in Cajamar on May 21, 1996 attended by the authors there were more than eighty peasant women leaders from all regions of Brazil discussing issues such as gender equality in cooperatives, greater leadership roles, and greater acceptance of married women attending cadre schools. In

a seminar presented by Petras, the class-gender framework was generally accepted and the debate flowed within the parameters of a rejection of bourgeois (classless) feminism and class reductionist economism.

9. In Mexico the exclusion of the small- and middle-sized enterprises from the neoliberal model, led to the formation of a 750,000 strong organization of indebted farmers, *El Barzon*. Although in recent years, the dynamics of *El Barzon* has significantly declined in the 1990s it was a force to be reckoned with by the neoliberal regime.

10. Cf. interview with João Pedro Stedile of the MST, May 13, 1996.

1.1 This was partly the case at least in some industries and factories in Argentina. The Montoneros and Peoples Revolutionary Army did have influence in certain unions, particularly in Cordoba and Rosario. But this was generally not the case in the major metallurgical industries in the Greater Buenos Aires area.

12. Chile was the classic case during the late 1960s and early 1970s. See Veltmeyer (2010), Chapter 1.

13. A typical list of declarations from the Foro appears in *America Libre* (Buenos Aires), No. 7, July 1995, pp. 115–18.

14. This section and other discussions in this chapter are based on interviews, informal discussions, and seminars that took place between 1993 and 1996. In May and August 1996, Petras led seminars organized by the MST and CUT, the Miners' Union and coca peasant growers in Bolivia, the Peasant Federation in Paraguay, and the EZLN in Mexico. Thus, much of the discussion in this chapter reflects a "participant observer" perspective. Of course, the dynamics of the struggle waged by the MST both then and since have been the subject of a broad range of studies.

15. Interview with MST leader João Pedro Stedile, May 13, 1996.

16. An example of the redistributive and productionist approach of the MST—and a favorable response from the mass media—is found in "De sem-terra a productor rural," *A Noticia*, May 31, 1996, p. 1. On the data see *Brazil Report: Latin American Research Report*, September 19, 1996, pp. 6–7.

17. Based on interviews (May 13, 1996) with regional leaders of the MST, Santa Catarina.

18. Only three countries (Bolivia, Peru, and Venezuela) experienced a worse deterioration in the purchasing power capacity of incomes and wages than Ecuador over the course of two decades of structural adjustment. With an index of this capacity set at 100 in 1980, in 1998 it went up to 190 for Latin America as a whole while in Ecuador it fell to 85—60.2 in Bolivia and 59 in Venezuela (Veltmeyer and Petras, 1997, with CEPAL data).

19. Interview with Evo Morales, Cochabamba, June 12, 1996.

20. Based on a discussion with coca farmers in a leadership training school, La Paz, June 6, 1996.

21. Interview of Evo Morales with Carlos D. Mesa Gisbert, *De Cerca* (La Paz), 1994.

22. The debates and controversies with the Bolivian trade union congress are summarized in Estellano (1996).

23. Daniel Campos Ruiz and Dianisio Borda, *Las Organizaciones Campesinas en la Decada de Los 80*, Asunción n.d.; Guia de Organizaciones

Campesinas 1992–1993, Asunción 1994; Censo de Organizaciones Campesinas 1992–1993, Asunción 1994; Myriam Cristina Davalos and Jose Carlos Rodriguez, *Organizaciones Campesinas de Mujeres 1992–1993*, Asunción 1994.

24. In 1990 there were 49 land occupations and 51 evictions—at times the same land was occupied more than once; in 1991, 17 occupations and 23 evictions; in 1992, 16 and 16; in 1993, 14 and 17. In the same period, 1,600 peasants were arrested. The same pattern persisted in 1996: in April there were 11 occupied farms and 4 evictions. Monthly data is found in Informative Campesinas (Asunción), December 1993 and April 1996.

25. Interview with Alberto Areco, member of the executive committee of the National Peasant Federation (FNC), July 7, 1996.

26. Interviews with Eladio Flecha and Alfonso Cohere, July 1, 1996.

27. One of the best sources on popular struggles is the monthly *Madres de la Plaza de Mayo* published by the group with the same name. See also "El Fuego de Santiago," *America Libre*, No. 5, June 1994, pp. 92–100.

28. Interview with Hebe Bonafini, June 20, 1996.

29. Based on an interview with Marcos, July 29, 1996.

30. See, for example, Fonseca and Mayer, 1988, p. 187.

5   Turning the Social Movements: Civil Society to the Rescue

1. The term "civil society" dates back to the eighteenth-century French and Scottish enlightenment intellectuals who invented the term to distinguish more clearly between "society" and "government" in their writings on "progress." The idea of "progress" (the possibility of creating a better alternative form of society), and the notion of "civil society," were also used in the early nineteenth century by philosophers such as Hegel and his nemesis (and later social scientist), Karl Marx. However, the term "civil society" virtually disappeared from social scientific discourse; it was resurrected in the 1980s by a generation of social scientists concerned once again with creating a new and better form of society liberated from soviet authoritarianism this time, as opposed to the class-based and elitist monarchy of the *ancien regime*.

2. The institution of "good governance" implies a democratic regime in which the responsibility for human security and political order is not restricted to the government and other institutions of the state but is widely shared by different civil society organizations (World Bank, 1994).

3. The UNDP, the World Bank, and other agencies of international development adopted the term "civil society" in its discourse precisely because it is so inclusive, including within its scope the "private sector" (basically capitalist or multinational corporations governed by the logic of capital accumulation or profit-making). The incorporation of the "private sector" into the development process has been a fundamental aim of the UNDP, the World Bank,

and other "international financial institutions" and development associations that dominate the development process and lead the fight against world poverty (Mitlin, 1998). The advantages of the "civil society" concept is that it is more inclusive, allowing the UNDP and other ODAs and the IFIs to seek to incorporate the private sector in to the development process.

4. Thus, for example, in Chile and Brazil today the NGOs receive more than 50 percent of their funding from the state rather than the international organizations cooperating for development.

5. As noted and emphasized by Rafael Galindo Jaime, leader of the Central Campesina Independiente (CCI) in Mexico, the policy in practice (after fifteen years of experience) "results in a dispersal of resources and a duplication of functions as well as another layer of bureaucracy" (http://redalyc.uaemex.mx/redalyc/html/124/12401802/12401802.html.).

6. A classic example was the success of the World Bank in coopting Antonio Vargas, former maximum leader of CONAIE and a member of the short-lived triumvirate that took power in the wake of the 2000 January indigenous uprising (ICCI-RIMAY, 2001). Vargas represented the indigenous nationalities in the Amazonian region of Ecuador, which had been thoroughly penetrated by the evangelical churches, and because their interests were tied more to territorial autonomy and ethnic cultural identity than the land, it was not too difficult for World Bank officials to "turn" him away from the confrontational politics of the class and land struggle to a local micro-project development approach to "change." Vargas now heads PRODEPINE, an NGO well-financed by the World Bank, and a large staff that operates in the localities and communities of the rural indigenous poor to build on the social capital of the poor rather than mobilize the forces of resistance.

7. Formed in 1986 as a coordinating network of indigenous organizations such as ECUARUNARI (Confederación de los Pueblos de la Nacionalidad Quichua) and CONFENAIE (Confederación de los Pueblos y Nacionalidades de la Amazonía).

8. On this point see the various monthly issues of the *Boletín ICCI "RIMAY"* and *Revista Koeyu Latinoamericano,* a news and analysis outlet for the *Instituto Científico de Culturas Indígenas.*

9. A similar rebellion against the government's neoliberal programs of structural adjustment measures was launched by Ecuador's indigenous organizations in 1994, contemporaneous with the Zapatista rebellion.

6 A Turn of the Tide: The Center-Left Comes to Power

1. Despite Margolis's exceedingly ideological and erroneous assessment of the forces at play, he is right in this regard: that the electoral regimes formed in recent years, and the red or pink tide that has washed over the political landscape of national politics in recent years, reflects a very pragmatic turn toward what we would term "pragmatic neoliberalism."

2. Venezuela has its "misiones," Bolivia its "bonos" (Bono Juancito Pinto, Bono Juana Azurduy), and Ecuador its "Socio-País" program, but Brazil has its "Bolsa Familia," Colombia its "Familas en Acción" program, and Mexico its "Oportunidades" program. All of these and other such antipoverty programs in the region conform to the now dominant post-Washington Consensus.

3. Although no hard data are available on this, or on their impact on the poverty rate, there are indications that fiscal expenditures on social programs increased in Bolivia between 2008 and 2010. New fiscal measures of social expenditures introduced by the government in recent years include income transfers to households in the form of Bono Juancito Pinto ($29 a year per child attending school; $2.40 a month, 8 cents a day) and Bono Juana Azurduy (new mothers receive $7 per medical visit, $17 per birth, and $18 for each medical visit to year two); and an increase in pensions ranging from $258 to $344 a year (Renta Dignidad). However, even though no assessment as yet exists on the impact of these populist fiscal measures on the poverty rate, it is evident that the improvement is likely to be only marginal. A more substantial improvement regarding poverty would undoubtedly require more than increased social expenditures; they would require structural changes in access to means of social production, decent jobs, and productive resources other than education. There is no evidence of any such measures.

7   Social Movements in a Time of Crisis

1. Lula's prioritized concern to represent the economic interests of the country's agro-exporting capitalist class is reflected in the agro-export strategy pursued by his regime, and the project to convert Brazil into the "the Saudi Arabia of ethanol." Brazil used to be a relatively "closed" economy, with a low level of foreign trade. But, since 2000, Brazil's exports have expanded by an average annual rate of more than 13 percent and, as a result, its export-to-GDP ratio has increased from 13 percent in 2000 to nearly 19 percent in 2008. Farming played a huge role in this growth, given that agricultural and food products account for about 35 percent of the country's exports. Brazil is the world's top exporter of six key agricultural commodities—sugar, beef, chicken, orange juice, green coffee, and the "soya complex" of beans, meal, and oil. However, regarding the social relations of agricultural production, it is abundantly clear that at play in government policy have been the interests, demands, and pressures of the capitalist class in the sector, not those of the small producers and peasants. In this connection, Luciano Coutinho, president of Brazil's powerful economic development bank, BNDES, has repeatedly called for the formation of "Brazilian champions," the equivalent of South Korean *chaebols* and Japanese *keiretsu*. In 2008 (the last year for which figures are available), BNDES made loans worth R$128bn (US$80bn), most of it geared to building infrastructure for export and funding mergers and takeovers. The loans made by BNDES were worth more than the total amount lent by the World Bank, the Inter-American Development Bank (IDB), and the US Eximbank.

2. The battle is over the government's proposed use of accumulated foreign curency reserves to meet its external debt obligations. The president of the Central Bank is holding the line (as of February, and into March 15, 2010) in refusing to accede to this policy. The conservative-neoliberal right-wing parliamentary opposition has grabbed onto the issue as a means of gaining leverage over the government's legislative agenda. Fortunately for the president, the opposition strategy is beset by internal squabbles and a rather fragile political alliance.

3. We need to recall that, as in all cases of democratic government, Kirchner represents only certain fragments of the dominant capitalist and ruling class. Individuals and groups representing other fragments of this class inevitably are opposed. This is clearly illustrated in the current (February–early March 2010) clash between the government and the president of the Central Bank over the government's intention to use US$48 billion of international reserves to pay down the external debt.

4. Morales' first cabinet consisted of sixteen ministers (and forty-seven vice-ministers), of which seven were immediately called into question by the very movement that propelled Morales to the presidency. Eight were directly connected to NGOs such as CIPCA, ideologically disposed toward liberal democracy, indigenism, and the regime. For example, two ministers and two vice-ministers were drawn from CEJIS, an NGO focused on land issues and headquartered in Santa Cruz. All of the indigenous community representatives were also NGO-based or connected, as were the four Ministers identified by *Los Tiempos* as "leftist intellectuals." Representatives of "civil society" included Abel Mamami (Water), former leader of the Federation of Neighbourhood Councils (FEJUVE) in El Alto, the key organization that ignited the insurrections that toppled two former neoliberal presidents and gave Morales a resounding majority in El Alto; Walter Villaroel (Mining), ex-executive secretary of FENCOMIN—the Federation of Mining Cooperatives—who defected from the right-wing UCS to jump on the Morales bandwagon; Soliz Rada (Hydrocarbons), a former leader of the center-right CONDEPA party that cohabitated with former neoliberal presidents, even as he polemicized against the illegal sell-off of state petroleum resources; Casimira Rodríguez Romerom (Justice), leader of the *Trabajadoras del Hogar,* the Domestic Workers Union; Alex Gálvez (Labor), ex-Executive National Secretary of the Metallurgical Workers Union; Celinda Sosa (Economic Development), former Secretary General of the Federation of Women Peasants Bartolina Sisa, which was also brought into the ambit of democratic development engineered by CIPCA, FBDM, and CEJIS; Walker San Miguel Rodriguez (Defence), a lawyer and former director of Lloyd Bolivian Airline accused of covering up the illegal privatization of the former state airline, and a long-time member of the right-wing MNR as well as a former supporter of ex-President Sanchez de Lozada; David Choquehuanca (Foreign Affairs), former director of Nina, an NGO affiliate of UNITAS, and a close collaborator of neoliberal ex-President Jaime Paz Zamora, as well as a strong supporter of a free trade agreement with the United States, a policy that not even the previous neoliberal regime could pursue; and Luis Alberto

Arce (Finance), long connected with international financial institutions such as the IMF, World Bank, and Inter-American Development Bank, and a long-term supporter of their regressive structural adjustment programs. In addition, the Minister of the Presidency, Juan Ramón Quintana, was an associate member of RESDAL, a network for the defense and security of Latin America financed by George Soros, the founder of "Open Society," as well as the National Endowment for Democracy (NED).

5. This resolution followed a similar resolution of the 3rd National Congress of Ecuarunari in December 17, 2009. Ecuarunari is the most powerful indigenous grouping within CONAIE and was able in December to bring together over a thousand representatives of diverse highland indigenous peoples and peasant farmers such as the natabuelas, caranquis, pastos, otavalos, kayambis, kitukaras, panzaleos, chibuleos, paltas, salasacas, kisapinchas, tomabelas, warankas, puruhaes, cañaris, saraguro.

6. On the impact and significance of the Cuban Revolution for nationalists, revolutionaries and socialists in the Caribbean, see Girvan (2009).

7. This alliance includes the Coordinadora Andina de Organizaciones Indígenas (CAOI), the Coordinadora de Organizaciones Indígenas de la Cuenca Amazónica (COICA), the Consejo Indígena de Centro América (CICA), the Movimiento Sin Tierra del Brasil (MST), Vía Campesina; the organizations of the Unity Pact (Pacto de Unidad) of Bolivia, and diverse indigenous organizations of Colombia, Ecuador, and Peru—meeting most recently on the 26th of February 2009, in the locality of the Unity Pact in La Paz, Bolivia.

8. alba@movimientos.org.

9. *La Jornada* online, February 24, 2009.

10. This was in clear violation of a 1969 ILO-brokered agreement obligating the Peruvian government to consult and negotiate with the indigenous inhabitants over exploitation of their lands and rivers.

11. Predictably, the Obama regime did not issue a single word of concern or protest in the face of one of the worst massacres of Peruvian civilians in this decade perpetrated by one of America's closest remaining allies in Latin America. Taking his talking points from the US Ambassador, Garcia accused Venezuela and Bolivia of having instigated the Indian "uprising," quoting a letter of support from Bolivia's President Evo Morales sent to an intercontinental conference of Indian communities held in Lima in May as "proof."

12. Alan García was no stranger to government-sponsored massacres. In June 1986, he ordered the military to bomb and shell prisons in the capital holding many hundreds of political prisoners protesting prison conditions, resulting in over 400 known victims. Later, obscure mass graves revealed dozens more. This notorious massacre took place while García was hosting a gathering of the so-called Socialist International in Lima. His political party, APRA (American Popular Revolutionary Alliance), a member of the "International," was embarrassed by the public display of its "national-socialist" proclivities before hundreds of European Social Democrat functionaries. Charged with misappropriation of government funds and leaving office with an inflation rate of almost 8,000 percent in 1990, he agreed to support presidential candidate Alberto Fujimori in exchange for amnesty.

When Fujimori imposed a dictatorship in 1992, García went into self-imposed exile in Colombia and, later, France. He returned in 2001 when the statute of limitations on his corruption charges had expired and Fujimori was forced to resign amidst charges of running death squads and spying on his critics. García won the 2006 presidential elections in a run-off against the pro-indigenous nationalist candidate and former army officer Ollanta Humala, thanks to financial and media backing by Lima's right-wing, ethnic European oligarchs, and US overseas "aid" agencies.

8   Latin America in the Vortex of Social Change

1. On the dynamics of the global crisis in Latin America, and the strategic responses of governments and the social movements see Veltmeyer (2007. The country most seriously affected by the financial crisis is Mexico (an anticipated contraction of 7.5 percent in national output), due to its closeness to the United States and the openness to the US economy. The least affected countries are Bolivia, Ecuador, and Venezuela, although the latter, together with the countries in the southern cone and the Andes, did share the negative impact of the sharp fall in commodity prices and the downturn in the associated export earnings. Almost all governments in the region, according to ECLAC (2009), regardless of ideological orientation or regime type, had the same strategic response to the crisis: a program of countercyclical policies. It is too early to tell at this point how the crisis itself, and the responses to it by governments in the region and at the center of the world capitalist system, will impact on US-Latin American relations and the dynamics of imperialism in the region.

2. An exception to this proposition can be found in the US war on drugs, particularly the operations of this war in Colombia. In fact, it has even been argued in this context that US military presence if not power has increased. In a week that saw the official end of the US military presence in Panama in terms of bases and the southern command, the Pentagon's activities throughout Latin America, he argues, remained on the rise. According to a report released that week and summarized by Lobe, even as the last US military bases were handed over to the Panamanian government, Washington was actively establishing new military capabilities, called "Forward Operating Locations" (FOLs) on bases in Puerto Rico, Ecuador, Honduras, the Dutch Antilles, and possibly even Costa Rica—all in pursue of the "war against drugs." In fact, Adam Isacson, coauthor of the report (*Just the Facts: A Civilian's Guide to US Defense and Security Assistance to Latin America and the Caribbean*), stated that "the handover of the Canal Zone doesn't signal any shift in US military priorities and presence in Latin America." "It's not ending; it's just moving around," he added. In this connection, he noted that in 1998 nearly 50,000 US troops were deployed in the region, mostly for antidrug as well as counterinsurgency training rather than for military operations. In the context of the State Department's continued antidrug war

operations since, both in Colombia and elsewhere, it is likely that US military "aid" and sales, as well as military training at home and in the region
(of "some of the region's worst human rights abusers," according to a recent
US House-Senate Conference Committee) have continued to increase (US
Senate, 106th Congress (1999).

3. Based on the principles of the Bolivarian Revolution, ALBA is much more
than a simple trade agreement. It has diverse social and economic dimensions, including cooperative programs of health and education, as well as
projects related to development finance (the Bank of the South) and energy
(Petrocaribe). On the significance of ALBA to the regional resistance against
neoliberalism and US imperialism see Girvan (2009).

4. The US ambassador to Colombia, William Brownfield, refused to make
any declarations regarding stepped-up support and expansion of "Plan
Colombia," which entails the biggest outlay of funds for maintaining the
empire in the region. However, he did insist that the United States would
not construct any new military bases in Colombia. The policy was to "modernize" existing bases. Brownfield was ambassador to Venezuela in 2002
when the US-supported conspiracy to oust Chávez failed. In the context of
this failure Colombia has become increasingly central to the US strategy of
"containing" the forces of revolutionary change in the region. In this connection Colombia's immediate neighbors Venezuela and Ecuador have been
the objects of diverse provocations from both Colombia and Washington.

5. In this connection, Marco Gandásegui, of the University of Panama, makes
reference (http://marco agandasegui.blogspot.com) to recent reports that
show that at the end of the month the United States was to sign an agreement on military bases. The Minister of Defence, General Freddy Padilla,
announced that the agreement will have an initial term of ten years. The
principal base will be at Palanquero, barely 100 kilometers from Bogotá.
The agreement includes an increase of visits by US warships to the Pacific
Ocean port of Málaga and the Caribbean port of Cartagena. Colombian
government spokesmen also noted that the new agreement would allow the
United States to replace the military base in Manta, closed down by the
Ecuadorian government under President Correa The agreement will also
allow the United States to extend its military occupation of Colombia by
up to 1,400 troops in addition to those already assigned to the "war against
drugs" (i.e., FARC). In this connection, a Pentagon report presented in April
2009 at the Maxwell airbase in Alabama is clear enough. Palanquero can
serve as a "base for cooperative security" and the execution of "mobile
operations."

6. See Gandin (2010) re [recent] challenges to US authority that have led the
Council on Foreign Relations to pronounce the Monroe Doctrine "obso-
lete." But that doctrine, according to Gandin, has not expired so much
as slimmed down, with Obama's administration disappointing potential
regional allies by continuing to promote a volatile mix of militarism and
free-trade orthodoxy in a corridor running from Mexico to Colombia. The
anchor of this condensed Monroe Doctrine is Plan Colombia. Heading
into the eleventh year of what was planned to phase out after year five,

Washington's multibillion-dollar military aid package has failed to stem the flow of illegal narcotics into the United States. More Andean coca was synthesized into cocaine in 2008 than in 1998, and the drug's retail price is significantly lower today, adjusted for inflation, than it was a decade ago. But Plan Colombia is not really about drugs; it is the Latin American edition of GCOIN, or Global Counterinsurgency, the current term used by strategists to downplay the religious and ideological associations of George W. Bush's bungled "global war on terror" and focus on a more modest program of extending state rule over "lawless" or "ungoverned spaces," in GCOIN parlance. Starting around 2006, with the occupation of Iraq going badly, Plan Colombia became the counterinsurgent marquee, celebrated by strategists as a successful application of the "clear, hold and build" sequence favored by theorists like Gen. David Petraeus. Its lessons have been incorporated into the curriculums of many US military colleges and cited by the Joint Chiefs of Staff as a model for Afghanistan. Not only did the Colombian military, with support from Washington, weaken the Revolutionary Armed Forces (FARC), Latin America's oldest and strongest insurgency, but according to the Council on Foreign Relations, it secured a state presence in "many regions previously controlled by illegal armed groups, reestablishing elected governments, building and rebuilding public infrastructure, and affirming the rule of law." Plan Colombia, in other words, has offered a road map to success as well as success itself. "Colombia is what Iraq should eventually look like," wrote Atlantic contributor Robert Kaplan, "in our best dreams."

7. Peru's President Alan Garcia himself wrote a newspaper article designed to further polarize Peruvian society and deepen the class struggle. He wrote that behind the indigenous protest was a small group of Peruvians, some 50,000, who represented the interests of a small minority as against the vast majority, virtually everybody else, who supported the neoliberal model of government policy.

8. On this see Petras et al. (2004).

9. On the actual and apparent dynamics of US policy on this issue, and the opportunity and dilemma presented by the coup, there is a large and growing literature, much of it from the coordinated voice of the popular movement in the country and region.

10. On the dynamics of this response see, inter alia, Saney (2004).

11. In this connection, the meaning of "socialism" is still very much at issue, as is the question of what forms it might or should take. In Latin America an emerging debate on this issue has centered on developments in Venezuela under Chávez ("the socialism of the 20th Century") as well as communalism, the so-called communalist socialism of Evo Morales.

12. The major Internet-based forum, source of information and communications tool for communications about and among Latin American social movements is the Agencia Latinoamericana de Información (ALAI), formed in Ecuador in 1983 as a communications and information-sharing tool for the social movements. More recently, in 2004, ALAI expanded its intervention in the CT social movement field (Phase II') with the establishment (funded

inter alia by IDRC) of the "Minga Informativa de Movimientos Sociales," a programme of *"colaboración informativa, práctica de difusión en Internet, intercambio y reflexión entre las organizaciones participantes."* As such it has become an important Web-based IT communications tool for the social movements in advancing intramovement communications, organizing events and coordinating collective action.

13. The CMS, by its own definition is "a space for the broad alliance of Ecuadorian social movements in the countryside and the cities.' It groups more than 80 national, 250 provincial, and 3,000 local organizations that represent a large part of Ecuadorian society. In this organizational grouping, can be found groups affiliated with Seguro Social Campesino, neighborhood associations, NGOs concerned with human rights, the environment, women's equality, public sector workers, small merchants, artisans, teachers, youth organizations, and ecclesiastical base communities.

14. See, for example, the "Minga Informativa de Movimientos Sociales" and the journal ALAI *América Latina en Movimiento*, especially No. 449, in which are published diverse reflections on the debates and issues that surround the challenges faced by the social movement in the current conjuncture—"los nuevos escenarios."

15. In this connection we appreciate the critical comments on our "NGO analysis" by Darcy Tetreault, who is concerned that this analysis "essentially paints all NGOs with the same brush: as Trojan horses that (unwittingly or consciously) support the neoliberal agenda, undermine popular organizations and steer social movements away from confrontational politics." This, as Tetreault rightly points out, suggests "an overly simplistic dichotomy between NGOs and popular organizations (or worse, vs. social movements)." Tetreault adds: "While the gist of this argument and analysis is [certainly] valid... it fails to capture the diversity of the collective actors that drive social movements." Point taken.

16. In July 2004 Mecnam divided into two distinct currents: a majority grouping of CNOC, ANEC, AMUCSS, Red Mocaf, UNOFOC, FDC, and CEPCO that constituted a leftist Unión General Obrero Campesino Popular (UGOCP); and a minority ideologically heterogeneous movement formed by CIOAC, UNORCA, CNPA, and CODUC, in alliance with El Barzón, and accompanied by UNTA and the Central Campesina Cardenista (CCC) and CAP, a grouping of "independientes," Priistas and agrarian gangsters.

17. In a series of recent conferences and assemblies (see, e.g., the various dispatches in diverse issues of *América Latina en Movimiento*) the popular movement managed to maintain a strategic focus on anti-capitalism, antineoliberalism and anti-imperialism, within a program that included themes ranging from the preservation of water, forests, land, subsoil, traditional territories, and air; the political system and popular sovereignty; culture; justice; autonomy; sexual diversity; health; communications; foreign policy and international relations; antipatriarchal struggles; antiracism; national security; work and workers' rights; the economic system; indigenous and black communities; youth; fighting corruption; and learning about popular accounting.

Bibliography

Abya Yala—Movimientos Indígenas, Campesinos y Sociales (2009). "Diálogo de Alternativas y Alianzas," *Minga Informativa de Movimientos Sociales*, La Paz, 26 de Febrero.

Aglietta, M (1979). *A Theory of Capitalist Regulation: The US Experience*. London: New Left Books.

———(1982). "World Capitalism in the 1980s," *New Left Review*, Vol. 137.

Álamos, Rodrigo (1987). "La modernización laboral," *Estudios Públicos* [Santiago], núm. 26, otoño.

Alex Contreras Baspineiro Alex (1994). *La Marcha Historica*. Cochabamba.

Alimir, Oscar (1994). "Distribución del Ingreso e incidencia de la pobreza a lo largo del ajuste," *Revista de CEPAL*, 52, abril: 7–32.

Amalric, Frank (1998). "Sustainable Livelihoods, Entrepreneurship, Political Strategies and Governance," *Development*, 41 (3): 31–38.

Amsden, Alica and Ralphj Van der Hoeven (1994). "Manufacturing Output and Wages in the 1980s: Labor's Loss towards Century's End," *Working Paper* No. 3, University of Wisconsin-Madison, Global Studies Program.

Annan, Kofi (1998). "The Quiet Revolution," *Global Governance*, 4 (2): 123–38.

Arrida Palomares, Joaquín (1995). "Economía y sindicalismo. Significado económico del marco de relaciones laborales Salvadoreño," *ECA 551*.

Arrighi, Giovanni (1990). "Marxist Century—American Century: The Making and Remaking of the World Labour Movement," in Samir Amin, Giovanni Arrighi, Andre Gunder Frank, and Immanuel Wallerstein. *Transforming the Revolution*. New York: Monthly Review Press.

Atal, Yogesh and Yen, Else (eds.) (1995). *Poverty and Participation in Civil Society*. Proceedings of A UNESCO/CROP Round Table, World Summit for Social Development. Copenhagen: Denmark, March.

Atria, R., M. Siles, M. Arriagada, L. Robison, and S. Whiteford (eds.) (2004). *Social Capital and Poverty Reduction in Latin America and the Caribbean: Towards a New Paradigm*. Santiago: ECLAC.

Bárcena, A., (2009). *Preliminary Overview of the Economies of Latin America and the Caribbean*. Santiago: ECLAC.

Baros Horcasitas, José Luis, Javier Hurtado, and Germán Pérez Fernández del Castillo (eds.) (1991). *Transición a la democracia y reforma del Estado*.

FLACSO-Universidad de Guadalajara/ México: Grupo ed. Miguel Ángel Porrua.

Barrett, Patrick, Daniel Chávez, and César Rodríguez-Garavito (eds.) (2008). *The New Latin American Left*. London: Pluto Press.

Bartra, Roger (1976). "¿Y si los campesinos se extinguen...?" *Historia y Sociedad*, Vol. 8 (Winter).

Bartra Armando (2005). "Los apocalupticos y los integrados, indios y campesinos en la crucijada." Aporrea.org.

Bebbington, A., Michael Woolcock, and Scott E. Guggenheim (2006). *The Search for Empowerment: Social Capital as Idea and Practice at the World Bank*. West Hartford, CT: Kumarian Press.

Behrman, J, A. Gaviria and M. Székely (eds.) (2003). *Who's In and Who's Out: Social Exclusion in Latin America*. Washington DC: Inter-American Development Bank.

Beinstein, Jorge (2009). "Acople depresivo global (radicalización de la crisis)," *Servicio Informativo Alai-Amlatina*, 13/0409 [Buenos Aires].

Bell Lara, José (2002). *Globalization and the Cuban Revolution*. Havana: Editorial Jose Marti.

Bello, Walden (2009), "The Global Collapse: A Non-Orthodox View," *Z Net*, February 22. [http://www.zmag.org/znet/viewArticle/20638].

Bernanke, Ben (2000). *Essays on the Great Depression*. Princeton, NJ: Princeton University Press.

Bessis, Sophia (1995). "De la exclusion social a la cohesion social," Síntesis del Coloquio de Roskilde, World Summit for Social Development, Copenhagen, Denmark, March.

Blair, H. (1995). "*Assessing Democratic Decentralization*," A CDIE Concept Paper. Washington DC: USAID.

Blanco, Hugo (1972). *Land or Death: The Peasant Struggle in Peru*. New York: Pathfinder Press.

Boisier, Sergio, Francisco Sabatini, and Verónica Silva (1992). "La descentralización: el eslabón perdido de la cadena Transformación Productiva con Equidad y Sustentabilidad," *Cuadernos de CEPAL* [Santiago].

Boom, Gerard and Alfonso Mercado (eds.). (1990). *Automatización flexible en la industria*. Mexico: Editorial Limusa Noriega.

Botero, Libardo (1992). "Apertura economica y reforma laboral," in Botero et al. *Neoliberalsimo y subdesarrollo*. Bogota: El Áncora.

Botz, Dan (1996), "Mexico at the Turning Point, Part I: Rebellion and Militarization," *Againt the Current*, No. 65, November–December.

Boyer, Robert (1986). *La teoría de la regulación: un analísis crítico*. Buenos Aires: Ed. Humanitas.

Boyer, Robert and J. Mistral (1983). *Acumulacion, Inflation et Crise*. Paris: PUF.

Brass, Tom (1991). "Moral Economists, Subalterns, New Social Movements and the (Re)Emergence of a (Post) Modernised (Middle) Peasant," *Journal of Peasant Studies*, 18, 2.

——— (2000). *Peasants, Populism and Postmodernism: The Return of the Agrarian Myth*. London and Portland OR: Frank Cass.

Brenner, Robert (2000). *The Economics of Global Turbulence*. London: Verso.

Brockett, Charles D. (1998). *Land, Power and Poverty: Agrarian Transformation and Political Control in Central America*. Boulder, CO: Westview Press.

Brodsky, Melvin (1994). "Labor Market Flexibility: A Changing International Perspective," *Monthly Labor Review*, November.

Brown, Flor and Lilia Dominguez (1989). "Nuevas tecnologias en la industria maquiladora de exportación," *Comercio Exterior* [Mexico], Vol. 39, Num. 3, Marzo.

Bruce, Iain (2008). *The Real Venezuela*. London: Pluto Press.

Bulmer-Thomas, Victor (1996). *The Economic Model in Latin America and Its Impact on Income Distribution and Poverty*, New York, St. Martin's Press.

Burbach, Roger (1994). 'Roots of the Postmodern Rebellion in Chiapas,' *New Left Review* 205.

Bustillo Inés and Helvia Helloso. (2009). *The Global Financial Crisis: What Happened and What's Next*. Washington DC: ECLAC Washington Office, February.

Campos Ruiz, Daniel, et al. *Las Organizaciones Campesinas*

Cancian, Frank (1987). "Proletarianization in Zinacantan 1960–83," pp.11–36 in Morgan Maclachan (ed.), *Household Economies and Their Transformation*. Lanham MD: University Press of America.

Carothers, T. (1999). *Aiding Democracy Abroad*. Washington DC: Carnegie Endowment for International peace.

Carroll, T. (1992). *Intermediary NGOs. The Supporting Link in Grassroots Development*. Hartford, CT: Kumarian Press.

Castañeda, Jorge G (1993). *Utopia Unarmed: The Latin American left after the Cold War*. New York: Alfred Knopf

Castañeda, Jorge G. and Marco A. Morales (2009). "The Emergence of a New Left," in *Which Way Latin America? Hemispheric Politics Meets Globalization*. United Nations University Press.

Castañeda, Jorge G. and Marco A. Morales (eds.) (2008). *Leftovers: Tales of the Latin American Left Democracy*. New York: Routledge.

Castells, Manuel (1976). *Movimientos sociales urbanos en América Latina: Tendencies históricas y problemas teóricos*. Lima: Pontífica Universidad Católica.

CEPAL (1992a). *Social Equity and Changing Production Patterns: An Integrated Approach*. Santiago de Chile: CEPAL.

——— (1992b). *Focalización y Pobreza: nuevas tendencias en la política social*. Santiago de Chile.

——— (1995). *Panorama Social de America Latina*. Santiago de Chile.

——— (2009). "Crecimiento de América Latina y el Caribe retrocedería a -0.3% en 2009, según la CEPAL," 6 de abril, en: http://www.eclac.org.

CEPAL—UN Economic Commission for Latin America (1990). *Productive Transformation with Equity*. Santiago: CEPAL.

CEPAL/CLAD/SELA (1996). *Desarrollo con equidad*. Caracas: Ed. Nueva Sociedad.

Chambers, R. (1997). *Whose Reality Counts?* London: IT Publications.

Chambers, Robert and Gordon Conway (1998). "Sustainable Rural Livelihoods: Some Working Definitions," *Development*, 41 (3), September.

Chávez, Hugo R. (2007). "El socialismo del siglo XXI," pp.245–48 in Néstor Kohan (ed.) *Introducción al pensamiento socialista*. Bogotá: Ocean Sur.

Chotray, V. (2004). "The Negation of Politics in Participatory Development Projects, Kurnool, Andhra Pradesh," *Development and Change*, 36 (2).

Contreras Baspineiro, Alex (1994). *La Marcha Historica*, Cochabamba 1994; Interview with Evo Morales, in Carlos D. Mesa Gisbert, *De Cerca*, La Paz.

Cockcroft, James (2008). *Latinos en la construcción de los Estados Unidos*. La Habana: Instituto del libro, Ciencias Sociales.

Cook, Maria Lorena, Kevin Midlebrook, and Juan. Molinar (eds.) (1996). *Las dimensiones políticas de la reestructuración económica*. México: UNAM.

Cornia, Andrea, Richard Jolly, and Frances Stewart (eds.) (1987). *Adjustment with a Human Face*. Oxford: Oxford University Press.

Court, J., Hyden, G. and Meese, K. (1984). "Governance Performance: The Aggregate Picture," *World Survey Discussion Paper*. Tokyo: UNU, 2002.

Crabtree, John (2003). "The Impact of Neo-Liberal Economics on Peruvian Peasant Agriculture in the 1990s," in Tom Brass (ed.), *Latin American Peasants*, pp. 131–61. London: Frank Cass.

Crouch, C. and A. Pizzorno (1978). *Resurgence of Class Conflict in Western Europe since 1968*, London: Holmes and Meier.

Dandler, Jorge (1969). *El Sindicalismo Campesino en Bolivia*. México: Instituto Indigenista Interamericano.

Dataluta–Banco de dados de luta pela terra, 2002, *Assentamentos rurais*. Sao Paulo: UNESPI/MST.

Davis, Mike (1984). "The Political Economy of Late-Imperial America," *New Left Review* 143, January–February.

——— (2006). *Planet of Slums*. London: Verso.

De Janvry, Alain (1981). *The Agrarian Question and Reformism in Latin America*. Baltimore, MD: Johns Hopkins University Press.

De Janvry, Alain, Gustavo Gordillo, and Elisabeth Sadoulet (1998). *Mexico's Second Agrarian Reform*. La Jolla CA: Center for US-Mexican Studies, University of California, San Diego.

De Paula Leite, Marcia (1993). "Innovación tecnológica, organización del trabajo y relaciones industriales en el Brasil," *Nueva Sociedad*, núm. 124, marzo-abril.

De Soto, Hernando (1989). *The Other Path*. New York: Basic Books.

Deininger, Klaus (1998). "Implementing Negotiated Land Reform: Initial Experience from Colombia, Brazil and South Africa," in *Proceedings of the International Conference on Land Tenure in the Developing World with a Focus*.

Delgado Jara, Diego (2000). *Atraco bancario y dolarización*. Quito: Ediciones Gallo Rojo.

Delgado Wise, Raúl and James Cypher (2005). "The Strategic Role of Labour in Mexico's Subordinated Integration into the US Production System Under NAFTA," *Working Document*, Doctorado en Estudios del Desarrollo, Universidad Autónoma de Zacatecas.

Diaz, Alvaro (1989). "Chile: reestructuracion y modernizacion industrial auto-riatoria. Desafios para el sindicalismo y la oposición, in *Industria, Estado y sociedad," Nueva Sociedad* [Caracas].

Dominguez, Francisco (2006). "ALBA: Latin America's Anti-Imperialist Economic Project," August 10, 2006, http://21stcenturysocialism.com.

Dominguez, J. and Lowenthal, A. (eds.) (1996). *Constructing Democratic Governance.* Baltimore, MD: Johns Hopkins University Press.

Dunkerley, James (1984). *Rebellion in the Veins: Political Struggle in Bolivia 1952–82.* London: New Left Books.

Durston, John (1999). "Building Community Social Capital," *CEPAL Review,* 69: 103–18.

Dutrénit, Gabriela and Mario Capdevielle (1993). "El perfil tecnológico de la industria mexicana y su dinámica innovadora en la decada de los ochenta," *El trimestre Económico* [México,] vol. LX, num. 239, julio-Septiembre.

ECA (Estudios Centroamericanos) (1994, 1995). Nos. 551, September; 564, October.

ECLA (2008). *Social Panorama of Latin America.* Santiago: Chile.

ECLAC (2007). *The Social Panorama of Latin America.* Santiago: United Nations.

ECLAC (2009a). *The Reactions of Latin American and Caribbean Governments to the International Crisis: An Overview of Policy Measures up to 30 January 2009.* Santiago: United Nations.

ECLAC (2009). *The Social Panorama of Latin America.* Santiago: United Nations.

ECLAC (2010). *Time for Equality: Closing Gaps, Opening Trails.* Santiago de Chile.

ECLAC—Economic Commission of Latin America and the Caribbean (1990). *Productive Transformation with Equity.* Santiago: United Nations.

Engdahl F. William (2007). "Seeds of Destruction," *Global Research,* May.

Escobar, A. and Alvarez, S. (eds.) (1992). *The Making of Social Movements in Latin America:* Identity, Strategy, and Democracy. Boulder, CO: Westview Press.

Estellano, Washington (1996). "El Congreso Interrumpido," *Punto Final* [Santiago], July 15.

Esteva, Gustavo (1983). *The Struggle for Rural Mexico.* Westport, CT: Bergin and Garvey.

Ferrer, Aldo (1993). "Nuevos paradigmas tecnológicos y dersarrollo sostenible: perspectiva Latinoamericana," *Comercio Exterior,* Vol. 43, Núm. 9, Setiembre.

Figueroa, Victor (1986). *Reinterpretando el Subdesarrollo. Trabajo general, clase y fuerza productivo en America Latina.* Mexico DF: Siglo XXI.

Finan, Ann (2007). "New Markets, Old Struggles: Large and Small Farmers in the Export Agriculture of Coastal Peru," *Journal of Peasant Studies,* 34 (2).

Fine, Ben (2001). *Social Capital versus Social Theory: Political Economy and Social Science at the Turn of the Millennium.* London and New York: Routledge.

Fogel, Ramon Bruno (1986). *Movimientos Campesinos en el Paraguay*. Asunción: Centro Paraguayo de Estudios Sociológicos (CPES).

Foley, Michael (1991). "Agenda for Mobilization: The Agrarian Question and Popular Mobilization in Contemporary Mexico," *Latin American Research Review*, 26 (2).

Foley, M. W. and Edwards, B. (1999). "Is It Time to Disinvest in Social Capital?" *Journal of Public Policy*, 19 (2): 141–73.

Fonseca, Cesar and Enrique Mayer (1988). *Comunidad y Producción en el Peru*. Lima: Ediciones FOMCIENCIAS.

Foster, John Bellamy and Fred Magdoff (2008). "Financial Implosion and Stagnation: Back to the Real Economy," *Monthly Review*, 60 (6), December: 1–10.

——— (2009). *The Great Financial Crisis: Causes and Consequence,* New York: Monthly Review Press.

Fröbel, Folker, Jurgen Heinrichs, and Otto Kreye (1980). *The New International Division of Labour: Structural Unemployment in Industrialised Countries and Industrialisation in Developing Countries*. Cambridge: Cambridge University Press.

Fuentes, Federico (2010). "Venezuela's Revolution Faces Crucial Battles," The Bullet—Socialist Project, E-Bulletin No. 316, February 22.

Fuentes, Marta and Andre Gunder Frank (1989). "Ten Theses on Social Movements," *World Development*, 17 (2): 179–91.

Fundación José Peralta (2003). *Ecuador: su realidad*. Quito: Fundación de Investigación y Promoción Social José Peralta.

FUSADES (1996). *Boletin Economico y Social*, No. 128, Julio [San Salvador].

Geller, Lucio (1993). *Cambio tecnológico, trabajo y empleo: industria manufacturera del Gran Santiago, 1988–1990*. Santiago: PREALC.

George, Susan (1999). *The Lugano Report: On Preserving Capitalism in the 21st Century*, London: Pluto Press.

Ghimire, Krishna B. (ed.) (2001). *Land Reform and Peasant Livelihoods: The Social Dynamics of Rural Poverty and Agrarian Reform in Developing Countries*. London: ITDG.

Girvan, Norman (2009), "La deuda es impagable," Keynote Address, Conference on "Latin American Transformations," Saint Mary's University, Halifax, October 3.

Gledhill, J. (1988). "Agrarian Social Movements and Forms of Consciousness," *Bulletin of Latin American Research*, 7 (2).

Glynn, A., Hughes, A. Lipietz, and A. Singh (1990). "The Rise and Fall of the Golden Age," in Stephen Marglin and Juliet Schor (ed.) *The Golden Age of Capitalism: Re-interpreting the Post-War Experience*. Oxford: Clarendon Press.

Goss, Sue (2001). *Making Local Governance Work: Networks, Relationships and the Management of Change*. New York: Palgrave Macmillan.

Gould, Jeffrey L. (1990). *To Lead as Equals: Rural Protest and Political Consciousness in Chinandega, Nicaragua, 1912–1979*, Chapel Hill, NC: University of North Carolina Press.

Grandin, Greg (2010). "Muscling Latin America," *The Nation,* February 8.

Green, Duncan (1995). *Silent Revolution: The Rise of Market Economics in Latin America.* London: Cassell.

Guerrero de Lizardi, Carlos and Alejandro Valle (1995). "Salario, participación del salario en el producto y productividad," in L.A. de la Garza and Enrique Nieto (ed.). *Distribución del ingreso y política sociales.* Tomo I. México: Juan Pablo Ed.

Guillén, Arturo (2009). "En la encrucijada de la crisis global," *Alai Amlatina,* Junio 18.

Guimarães, Roberto (1997). "The Environment, Population and Urbanization," in R. Hillman (ed.), *Understanding Contemporary Latin America,* Boulder CO: Lynne Rienner.

Harnecker, Marta (2010). "Latin America and Twenty-First Century Socialism: Inventing to Avoid Mistakes," *Monthly Review Press,* 62 (3), July–August.

Harriss, J. (2001). *Depoliticising Development: The World Bank and Social Capital.* New Delhi: Left Word Books.

Harvey, David (2005). *A Brief History of Neoliberalism,* Oxford: Oxford University Press.

Harvey, Neil (1998). *The Chiapas Rebellion: The Struggle for Land and Democracy.* London and Durham, NC: Duke University Press.

Hayden, Robert (2002). "Dictatorships of Virtue," *Harvard International Review,* Summer.

Helmore, Kristen and Naresh Singh (2001). *Sustainable Livelihoods: Building on the Wealth of the Poor.* West Hartford, CT: Kumarian Press.

Henriquez, Helia and I. Reca (1994). "La mujer en el trabajo: la nueva puesta en escena de un tema antiguo," *Economia y trabajo en Chile 1993–1994.* Cuarto Informe Anual. Santiago de Chile: Programa de Economía del Trabajo (PET).

Hernandez, Luis (1992). "La UNORCA: doce tesis sobre el nuevo liderazgo campesino en Mexico," in J. Moguel Botey & L. Hernandez (coord.), *Autonomia y nuevos sujetos sociales en el desarrollo rural.* Mexico.

Hernandez Montoya, Leticia (1996). "Rechazamos el Dialogo; Derrocar al Estado, Nuestro Objetivo: EPR," *Excelsior,* August 10.

Herrera, Gonzalo (1995). "Tendencias del cambio tecnológico en la industria Chilena," *Economía y Trabajo en Chile 1994⊠1995.* Santiago: Programa de Economía del Trabajo (PET).

Hobsbawm, Eric (1994). *The Age of Extremes: The Short Twentieth Century, 1914–1991.* London: Abacus.

Holloway, John (2002). *Change the World tithout Taking Power: The Meaning of Revolution Today.* London: Pluto Press.

Hristow, Jasmin (2009). *Blood & Capital: The Paramilitarization of Colombia.* Toronto: Between the Lines.

Huizer, Geritt (1999). "Peasant Mobilization for Land Reform: Historical Case Studies and Theoretical Considerations," *Discussion Paper 103,* Geneva: UNRISD.

Hyden, G.; Court, J. and Meese, K. (2003), "Making Sense of Governance: the Need for involving Local Stakeholders," *Development Dialogue*. London: IDI.

ICCI-RIMAY (2001). "Banco Mundial y PRODEPINE: Hacia un neoliberalismo étnico?" *Bolétin ICCI 'RIMAY*, III (25), Abril.

IDB—Inter-American Development Bank (1993). *Reforma social y pobreza: hacia una agenda integrada de desarrollo*. Washington: BID.

International Labour Office (ILO) (1995). *World Employment 1995*. Geneva: ILO.

Jazairy, Idriss et al. (1992). *The State of World Rural Poverty*. London: Intermediate Technology Publications (for IFID).

Jones, Bart (2007). *¡Hugo!: The Hugo Chávez Story from Mud Hut to Perpetual Revolution*. New Hampshire: Steerforth Press.

Kamat, S. (2003). "NGOs and the New Democracy: The False Saviours of International Development," *Harvard International Review*. Spring.

Katz, Claudio (2005). "Strategies for the Latin American Left. Problems of Autonomism," *International Socialist Review*, Issue 44, November–December.

——— (2008). *Las disyuntivas de la izquierda en América Latina*. Buenos Aires: Ediciones Luxemburg.

Katz, Friedrich (1988). *Riot, Rebellion, and Revolution: Rural Social Conflict in México*. Princeton NJ: Princeton University Press.

Kay, Cristóbal (1999). "Rural Development: From Agrarian Reform to Neoliberalism and Beyond," in Robert Gwynne and Cristóbal Kay (ed.), *Latin America Transformed*. New York: Oxford University Press.

——— (2000). "Latin America's Agrarian Transformation: Peasantisation and Poletarianisation," pp. 123–38 in D. F. Bryceson, Cristóbal Kay, and Jos Mooij (ed.), *Disappearing Peasantries? Rural labour in Africa, Asia and Latin America*. London: Intermediate Technology Publications.

——— (2008). "Reflections on Latin American Rural Studies in the Neoliberal Globalization Period: A New Rurality?" *Development and Change*, 39 (6): 915–43.

Kearney, Michael (1996). *Reconceptualizing the Peasantry*. Boulder CO: Westview Press.

Landim, Leilah (1988). "Non-Governmental Organizations in Latin America," *World Development*, 15 (Supplement): 29–38.

Landsberger, Henry A., ed. (1969). *Latin American Peasant Movements*. London and Ithaca, NY: Cornell University Press.

Landsberger, Henry A. (ed.) (1974). *Rural Protest: Peasant Movements and Social Change*. London: Macmillan.

Larrea, Carlos (2004). *Pobreza, dolarización y crisis en el Ecuador*. Quito: Editorial Abya-Yala.

Laserna, Roberto and Miguel Villaroel (2008). *38 años de conflictos sociales en Bolivia*. Cochabamba: CERES.

Latin America (1997). MST—Direccion Nacional (1991). *Como Organizar a la Masa. Documento Basico do MST*. São Paulo, September.

Lehmann, David A., ed. (1974). *Peasants, Landlords and Governments: Agrarian Reform in the Third World.* NY: Holmes and Meier.

Leiva, Fernando (1996). "Flexible Labor Markets, Poverty and Social Disintegration in Chile, 1990–1994," unpublished manuscript, CETES. Santiago de Chile, March.

Leiva, Fernando and James Petras, with Henry Veltmeyer (1994). *Democracy and Poverty in Chile.* Boulder, CO: Westview Press.

Leiva, Fernando and Rafael Agacino (1994). *Mercado de trabajo flexible, pobreza y desintegración social en Chile, 1990⊠1994.* Santiago: OXFAM/ Universidad ARCIS.

Lerner, Bertha (1996). *Los debates en política social, desigualdad y pobreza.* Mexico DF: Fideicomiso-Banco Internacional/UNAM.

Lesbaupin, Ivo (2000). *Poder local X Exclusão social.* Petrópolis: VOZES.

Levitt, K. (1990). "Debt, Adjustment and Development: Looking to the 1990s," *Economic and Political Weekly,* July 21: 1585–94.

Levitt, K. (2001). "Development in Question," Keynote Address. Canadian Association for International Development Studies, Toronto, May 31.

Lewis, W. A. (1954). "Economic Development with Unlimited Supply of Labour," *The Manchester School of Social and Economic Studies,* 22 (2): 139–91.

Lievesley, Geraldine and Steve Ludlam (2009). *Reclaiming Latin America: Experiments in Radical Social Democracy.* London: Zed Books.

Lipietz, Alain (1982). "Towards Global Fordism," *New Left Review,* 13, March–April.

—— (1987). *Mirages and Miracles: The Crisis in Global Fordism.* London: Verso.

Lohman, Maria (1994). "Guerra a las Drogas: Una Vision desde las Andes," Cochabamba: CEDIB.

Lopez, Nestor and Alberto Minujin (1994). "Nueva Pobreza y exclusion: El caso Argentino," *Nueva Sociedad,* No. 131, May–June, 88–105.

Magdoff, Harry and Paul M. Sweezy (1988). *The Irreversible Crisis.* New York: Monthly Review Press.

—— (1990). "The Editors Comment," *Monthly Review* 42 (7), December: 37–38.

Mansilla, H. F. C. and Maria Teresa Zegada (1996). *Politica, Cultura y Etnicidad en Bolivia.* La Paz. CEBEM.

Marcos, Jaime (1996). "Las comunidades campesinas en el proceso de regionalización del Peru," *Nueva Sociedad,* 142, Abril–Mayo.

Marglin, Stephen and Schor, Juliet (1990). *The Golden Age of Capitalism: Reinterpreting the Postwar Experience.* Oxford: Clarendon Press.

Margolis, Mac (2009). "Latin America isn't tilting left, it's tilting right," *Newsweek* Web Exclusive, August 7.

Marini, Ruy Mauro (1981). *Dialéctica de la dependencia.* Mexico DF: Era.

McEwan, Arthur (1981). *Revolution and Economic Development in Cuba: Moving Towards Socialism.* New York: St. Martin's Press.

Mead, Walter (1991). *The Low Wage Challenge to Global Growth.* Washington DC: Economic Policy Institute.

Meillasoux, Claude (1978). *Mujeres graneros y capital*. Mexico: Editorial Siglo XXI.

Melucci, Alberto (1992). "Liberation or Meaning: Social Movements, Culture and Democracy," pp.43–77 in J, Nederveen Pieterse (ed.) *Emancipations, Modern and Postmodern*. London: Sage.

Mercado, Alfonso (1990). "La adquisición de máquinas-herramientas de control numérico en América latina," pp.87–115 in Gerard Boom and Alfonso Mercado (ed.), *Automatización flexible en la industria*. Mexico D.F.: Ed. Limusa Noriega.

Mitlin, D. (1998). "The NGO Sector and Its Role in Strengthening Civil Society and Securing Good Governance," pp.81–96 in Armanda Bernard, Henry Helmich, and Percy Lehning (ed.), *Civil Society and International Development*. Paris: OECD Development Centre.

Montesinos, Mario and Roberto Góchez (1995). "Salarios y productividad," *ECA* 564, octubre.

Morales, Evo (2003). "La hoja de coca, una bandera de lucha," Interview with *Punto Final* [Santiago], May.

Morales, Josefina (1992). "La reestructuración industrial," in J. Morales et al. (ed.), *La reestructuración industrial en México: cinco aspectos fundamentales*. Mexico DF: Editorial Nuestro Tiempo.

Morley, Samuel (1995). "Structural Adjustment and Determinants of Poverty in Latin America," in Nora Lustig (ed.), *Coping with Austerity: Poverty and Inequality in Latin America*, pp. 42–70. Washington DC: Brookings Institution.

Morton, A. (2001). "La Resurrección del Maíz: Some Aspects of Globalisation, Resistance and the Zapatista Question," Paper presented at the 42nd Annual Convention of the International Studies Association. Chicago, February 20–24.

Movimento dos trabalhadores rurais sem terra (1994). *Documento Basico do MST*. São Paulo. *Documento Basico do MST*. São Paulo.

Muñoz, Oscar (1989). *Industria, Estado y sociedad, la reestructuración industrial en América Latina y Europa*. Caracas: Editorial Nueva Sociedad.

Narayan, Deepa (2002). *Empowerment and Poverty Reduction: A Sourcebook*. Washington DC: World Bank.

Nash, R., A. Hydson, and C. Luttrell (2006). *Mapping Political Context: A Toolkit for Civil Society Organizations*. London: ODI.

Nugent, Daniel (1994). "Social Class and Labor Process in the Determination of a Peasantry in Mexico," *Critique of Anthropology*, 14 (3): 285–313.

Ocampo, J. A. (1998). "Beyond the Washington Consensus: An ECLAC Perspective," *CEPAL Review* (66), December, 7–28.

——— (2006). "Latin America and the World Economy in the Long Twentieth Century," pp.342–72 in K.S. Jomo (ed.), *The Great Divergence: Hegemony, Uneven Development, and Global* Inequality. New York: Oxford University Press.

——— (2007). "The Macroeconomics of the Latin American Economic Boom," *CEPAL Review* 93.

Ocampo, J. A., K. S. Jomo, and Sarbuland Khan (eds.) (2007). *Policy Matters: Economic and Social Policies to Sustain Equitable Development.* London: Orient Longman; New York and Penang: Third World Network,

OECD (1994). *The OECD Jobs Study: Facts, Analysis, Strategies.* Paris: OECD.

——— (2010). *Perspectives on Global Development: Shifting Wealth.* Paris: OECD.

Olave, Patricia (1994). "Reestructuración productiva bajo el nuevo patrón exportador," in Juan Arancibia Córdova (ed.), *América latina en los ochenta: reestructuración y pespectivas.* Mexico DF: IIEC-UNAM.

Oliviera, Francisco de and Leida Maria Paulini (2007). "Financialization and Barbarism: A Perspective from Brazil," in P. Bowles et al., (ed.), *National Perspectives on Globalization: A Critical Reader,* Basingstoke, London: Palgrave Macmillan.

Omae, Kenichi (1990). *The Borderless World: Power and Strategy in the Interlinked World Economy.* New York: Harper Business.

Ominami, Carlos (ed.) (1986). *La tercera revolución industrial. Impactos internacionales el actual viraje tecnológico.* Mexico: RIAL-Anuario-Grupo Ed. Latinoamericano.

Ortega, Eduardo (2008). "Lanza Felipe Calderón cinco medidas para enfrentar la crisis," *El Financiero,* 9 de Octubre.

Otero, Gerardo (1999). *Farewell to the Peasantry? Political Formation in Rural Mexico.* Boulder, CO: Westview Press.

Ottaway, M. (2003). *Democracy Challenged:* The Rise of Semi-Authoritarianism. Washington DC: Carnegie Endowment for International Peace.

Palorames, Laura and Leonard Mertens (1993). "Empresa y trabajador ante la automatización programable," in Leonel Corona (ed.), *Mexico ante las nuevas tecnológias.* CIIH-UNAM.

Panitch, Leo and Sam Gindin (2009). "From Global Finance to the Nationalization of the Banks: Eight Theses on the Economic Crisis," The Bullet <www.socialist project.ca/bullet/bullet210.html>

Patomäki, H. and T. Teivainen (2004). *A Possible World: Democratic Transformation of Global Institutions.* London: Zed Books.

Paugam, Serge, ed. (1996). *L' exclusion. L'Etat des savoirs.* Paris: Ed. La Découverte.

Pérez Caldentey, Esteban and Matías Verneng (2008). *Back to the Future: Latin America's Current Development Strategy.* New York: Monthly Review Press.

Petras, J. and H. Veltmeyer (2001). *Globalization Unmasked: Imperialism in the 21st Century.* Halifax: Fernwood Publications; London: ZED Books.

——— (2002). *Argentina: Entre desintegración y la revolución.* Buenos Aires: Editorial la Maza

——— (2005). *Empire with Imperialism.* London: Zed Books.

——— (2009). *Espejismos de la izquierda en América Latina.* Buenos Aires: Editorial Lumen.

——— (2009). *What's Left in Latin America.* Aldershot: Ashgate.

Petras, J., H. Veltmeyer, L. Vasapollo, and M. Casadio (2004). *Imperio con Imperialismo*. Havana: Editorial de Ciencias Sociales.

Petras, J. (2007). "The Great Financial Crisis or Who's Got a Turd in his Briefcase?" James Petras Web site, August 24.

Petras, J. and H. Veltmeyer (1995). "La Recuperación Económica en America Latina: El Mito y la Realidad," *Nueva Sociedad*, No. 137, Mayo–Junio.

—— (2003). "The Peasantry and the State in Latin America: A Troubled Past, an Uncertain Future," in Tom Brass (ed.), *Latin American Peasants*, London: Frank Cass.

—— (eds.) (2004). *Las privatizaciónes y la desnacionalización en América Latina*. Buenos Aires: Libros Prometeo.

Pilger, J. (2003). *The New Rulers of the World*. London: Verso.

Pior, Michael and Charles Sabel (1984). *The Second Industrial Divide*. NY: Basic Books.

Pochmann, Marcio (2004). *Atlas da exclusâo no mundo*, 5 vols. Sao Paulo: Cortez Editora.

Portes, Alejandro (1998). "Social Capital: Its Origins and Applications in Modern Sociology," *Annual Review of Sociology*, 24: 1–2.

Portes, Alejandro, Manuel Castells, and Lauren Benton (eds.) (1989). *The Informal Economy: Studies in Advanced and Less Developed Countries*. Baltimore, MD: Johns Hopkins University Press.

Porzecanski Arturo (2009). "Latin America: The Missing Financial Crisis," *Studies and Perspectives* No. 6, Washington DC, ECLAC.

PREALC (1990). *PREALC Informe*. Santiago, Chile: ILO-PREALC.

PREALC—Programa Regional de Empleo de America Latina y el Caribe (1988). *La evolucion del mercado laboral entre 1980 y 1987*. Santiago, Chile: ILO-PREALC/328.

Rao, V. (2002). *Community Driven Development: A Brief Review of the Research*. World Bank, Washington DC for Environment and Development.

Rice, J. and M. Prince (2000). *Changing Politics of Canadian Social Policy*. Toronto: University of Toronto Press.

Rifkin, Jeremy (1996). *The End of Work*. New York: G.P. Putnam's Son's.

Rondinelli, D. A., J. McCullough, and W. Johnson (1989). "Analyzing Decentralisation Policies in Developing Countries: A Political Economy Framework," *Development and Change*, 20 (1): 57–87.

Roseberry, William, Lowell Gudmundson, and Mario Samper Kutschbach, eds. (1995). *Coffee, Society, and Power in Latin America*. Baltimore, MD: Johns Hopkins University Press.

Rosenbluth, Guillermo (1994). "Informalidad y pobreza en America Latina," *Revista de CEPAL*, 52, Abril: 57–78.

Sagasti, Francisco and Gregorio Arevalo (1992). "América Latina en el nuevo orden mundial fracturado: perspectivas y estrategias," *Comercio Exterior* [Mexico], 42 (12), December.

Sandbrook, Richard, Marc Edelman, Patrick Heller and Judith Teichman (2007). *Social Democracy on the Periphery*. Cambridge, UK: Cambridge University Press.

Saney, Isaac (2003). *Cuba: A Revolution in Motion*. Halifax: Fernwood Publishing.

Sanfuentes, Alejandro (1987). "Effects of the Adjustment Policies on the Agriculture and Forestry Sector," *CEPAL Review*, No. 3, December.

Saxe-Fernández, John (2002). *Globalización: Crítica a una paradigma*, Barcelona: Plaza Janés Editores.

Saxe-Fernández, John and Omar Núñez (2001). "Globalización e Imperialismo: La transferencia de Excedentes de América Latina," pp.87–166 in Saxe-Fernández (ed.), *Globalización, Imperialismo y Clase Social*, Buenos Aires/ México: Editorial Lúmen.

Scott, James C. (1985). *Weapons of the Weak: Everyday Forms of Peasant Resistance*. New Haven, CT: Yale University Press.

Slater, David (1985). *New Social Movements and the State in Latin America*. Amsterdam: CEDLA.

Solow, R. (2000). "Notes on Social Capital and Economic Performance," in Partha Dasgupta and Ismail Serageldin (ed.), *Social Capital: A Multi-Faceted Perspective*. Washington DC: World Bank.

Sotelo Valencia, Adria (1995). "La reestructuración del trabajo y el capital en América latina," in Ruy Mauro Marini and Márgara Millán (ed.), *La teoría social Latinoamericana: cuestiones contemporáneas,* Vol. IV. Mexico DF: Ediciones El Caballito/UNAM.

Stavenhagen, Rodolfo (1970). *Agrarian Problems and Peasant Movements in Latin America*. New York: Anchor Books.

Stedile, João (1998), "The Class Struggles in Brazil: The Perspective of the MST." *Socialist Register.*

Stedile, João and Frei Sergio (1996). *A Luta pela Terra No Brazil*. São Paulo: Scritta.

Sunkel, Osvaldo and Ricardo Infante (2009). *Hacia un desarrollo inclusivo: el caso de Chile*. Santiago: CEPAL.

Tabera Soliz, Gabriel (1996). "Mineria boliviana en manos de Comsur e Inti Raymi," *La Razon* (La Paz), January 21: d8, 9.

Tannenbaum, Frank (1968) [1929]. *The Mexican Agrarian Revolution*. New York: Anchor Books.

Taylor, Lance (1988). *Varieties of Stabilization Experience*. Oxford: Clarendon Press.

Thiesenhusen, William (ed.) (1989). *Searching for Agrarian Reform in Latin America*. Winchester, MA: Unwin Hyman.

Thiesenhusen, William (1995). *Broken Promises: Agrarian Reform and the Latin American Campesino*. Boulder, CO: Westview Press.

UNCTAD, Secretariat to the VIIIth Conference (1990*). Analytical Report*. New York: UNCTAD Conference secretariat.

UNDP (1996). *"Good Governance and Sustainable Human Development," Governance Policy Paper.* http://magnet.undp.org/policy.

―――― (1997). "The Shrinking State: Governance and Sustainable Human Development," *Policy Document*. New York: UNDP.

―――― (2000). The UNDP Role in Decentralisation and Local Governance. UNDP Evaluation Office, February.

UNIDO—UN Industrial Development Organization (1991, 1992). *Industry and Development Global Report*. Vienna: UNIDO.

United Nations (1996). *Estudio Económico y Social Mundial 1996: Tendencias y Políticas en la Economia Mundial*. New York: UN.

US Senate, 106th Congress (1999). *Private Banking and Money Laundering: A CaseStudy of Opportunities and Vulnerabilities Hearings before the Permanent Sub-Committee on Investigations of the Committee on Governmental Affairs*. Report,November 9–10.

Uphof, N. (1994), "Social Capital and Poverty Reduction," pp.105–32. in R. Atria, et al (ed.), *Social Capital and Poverty Reduction in Latin America and the Caribbean: Towards a New Paradigm*. Santiago: ECLAC

Veltmeyer, Henry (1983). "Surplus Labour and Class Formation on the Latin American Periphery," in Ron Chilcote and Dale Johnson (ed.), *Theories of Development*. Beverly Hills, CA: Sage.

———— (1996). "La búsqueda de un desarrollo alternativo," Working Paper, Maestria en Ciencia Política, Universidad Autónoma de Zacatecas.

———— (1997a). "Latin America in the New World Order," *Canadian Journal of Sociology*, 22: 2 (June).

———— (1997b). "The World Bank's Report on Labour: A Capitalist Manifesto," *Transition* [Georgetown].

———— (2005), "The Dynamics of Land Occupation in Latin America," pp.285-316 in edited by Sam Moyo and Paris Yeros (ed.), *Reclaiming the Land: The Resurgence of Rural Movements in Africa, Asia, and Latin America*. London: Zed Books.

———— (2007). *Illusions and Opportunities: Civil Society in the Quest for Social Change*. Halifax: Fernwood.

———— (ed.) (2010). *Imperialism, Crisis and Class Struggle: The Verities of Capitalism*. Leiden and Boston: Brill Publishers.

Veltmeyer, H. and J. Petras (1997). *Economic Liberalism and Class Conflict in Latin America*. London: Macmillan Press/New York: St. Martin's Press.

———— (2005). "Foreign Aid, Neoliberalism and Imperialism," in A. Saad-Filho and D. Johnston (ed.), *Neoliberalism: A Critical Reader*. London: Pluto Press.

Vicuña Izquierdo, Leonardo (2000). *Política económica del Ecuador: Dos décadas perdidas. Los años 80-90*. Guayaquil: ESPOL.

Vieira, Pedro Antonio (1994). *Luchas obreras, control de la fuerza de trabajo y automatizacion de los medios de trabajo*. Doctoral Thesis, Economics Faculty, UNAM, Mexico.

Wallace, Tina (2003). "NGO Dilemmas: Trojan Horses for Global Neoliberalism?" *Socialist Register*. London: Merlin Press.

Webber, J. R. (2007). "Bolivia's Neoliberal Labyrinth," *Latin American Perspectives*, 34: 162–64.

Weisbrot, Mark (2009). "Economic Rebels," guardian.co.uk, Wednesday, October 28, 2009.

Weisbrot, Mark, Rebecca Ray, and Jake Johnston (2009). *Bolivia: The Economy during the Morales Administration*, CEPR, December 3.

Whetten, Nathan (1948). *Rural Mexico*. Chicago: University of Chicago Press.

Williamson, J. ed. (1990). *Latin American Adjustment. How Much Has Happened?* Washington DC: Institute for International Economics.

Wolfe, Marshall (1994). "Some Paradoxes of Social Exclusion: International Institute for Labour Studies," *Discussion Paper 63*. Geneva.

World Bank (1994). *Governance and Development*. Washington, DC: World Bank.

———(1993). *Latin America and the Caribbean: A Decade after the Debt Crisis*. Washington DC: World Bank.

——— (1994). *Governance*. The World Bank Experience. Washington DC: World Bank.

——— (1995). *Workers in an Integrating World*. New York: Oxford University Press.

——— (1996, 1997). *World Development Report*. Washington, DC: World Bank.

———(2000). *World Development Report 2000/2001: Attacking Poverty*. New York: Oxford University Press.

——— (2004). *Partnerships in Development: Progress in the Fight against Poverty*. Washington DC: World Bank.

——— (2008). *Latin America and the Global Crisis*. Washington DC.

Yepe, M. E. (2008). "Cuba Reforms Its Food Production Process," *Political Affairs*, Online Edition, July 28 <http://political affairs.net/article/articleview/7184.>

Index